A WORLD WITHOUT HEROES

A WORLD WITHOUT HEROES

The Modern Tragedy

George Roche

George Roche and the
Hillsdale College Press

Books by the Hillsdale College Press include: volumes by George Roche, President of Hillsdale College; *Champions of Freedom* series on economics; *The Christian Vision* series; and other works.

A WORLD WITHOUT HEROES: THE MODERN TRAGEDY

First Printing 1987
Library of Congress Catalog Card Number: 87–080235
ISBN 0–916308–89–8

Cover Design by Carl Benkert

Contents

To my mother

Foreword

A hero, as the old Century Dictionary puts it, is "a man of distinguished valor, intrepidity, or enterprise in danger; a prominent or central personage in any remarkable action or event; one who exhibits extraordinary courage, firmness, fortitude, or intellectual greatness in the course of action."

Dr. Roche—who in recent years displayed considerable fortitude in his resistance to "affirmative action" zealots—is the president of Hillsdale College, where the heroic is not mocked by many. The man of letters who influences him most is C. S. Lewis. This latest Roche book reminds us strongly of Lewis's grim witticism, in *The Abolition of Man,* that modernists (whom Roche calls anti-heroes) "castrate, and bid the geldings be fruitful."

George Roche knows that in truth not a few heroes still live and move and have their being nowadays. We mock our own national failure in the Indo-Chinese war; yet there were many heroes among our men in Asia, and they fought with high courage, as one may learn by turning to the graphic books of S. L. A. Marshall about those campaigns. The title of his book suggests, rather, the significance of Nathaniel Hawthorne's observation: "A hero cannot be a hero unless in an heroic world." If the shapers of public opinion deny the reality of heroism—why, presently Everyman may be unable to perceive the intrepidity of those who give their lives that others may live.

Dr. Roche reminds us that heroism is a flowering of the spirit. One thinks of what Amiel wrote in his journal in 1849: "Heroism is the brilliant triumph of the soul over the flesh: that is to say, over fear; fear of poverty, of suffering, of calumny, of sickness, of isolation, and of death." Just so; and folk who deny the existence of souls come to the conclusion, logically enough, that heroism is mere fable.

Why has the belief in heroism decayed? Because of intellectual errors, Dr. Roche argues; and the errors of scientism in particular. (*Scientism*, an ideology, is a far cry from genuine science, or systematic knowledge.) For many—especially for that class which prides itself upon its intellectuality—Christian belief now seems a mass of the superstitions of the childhood of the race; and a naïve naturalism supplants two thousand years of insight into the human condition. A dogmatic Darwinism, insistent that biological assumptions of the mid-nineteenth century cannot be improved upon, corrupts the modern temper. Like Benjamin Disraeli, George Roche sides with the angels, not with the apes. A ruinous egalitarianism is one consequence of the premise that we human beings are nothing more than products of heredity and circumstance.

With considerable intellectual boldness, George Roche touches upon the power of "the wiles of hell striving against the spirit." That diabolical power is one possible cause for the assault upon heroism, he suggests. Amen to that. What T. S. Eliot called the operations of the Evil Spirit upon the imagination no longer can be disregarded by those who would maintain some tolerable private and public order.

There exist other explanations for the decay of belief in the heroic than George Roche's. Henry Adams and Brooks Adams argued that human destiny moves ineluctably through phases; that the age of chivalry is succeeded by the age of commerce, the gentleman with his sense of honor giving way to the usurer with his eagerness for gain; and the capitalist, in turn, being undone by the communist. And after that consummation? Why, then human society will rot out, the life of collectivism not being worth living.

Yet George Roche lets cheerfulness break in, near the end of this book. The politics of prudence may yet prevail over ideology; right reason may regain its seat, ousting scientism; and the adulation of mediocrity may be swept away, at crisis, by a renewed popular apprehension of the heroic.

Nearly half a century ago I wrote an essay on tragedy, one of my earlier publications. True tragedy requires heroes—even if those heroes have flaws. I venture to quote here some sentences from this piece of juvenalia.

Perhaps every age has weighed the qualities of its men against the virtues of men of other ages and has thought the worth of the living less than the worth of the dead. In this vein it is the assertion of certain critics of our day, among them Joseph Wood Krutch, that we moderns cannot write and cannot appreciate tragedies. Ours is too materialistic an age, too deeply affected by a new psychology and a new philosophy, for understanding or recording or doing noble deeds. A real tragedy must show some purpose in life, some pattern to the eternal struggle, it is said; our attempts at tragedy lack such elements. Tragedy must picture the losing fight of a noble character against elemental forces; we neither possess the noble characters nor believe in the elemental forces. The classic tragedy is as lost as the culture that called forth its heroes.

But do adherents to these views hold the right concept of the essentials of tragedy and of the nature of our world? Are they not attempting to mourn over the corpse of a tragic spirit which has not perished but has only changed its somber garments? ... Materialist critics and philosophers and psychologists have woven about themselves a net of dismaying elaborations so thick that they cannot see through its stifling strands to the realities of life. For in the world men still fight for the things they always have fought for, and often fight in vain—for their honor and for a defense of others.

Not repenting of those phrases of a callow youth, I do commend to you *A World Without Heroes,* for therein you will find comparable sentiments, more maturely expressed. Say not the struggle naught availeth.

Russell Kirk
Mecosta, Michigan

Preface

Let me offer you in sacrifice the service of my thoughts and my
tongue, but first give me what I may offer you.
                                        —St. Augustine's prayer

I believe I have been given the central understandings of this
book in exactly the sense of Augustine's prayer. If not, I might
as well have been engaged in some Soviet-style five-year plan,
with equal futility. Over and again this book has surprised its
author, always, and unerringly, turning down paths unsuspected or little known to me.

   Certainly it did not go according to plan, and I have four
or five chapters' worth of material, discarded as insufficient, to
show for it. I had had the title from the outset, along with
strong concepts of the heroic and the anti-heroic. Over years
of reading wise and fortifying books, I had assembled, copied
and organized thousands of passages—the stack of these
excerpts is over a foot high. The number of my source books
soared during two years of writing. I relate these matters
merely in evidence; for whatever my crystalline ideas of

heroism had been—and I can scarcely recall now—they were soon shown to be badly wanting. It was not so much misdirection; my illustrious mentors had spared me that. Rather, my understandings, and at times theirs, fell far short of the truth.

We had all adjudged heroism to be something "larger than life." Informed thus by heroic acts, we may say: "Here is proof that we can rise above ourselves." But at the same time we almost automatically add a reservation: "This way is open only to the few, the courageous, the bold. I could never be a hero. It is not asked of me. The way is not open to all."

But it is; and we are all asked to be heroes, each in his own circumstances.

We are misled by our perspective. In seeing the heroic as too large for ourselves, we have been deceived and cheated by man-made philosophies that see human purpose as far too small. These anti-heroic philosophies, of which we have much to say in this book, have been woven of scientific errors and prideful cravings, in rebellion against God. In sum, they constitute a sweeping denial of value and purpose to human life, setting us adrift in an existence without meaning or hope. They hate life. Over six centuries they have gained force, reaching a malignant ascendance in modern times, our times, that is destroying civilized life. They are against us. This—not conflict between classes, nations, economic systems or forms of government—is the nature of the struggle in the West. In the end, we cannot win it, save by fighting for our souls.

The struggle, in microcosm, might be conveyed in the meaning of two outwardly identical acts. From external observation, with all the instruments at our disposal and the utmost of scientific rigor, we cannot tell them apart. A consistent Darwinism must deny that either of these acts could occur at all; but they do. The anti-heroic view simply denies that either has meaning. Yet any six-year-old can easily distinguish between them. In effect, our fate depends on our willingness to believe that the distinction is real.

The acts are these: two men plunge into a river. The first intends suicide, hoping to find oblivion in death. The second, in peril of his life, leaps to save a drowning child.

Of course we distinguish these by their purposes, which are opposite. The one is an act of cowardice, the other of heroism. The first is a denial of all human values, the second is the highest affirmation of human worth. The one rates life less than nothing; the other, braving death, raises life to transcendent meaning. Both men may fail in their purpose: the would-be suicide may live, the hero may drown in his rescue attempt. Yet our judgment would not change an iota the truth that the one act is base and the other noble and supremely right. Every one of us knows this in his heart.

The anti-heroic dismisses all purpose as illusion. It sees us as helpless pawns, unable to act or even think on our own, fully shaped and determined by outside forces. It reaches this position with tortuous chains of inference, with misused "scientific assumptions" and fanciful formulas that dare to tell us what we can and cannot know, what is and is not real. But all this is contrivance, serving not the search for knowledge and truth, but the rebel's own dark purposes. And it is all belied in an instant by that one purposeful, death-defying act of a hero. That act, a reality known to us all, tells us more about the human condition than all of the empty and life-hating mutterings of modernist philosophies. It serves a Good we all may turn to for fulfillment in our lives.

The anti-hero daily, instinctively, intolerantly, in bad faith, mounts his attack on every aspect of civilized community. He attacks with twisted words and innuendos and legal persecution; increasingly his disciples turn to violence. Often he speaks to us from seemingly respectable positions: from the pulpit, in the media, in Academe. He has high-sounding arguments aplenty for his actions; it's a very easy trick. But it's a cheat. He serves not noble but reductionist and evil ends. Strip away his rationales and his hates are laid bare. In what he won't say as much as in what he will, we find him siding invariably with America's enemies, with measures that bring us into bondage, with every assault on Western liberty and religious belief. His campaign, reaching its crest over the past century, has changed us from a serene, joyful, proud, free nation to a vast, suffering bureaucracy, consumed by its "guilt" and festering "problems." The individual, denied his birthright thus, feels increasingly lost, thwarted and helpless. Where can one turn when the faith of our fathers and the goodness of this land are treated with anti-heroic contempt?

Author Marc Simmons, addressing the Western Writers of America, reached this conclusion about the group's anti-hero critics: "You see, they must discredit the Western hero because if just one person can be shown to have achieved wholeness, then it becomes evident that the possibility is open to all." It is a keen insight, addressing the whole of Western civilization, not alone the American West. Anti-heroism is precisely this, a war from withered and one-sided perspectives against all that is whole and healthy. The anti-hero, shrunken in the misery and guilt of his dissimulations, must perforce cast us all in his own image and try to bring us down to his own level. He must jeer at the hope of a better life. He must denigrate mind and morality to make bearable his own intellectual and spiritual barrenness. He must "debunk" Western literature and history and tradition, for they are stern witnesses against his rebellion. His complaints are ceaseless; we hear them everyday. He is lost, the slavering servant of the Dark Lord like Tolkien's character, Grima Wormtongue, his soul in dread of a just God, and he would bring us all to this. He shall not prevail.

There is a better life, and it is free for the asking. The value of a life well lived can only be denied, never diminished, by the anti-hero. It is still there, that satisfaction of a good life that we so hunger for now. It can be and still is claimed, as ever, by those who will have it, and in the teeth of adversity. If it is glorified by the hero, it is affirmed by every thought and act in defiance of Baal.

"A writer grimly controls his work to his peril," observed Madeleine L'Engle in *The Irrational Season*. "Slowly, slowly, I am learning to listen to the book, in the same way I listen to prayer. If the book tells me to do something completely unexpected, I heed it; the book is usually right." This has been true for me, and to it I add my own discarded chapters, a pile of wasted words, with gratitude. In seeking a whole life in a heroism larger than life, I was turned aside and gently led to see that the heroic is a seamless garment. It is as much the substance of our response to everyday tribulations—and every person faces his share of them—as to the extraordinary. If the heroic is the thunder of the great, it is also the meat and bread and wine of life in the comforting human dimension. It shines as surely in a tiny act of kindness as in the gallant defense at Thermopylae. We may seek it in the courage or fortitude of dictionary definitions of heroism; we will find it in obedience to the words, "Thy will be done."

Truly, this way is open to all.

In addressing heroism, it is my hope that we can test our latter-day beliefs from fresh and revealing perspectives. Political and economic analyses we have in surfeit. In these, the vocabulary of public affairs has become so snarled and tendentious it is virtually unusable. Empty labels pose as political theories and slogans pass for thought. More importantly, none of it cuts to the deeper level of belief that informs the modern world and is the source of our activity and direction.

Heroism is the lens we need to look at the inner human world of belief. Here we will find meanings so often lost under the roll of external events. Here, too, we will learn what we ourselves really stand for. It is not easy to look. It takes a bit of—heroism. But it is necessary that we do so, and it is worthwhile. To test our beliefs is to strengthen them. And we will need all our strength to keep the dark at bay: for a World Without Heroes is not inhabitable by men.

Writing a testamental book, Malcolm Muggeridge once suggested, may be a sign of advancing middle age. But then, it takes time to temper one's ideas against experience, and maturity to pitch out the ideas that fail. Only fools, knaves and the very young go on professing faith in utopian nostrums which, in all practical application, prove disastrous. There have been a hundred Brave New Worlds in this wretched century, seeking heaven and building hell on earth. Can we blind ourselves forever to what we do? But perhaps an end is in sight. An exhausted world wants to find its way home, and needs light to find its way. Let us, then, thank the passing years for protection against our own follies, and light what candles we can with what we have been given. At some point we learn, too, that we live as a sparrow in the hand of God. This is reason enough to say what we have to, while the time is still good, and the more reason to concern ourselves only with the true and enduring.

I am only too aware how little of one's experience and conviction one book can convey. It is but a small part of life that can be put into words, and not necessarily the best part. Charles Lindbergh observed in his *Wartime Journals,* "you write about the unusual rather than the usual, the abnormal rather than the normal. The normal in life is the most difficult to see." This is the more unfortunate, for the normal, productive, untroublesome side of life is exactly what we need to draw upon most when the world goes haywire. Yet a book may be a great comfort. It is scaled to our own pace. It takes us away from the daily duststorm of news. We read it at leisure, with time to contemplate. There is no pressure; we are free to agree or disagree as we will, and as an author, I would have it no other way. No one savors more than I a chance to push the papers aside, turn off the TV, and curl up with a book. And, for matters such as we explore in this work, only the measured pace of a book will do.

Best of all, a book fits the hands of one, where all things in life begin. Nowhere are we summoned to save the world. That has been done for us. It is a deception to think of "society" or other vast and fictitious classes of people; a conceit to demand mass "solutions" or "reforms." I am here to tell you there is no one-size-fits-all answer to our woes, and if there were, the politicians would ruin it before the day was out. Rather, if this tired old planet is to be healed, it will be the old-fashioned way, one by one, with each of us finding the best within us. We all have to be heroes!

But in this we are not alone, nor stumbling along unlit trails. The great writers of the past have prepared our way. I have, in admiration, derived much from their wisdom in this work, and acknowledge my debt to many. One of the most satisfying things about the written word is that it lets us choose our friends from any time. We are never less alone than in a library. Where I fail my mentors, the responsibility is, of course, my own.

One last virtue of a testamental book is that it reaches across generations. I write not only as a father but as an American saddened by the denial of our heritage, to the young, by anti-heroic indoctrinators. The anti-heroes, in the manner of conquerors, rewrite our history in their own vile image. Our children are being robbed of their roots and birthright, betrayed in the name of education by "activists" and "social engineers" who know no shame. There can be no greater crime against decency than abusing the young.

This too may be a sign of advancing years, that we face the eventual parting with our sons and daughters. Now this World Without Heroes threatens a parting more final than death. We must not leave our children defenseless. We must resolve to make the truth our richest legacy for them.

Toward the end of his life, Whittaker Chambers felt this need with urgency and great poignancy, watching his son leave his Maryland farm to register for military service. Chambers knew that his days were short, and that his last book, his testament, would have to say the things he had to, for his son. While I am not quite ready to call it a career, I have felt, in this work, what Chambers described so movingly in that remarkable book, *Cold Friday:*

> It seemed to me as I watched him leave that the most important thing I could do for him was to report for him how his father had viewed certain aspects of our reality, what I believed the forces of reality to be, and how I saw their origins and development, which pulverized individual men, and caught peoples, like shovelfuls of corn in a hammermill. My book should be something like what past ages used to call an enchiridion—a little dagger to arm him against the swarming night, a little dagger that might help him to cut his way among the enemies and perplexities of life. I meant no formidable treatise, for which I felt no confidence. What I had in mind was a little book to which he could turn in doubt or trouble, when he could no longer come to me.... My reward, never known by men, could be that he might one day say, "In the main, you spoke to me wisely."
>
> I have put off the task too long. Few tasks have been so difficult to begin as this book.... At the root of that feeling is the sense of hopelessness which besets most of those who have sought to carry on the struggle in our time.... The effort of recollection forces me to turn back to the horrors which no man can come through and live from day to day without putting them out of his mind.... They can be remembered only in a turmoil of the spirit that pushes the mind towards a longing for annihilation.
>
> But the greatest difficulty in writing this book is something else. It lies at the point where the book itself is a parting much more final than my son's walking up a path. I write consciously in the belief that this is probably the last effort of the kind that I shall make, a kind of summary testament, a backward reading of what I have learned from experience to this point. I am haunted by the need for truth, the fear of error, at the point of life when truth has become the one consuming need, since nothing else has real worth. My son must read this as the effort at truth, knowing that I could wish for him only what is good and true.

> I have a sense of leaving my son, that chapter by chapter puts
> us farther apart as if he were a figure compelled to watch from a
> shore another receding in a little boat.

There are things that perhaps should never be put into words—things to be felt and lived, too noble for our clumsy translation into ink on paper. The feelings that stir in us as we read these passages and share a father's feelings for his son are of this kind. We can only be grateful for them, and resolve, for our own children, to rekindle the light of the world.

This book is for all who watch from the shore.

George Roche

Introduction

"It is an unhappy country that has no heroes," says Andrea Sarti, puzzlingly, in Brecht's *Galileo*. Odder still is Galileo's reproach: "It is an unhappy country that needs heroes." What are we—dwellers in a World without Heroes—to make of this? Is there something Prince Valiant can do for us that is not being attended to by the Department of Health and Human Services?

Yet subtle clues may unlock great mysteries. And nothing is more mysterious than the dogged and pervasive unhappiness in our time. We cannot explain it. What has become of life on the human scale and the value of one life well lived?

It is bewildering. We have, after all, spent the whole of this century attacking human afflictions and social problems with the finest tools the modern mind can devise. We have applied the most enlightened theories, state-of-the-art science and advanced statecraft. We have fostered invention and built great engines of prosperity. Every source of discontent and injustice has been reformed to a fare-thee-well, and at no

1

niggardly expense. Our politicians openly beg for any new or original misfortune to overcome, and can hardly sleep nights for fear there are no disadvantaged groups left to aid or tax loopholes to plug. They have actually had to resort to solving the best problems in every session of Congress since the Great Depression. These problems are trotted out every year, faithfully, and new bureaus are created to take care of them, differing from the previous bureaus as one zebra differs from another. What more can be done? The historical record is sketchy, but I can only describe this as the greatest outpouring of caring, compassion and concern the world has ever seen. Its principal result is to make everybody cynical about politics, along with everything else. It leaves us unhappier than ever, and a good deal poorer.

But Americans are resourceful. When the system fails to provide happiness, we pursue it all the more resolutely with our own devices. To judge from cultural indexes, we are concerned with little else. The mighty mechanism we have erected to glut our senses and escape our unhappiness is a marvel to rival our science and industry. It puts at our fingertips everything from the soaps and sitcoms to hard-core porn, from fast foods to frozen beef Wellington to Club 21, from video arcades to Aspen and Cancun. Of our presumed 72 hours of leisure per week, we spend, on average, over 44 staring at the tube. Catering to every visual or tactile sensation, vicarious thrill and carnal urge, our culture promises happiness in every measure, for every purse, to every taste. We pursue it till we are weary, but can never hold it long.

For in the end there is no escape. Perhaps one day we wake up emptied, unable to try one more taste or seek one more liaison or even change channels, wondering what it was all about. Perhaps we will conclude, at last, that it is time to put the externals aside, and instead, seek to self-actualize our happiness from within. We will then find another subculture ready to cater to our new determination. It grinds out articles unending on self-betterment techniques and more meaningful relationships. It peddles its secrets at retreats, on cassettes, in seminars. It fills the paperback racks with how-to counseling. Every month another nostrum hits the market with a new, improved promise of Life Experience Enrichment. Like addicts, we swallow every one, no matter how inane, occult or bizarre. We scurry from self-analysis to group encounters to Eastern religions to alternative lifestyles to X-R-cycles to whatever's big in California. We make "getting it together" the national pastime. But again, the fixes wear off. And the maddening thing is, the more carefully and determinedly we follow each prescription, the quicker happiness dances out of reach—only to leave us more frustrated and miserable than ever.

We had better climb off the carousel and listen to Sarti. His statement about our condition is light years away from the things we usually hear: "It is an unhappy country that has no heroes." He is speaking of us.

But what are heroes, and how can they make us happier? The how-to books and counselors of holistic self-actualized OKness have nothing to say about this. If their theories are valid, indeed, heroes are of a kind with naiads, spooks and Mother Goose, and equally irrelevant. (There is nothing that would alarm the modern world quite so much as a real, mutually verifiable spook.) They would say the "real world" precludes heroism, and point to today's hero-less world as proof. But the same thinking would rule out Mother Teresa.

We'll have to explore these matters without counsel. In truth, the question is less about heroes than about the frameworks of belief in which they can, and cannot, flourish. In the end it concerns what we ourselves believe and ask of life. What the hero gives us is a completely fresh, unfailed way of looking at it. To honest seekers, it promises the answer to our pervasive, mysterious unhappiness.

Heroes are a fading memory in our times, but we can still recall a little about them. We know, at least, that what sets the hero apart is some extraordinary achievement. Whatever this feat, it is such as to be recognized at once by everyone as a good thing; and somehow, the achieving of it seems larger than life. Even by this sparse definition, the hero's deed rebukes us. We have been struggling frantically, merely to achieve the ordinary: that measure of happiness each of us is supposedly entitled to. The hero, in contrast, overcomes the ordinary and attains greatness, by serving some great good. His example tells us that we fail, not by aiming too high in life, but by aiming far too low. More, it tells us we are mistaken in supposing that happiness is a right or an end in itself. The hero seeks not happiness but goodness, and his fulfillment lies in achieving it. His satisfaction, such as it may be, is thus a result: a reward, if you please, for doing good. This path to happiness is open to all, not just heroes, and until modern times nobody believed there was any other. To pursue happiness for its own sake, it was believed, was the surest way to lose it.

Modern experience certainly bears this out. If nothing else, then, the hero yanks us out of the old rut and bids us to reexamine our values and goals. At the same time, he shows us by his own example that higher purposes in life, far from being an illusion, are the key to our richest potentials. This already is much more than the how-to books can promise. But you and I are not called on to be heroes—or are we? To see, we'll have to find the mainsprings of heroism.

Of course, not every extraordinary act is heroic, so it will help to see who is not a hero. I have in mind the most common "hero" in media usage, the mere high achiever: a rock idol, say, or the sports star who makes a key play. However fine the performance, there is simply nothing heroic in doing what one is exceedingly well paid to do. It bothers me no little that such as these are designated our finest. We have shabby ideals indeed if we have no nobler models for our young people to look up to; if we hunger for no more than glitter and easy money. But I don't think this is so at all. That we hunger for heroes at all is a good sign, even if it is only vicariously, through a great athlete or a Luke Skywalker on the screen.

Real heroism requires courage. It entails peril or pain. My dictionary says heroes are "distinguished by valor or enterprise in danger, or fortitude in suffering." One thinks of Lindbergh, who pitted his courage against the Atlantic and won, or Earhart, who pitted hers against the Pacific and lost. It was, precisely, bravery that exalted their acts. Still—and without detracting from their prodigious accomplishments— we know that both acted in calculated self-interest, and somehow this too seems to fall short of the heroic. Lindbergh and Earhart surely made our way easier through their courage in pioneering flight, but they did not make it nobler.

Plainly, heroism also has a selfless quality. The hero's deed is ennobled not alone by courage but by the call to duty or by service to others. In this it gains a larger symbolic value that can inspire and bind a whole nation. The hero acts for what is common and precious to all, and thereby replenishes the strength of our shared convictions. Our own courage grows larger just to recall John Hancock, who so deliberately risked all, or Dr. Joseph Warren and Nathan Hale, who gave all, for American independence. Lincoln, who suffered and died to end slavery and preserve the union, was a hero. The medal of honor winner touches our spirit, even as the champions of old, like Hector or Leonidas at Thermopylae. Fortitude equally uplifts the whole community. Helen Keller, overcoming impossible adversity, turned life into radiance. The fabulously gifted Simone Weil found joy in suffering and finally starved, lest she touch one crumb more than the ration in Nazi-occupied France.

These are heroes by any standard, and our debt to them is immeasurable. *Why do we honor none like them today?* Surely this is a clear sign of our own faltering convictions and failing courage. Our debt to heroes is no metaphor, but the substance of free society. It is our duty to one another and to moral law, a duty exemplified at its highest by the hero's own selflessness. We have not kept our end of the bargain. The very words we need to think about heroes—valor, magnanimity, fortitude, gallantry—rust from our disuse. How did we let things get so big, and life so small? When the Germans marched Pastor Bonhoeffer out to be executed (as they methodically recorded), his face was "shining with happiness." And happiness eludes us! The hero, turning life and even death into triumph, heralds the transcendent purpose to our lives that we have long ridiculed, and now sorely need. "A loss of courage may be the most striking feature which an outside observer notices in the West in our days," writes

Solzhenitsyn, adding: "Should one point out that from ancient times decline in courage has been considered the beginning of the end?"

Sarti is right. The moral relativism that saturates modern thought can produce neither heroes nor happiness. "A man who bows down to nothing," Dostoevsky observed, "can never bear the burden of himself." So too with nations. No civilization has ever arisen except on a religious basis, and none can maintain itself except as it is informed by absolute morality. It is faith held in common that civilizes, that holds men's animal self-interest at bay, and shapes a just law and community. Such freedom and security as we still enjoy are readily traced to the Judeo-Christian foundations of the West. But the central faith must be constantly guarded and renewed, not least by heroism, lest the bonds between men dissolve. Even barbarians know and yield to this. Carthage sought its cruel efficiency in demon worship, and threw its children into the glowering furnaces of Baal.* The "evil empire" denies God, but is very careful to preserve all the trappings of its Marxist pseudo-faith, and keeps its imitation savior, Lenin, on display in Moscow, stuffed like a prize tarpon. When belief dims, as it did at the end in Rome, no amount of force can hold the community together. Indeed, we will inevitably find that the amount of institutional coercion in any society is a perfect (and endlessly useful) measure of the falsity of its inner belief. The hero bespeaks these facts. He emerges only in that healthy community based on an objective moral order, and he

---

*It has been the unfailing practice of witchcraft and Devil worship throughout history to abuse innocent children. Can anyone be certain that the same impulse does not guide the abortion mills in this country, and the Soviet practice of dropping booby-trapped toys to maim children in Afghanistan?

in turn, by deed and symbol, replenishes its spiritual strength. We cannot evoke or even recognize heroism without a common faith.

The absent hero is thus a symptom of a paralyzing moral division in America. If our knight rode out and slew a dragon, half the editorials the next day would brand him "insensitive" if not an outright warmonger, and remind us that dragons are on the endangered species list. If we cannot agree that dragons are evil, we will have no dragon fighters. Unhappy the country that loses its moral bearings! Unhappy the many, bereft of spiritual leadership, who are doomed to cling to the self as the only reality in an unfathomable existence. Small wonder we fling ourselves on the treadmills of sensation, and turn for our redemption to the purveyors of clinically tested guilt-free "selfs."

For the same reasons, the whole of Western civilization in our times has been a World Without Heroes, in poor health and as unhappy as we. Diagnosing the ills of the West is a popular pastime, particularly among those who wish it ill. The patient has been pronounced terminal, or a candidate for euthanasia (if not summary execution), too many times to count. I think it is making a remarkable recovery, though not yet out of danger. And not being one who prefers the blessings of the Dark Ages to civilization, I count the news as nothing but good.

True enough, the West has long suffered an affliction of the spirit. Its most familiar carrier is secular humanism, that vision that has so strongly shaped this century and its "isms." Out of pride, it deified men's science and cut us off from the riches of life beyond the reach of laboratory instruments. Out of a lust for earthly power, it created a purely materialistic—

and entirely fictitious—conception of reality. To secure man's status as creator of the new reality, it dismissed the old Creator and announced that hereafter the universe belonged to the most intelligent of the anthropoid apes (a notion greatly cherished by some to this day). Human beings, in their quest for the stars, were therefore relegated to the status of beasts, and beasts, moreover, directed by nothing more than natural selection and economic principles. (Another notion still relished in some circles, not least the behavioral sciences.) The West is regaining its health in exact proportion to putting aside this whole banquet of utopian claptrap.

Is it any wonder that the pinnacle of philosophy for young manhood this past century has been "go get yours"? With Albert Jay Nock, I defy the whole of this utopian theory to produce any behavior higher than what can be explained by the formula of Tolstoy's peasant character, Yashvin: "He is after my shirt, and I am after his shirt." There, in a nutshell, is the sum philosophy of evolutionary theory, better remembered as the law of the jungle. If utopianism is to be believed, we animal-men cannot possibly rise above this, and therefore can have no complaint about the predatory statism and slavery of our time. Chesterton warned us, if men won't believe in God, the danger is not that they will believe in nothing, but that they will believe in anything.

Malcolm Muggeridge, surveying the wreckage of humanist utopianism in this century, offers a more specific fate: "When mortal men try to live without God, they infallibly succumb to megalomania, or erotomania, or both. The raised fist or the raised phallus; Nietzsche or D. H. Lawrence." So it has proven. The Soviets officially choose the one, and we informally the other, but it is only too obvious we both suffer the same infection. We misread our dilemma—and hugely underestimate our peril, I fear—if we suppose that the nature of world struggle is geographic, or economic, or one system of government versus another. The conflict is between our Christian heritage and secular power, between keeping the faith and having none, between God and clever monkeys who are astonished at their ability to add and subtract. The conflict is between irreconcilable conceptions of man, the universe, and ultimate reality. C. S. Lewis, as usual, put our choice in plain words: "The Christian and the materialist hold different beliefs about the universe. They can't both be right. The one who is wrong will act in a way which simply doesn't fit the real universe. Consequently, with the best will in the world, he will be helping his fellow creatures to their destruction." This is only too evident. And which has steered the modern world to Belsen and the Gulag?

Here Galileo demands to be heard, but he is one of the false claimants to the universal truth we seek. In few words he gets to the heart of just that humanist vision that has grown in the West since the days of the real Galileo Galilee: "It is an unhappy country that needs heroes." We can almost hear him add with a growl, "Grow up, you fools! Don't you know that you yourself possess the greatest power there is? You have the highest intelligence and the will to use it. You wallow in unhappiness because you are waiting for others to lead you and to do what is every man's duty. You need no heroes! It is your own reason and determination that must attack the ancient wrongs of mankind, and take control of man's destiny."

Here are the marching orders of Scientific Man to adherents of the humanist vision; or to put it less gently, the communist's remonstrations to liberals. How odd, and ironic, to hear them from one named Galileo—the biblical "Man from Galilee" versus the new, science versus superstition! Brecht must have been tickled. For the record, we should recall that the playwright finished *Galileo* in the late 1930s, during a period of peak revolutionary sentiment, that after the war he forsook his refuge in America (erotomania) to live out his years in East Germany (megalomania), and that he won a Stalin Peace Prize. There is no doubting the pedigree; not that we should judge Galileo's ideal on that account. From the empiricism and concept of absolute time of the original Galileo it grew; from Newton's infinite, dead, uncaring clockwork universe it gathered momentum; from classical mechanics, from positivist and "God-is-irrelevant" philosophies of the last century—from Feuerbach, Comte, Kant, Marx, Darwin, Hegel and Nietzsche, it reached flood stage. Ideas have consequences. The sentiment rapidly spread that "philosophers have explained the world; now men must change the world." Not heroes: all men of conviction.

Galileo's is an ancient faith, man's second oldest, as old as Eden, but reanimated by the seemingly invincible science of the nineteenth century: "ye shall be as gods." It is the vision of Man without God, of Man at the center of being, autonomous, free of external controls and in command of his own destiny. It is the promise of a new man and of a new world given purpose and plan by Man, the new creator. Its brutal strength lies in the dream of an avenging angel that will fill men's hunger for justice at last, not in any imaginary heaven but here and now, by sweeping away all that is weak and unclean. Its great commandment, Whittaker Chambers remarked, "is found, not in the Communist Manifesto, but in the first sentence of a physics primer: 'All of the progress of mankind to date results from the making of careful measurements.'"

Such a brew of science and vision is without historical parallel, and it struck the Western mind with tidal force. It purported to fit the older Christian foundations, both in the natural sciences, where the concept of an ordered cosmos was retained, and in the moral perceptions of justice and right that it borrowed from Christianity. The Marxists had only to substitute the power of the State for the authority of God and promise a socialist New Jerusalem in place of eternal life, to stay in business at the old stand. To a certain frame of mind it was, and is, irresistible. Men seized it with joy, and later yielded their conviction to reality with fierce reluctance or not at all—the signature of potent dogma. On its surface it seems a vision of good, and it has moved millions of good hearts. To a Christian, it is the original sin and the greatest of heresies.

By its own view and the Christian alike, "good" is the one thing the vision and its works cannot be. The natural universe, it holds, is all there is, and there is no good or evil in it; only natural events. Why, then, does Galileo exhort his flock to their duty? What drives men to suffer and die for communism and a better world, when their own doctrines deny any possibility of betterment? It is the fact, known to all men even if they deny it, that good does exist in this world. Every act of heroism affirms it; every act of kindness and mercy, charity and fair play affirms it. The naturalistic universe is built on contradiction. It is an irrational cosmos conceived by rational men. If they were right, we could have no reason to believe their reasoning. It is a dead, uncaring, amoral cosmos, conceived by living, moral men. If they were right they would destroy the basis of their preachments. We can no more deduce goodness from natural events than we can fathom the meaning of the Sistine Chapel by analyzing its component minerals. It is, finally, a determinist universe conceived by willful men. If they were right, how could they have chosen to study the universe and declare that we are all automatons, mindlessly responding to the dance of the atoms? That is what B. F. Skinner tells us, even now. By his own premises, he has no mind to say so.

The intellectuals of a century ago, presumably caretakers of reason and non-contradictory thought, believed this nonsense, and some believe it now. But time has passed them by. A brutal century has shown the insanity of their dreams. (The legal definition of insanity is the inability to distinguish between right and wrong: the central feature of Galileo's gospel.)

The vision is stone dead today, an empty husk. Its cherished "scientific" basis was destroyed seven decades ago—by science—and cannot be restored. It has no future whatever. Only its shadow survives, a suppurating malevolence toward the unconquered human soul. Everywhere its theories have been put into practice, its works have proven unspeakably cruel and murderous. Not once has even a hint of the secular New Jerusalem been created. The dumbfounding mystery for us is that this dark vision moves men still. We must find out why.

Somehow, Galileo's hopeless rebellion remains on the march. No, not in so many words; we all abjure expressions of our innermost faith. But we hear its echoes and theories from innumerable voices in the academy, in public life, and in the media; and from a thousand ostensibly Christian pulpits is preached the gospel of the godless cosmos. One can scarcely tune in the evening news without hearing the message half a dozen times. In fact, the remaining faithful share a private amusement, the thrill of covert preaching for "the cause," with no little success. Their media positions let them shape reality for millions who read their papers and magazines, and millions more glued to the tube. The vision is lifeless, but its institutions are intact, its armies remain in the field, and its superstitions still ricochet through public life, causing no end of trouble.

This is the sickness of the West. When I say that the patient is not out of danger, it is because there is no telling what embittered visionaries will do in the death throes of their drama. The world is bristling with conventional and nuclear arms, and Galileo's legions deny the one compelling reason not to use them: the moral basis of human life.

Future historians—if the "progressive" movement allows any future—may well date the demise of the humanist vision to 1917, the year Einstein published the last installment of his epochal theory, entitled "The Cosmological Considerations of General Relativity." Here was presented a new and eerie concept of the universe, shocking the scientific world with its finitude and its refutation of absolute measure of length, space or time. Newton's infinite clockwork was banished, and with it, any plausible basis for secular humanism. There is no naturalist explanation for Einstein's universe. Finite in all dimensions, it is the very essence of a contingent and purposefully created entity, dependent upon a supernature outside of itself for existence, and given order—the basis of scientific law—by a "Supreme Legislator." Scientists again began to speak of a created universe, albeit very clumsily. God, after a brief, and one hopes, refreshing death of 31 years, had reappeared. (Nietzsche had written the famous obituary in 1886, with some apprehension: "The greatest event of recent times—that 'God is Dead,' that the belief in the Christian God is no longer tenable—is beginning to cast its first shadows over Europe.") Men were relieved of their duty to be clever apes, and could once again look forward to uniquely human life, informed and fulfilled by its ability to look above itself.

It was not yet to be. Einstein's theory was badly misunderstood from the first by its would-be interpreters, with calamitous effects on thought that linger to this day. Its religious implications were simply ignored, being indigestible to utopian plans. Popularizers seized on the queer aspect of the theory, mistaking the "relativity" of space, time and length in the natural realm for "relativism" in the moral law. The public was soon reciting the mistake, which ludicrously reduced "Einstein" to seven words: "everything is relative" and "there are no absolutes." It was argued that good and evil, right and wrong, were therefore not absolute standards, or even real, but merely relative values to be juggled at the convenience of any culture. In truth, General Relativity is the most absolutist cosmological theory ever put forward. Einstein himself believed passionately in absolute right and wrong and detested the moral relativism which was attributed to his theory, and which he thought a disease. Nevertheless, moral relativism swiftly became pandemic through Europe and the West. It is at the heart of liberal theology and humanist doctrine even now. In this, I believe, we find the fatal collapse of the old vision into incoherence and evil.

Where once it had sought the good of man, albeit a good borrowed from Christianity and perverted, under moral relativism it gave itself, body and soul, to an insatiable will to power. It has been the pharaoh's harlot ever since.

The oracles of the day, peering at Relativity, declared that the world had gone mad and life was meaningless. Only the strong survive, said the ideologues, concluding that anything goes. Cultural decadence set in with startling speed. Wrote Albert Jay Nock, "The unmistakable mark of degeneracy which stood out on the period's attempts at artistic production was an intense and conscious preoccupation with the subjective. As Goethe remarked, all eras in a state of decline and dissolution are subjective...." Art turned surreal, and literature brewed Freud and the absurd to capture the "new reality," with Marcel Proust and James Joyce in the van. Historian Paul Johnson later observed, *"A la Recherche* and *Ulysses* marked not merely the entrance of the anti-hero but the destruction of individual heroism as a central element in imaginative creation, and a contemptuous lack of concern for moral balance-striking and verdicts." The whole humanist enterprise, since its unconditional surrender to moral relativism in the 1920s, has been, precisely, the world of the anti-hero, and hereafter I will use that term to refer to its adherents. All that they influence, build, or find is what I call a World Without Heroes.

Ironically, 1917 also marked the United States entry into the Great War, starting a trend to Old World-style statism that continues unchecked today. In the process, the old American values of individual responsibility and liberty have been pushed aside, to our enduring loss, by an immense, suffocating, bureaucratized central government. Someday we had better remember that strong government is for weak people and vice versa.

In a richer irony, it was in 1917 that Lenin seized power in Russia and put all that good, hungry utopian theory at the service of the state. Murders for ideological reasons began almost at once, continue every day even now, and may well have averaged 4,000 to 6,000 a day throughout the empire ever since (mass murderers do not oblige us with accurate bookkeeping, but this estimate has a good deal to recommend it). For such as these, a bag of 269 more innocent people on KAL Flight 007 is no big deal; but the pilot did get a medal. I have not counted the "heretic" member of the family, Germany, which borrowed Lenin's ideas about concentration camps, scientific oppression of the masses, and extermination of a hated class, and returned them with Teutonic efficiency to slaughter millions more. What else did anybody expect from regimes that mock God and declare that the only morality is their own self-interest? What great numbers of star-struck Western anti-heroes expected, in fact, was Utopia. In a steady stream throughout it all, even at the height of Stalin's purges or his "liquidation of the kulaks" (which murdered more people in one winter than Hitler's Holocaust), even today, they make their holy pilgrimages to Moscow, to see the wonders of the New Jerusalem with their own eyes, make obeisance to the reigning barbarian chieftain, and bring the good news (and a few cheap medals) back to their wavering comrades.

Visions die hard! It is a blessing and a great human strength that this is so. But political theories, however attractive, must pass the test of experience. If they are in harmony with human nature and the real world, they will bear good fruit; if not, they will reveal their error by the unending misery they cause. "Let me taste the dish," said Brillat-Savarin, "and you can spare yourself the rhetoric on how well you cook." The supreme folly is to make our theories magic and blind ourselves to their rank results. There is no utopia. What the pilgrims see, or believe from afar, is their heart's desire— not the drab life, food lines, police omnipresence and 2,000 slave labor camps of the Gulag; not the cold-blooded military dictatorship that actually exists.

The anti-hero congregation should be shattered by the scientific refutation of Galileo's vision, but it barely twitches. It is not even repentant when it ought to be in anguish over the unrelieved failure of "rationally planned society," engineered at such numbing human cost. How can it remain unmoved? Is it that to break faith now would confess an unbearable guilt? Do the anti-heroes still hope for the hopeless? This is the mystery we have to penetrate, for our own sake—to restore purpose and a human scale to our lives, and to minister to the West. For this, I'd like to call another hero as my last witness. His heroism is quite different from any we have examined, and he has something to say to each of us.

The heroes we have met all affirm, by their very deeds, the larger spiritual dimension to life. Simone Weil was not moved to joy in suffering by a vision of *homo oeconomicus*. The champion is not inspired to gallantry by his appreciation of differential equations. Materialist conceptions may purport to tell us what we are, but cannot touch our souls because, in last analysis, they cannot tell us what we should be. There is no "should" in the materialist cosmos: nor can it produce heroes. Galileo missed the point. If his world view had been true, there would be no arguments about needing heroes, because we would never have found out what heroism is.

My final hero tells us that life can be what it should be. It is a person who does not fit the heroic mold at all, and from whom, perhaps, we should least expect great or heroic deeds. This hero has been with us all along, and discharges his duty without giving a second thought to fashionable theories of the times. It could be anybody. It could be you. "Ordinary" people do heroic things every day that are simply unthinkable to the anti-hero conception of life. And we all know it. How else would we recognize Mother Teresa as a saint? J. R. R. Tolkien understood our extraordinary powers well in creating the *Lord of the Rings* trilogy. Hobbits, he said, "are made small . . . mostly to show up, in creatures of very small physical power, the amazing and unexpected heroism of ordinary men 'at a pinch.'"

My witness could be Lenny Skutnik. He may be the best known of my "ordinary" heroes because his heroism—indeed "amazing and unexpected"—was shown on television. You remember: the man who dove into the icy Potomac to rescue a survivor of an airplane crash a few years ago. It could be the man in that same crash who gave his life to be sure that rescuers picked up all the other survivors first. It could be the small boy who saved his father's life by lifting an automobile under which the man was pinned and dying. I think of the three-year-old who, instead of fleeing, went upstairs in a burning house to wake and save his mother. The young football pro who went to the aid of youngsters floundering in a gravel pit, knowing full well he himself could barely swim. He drowned. The paperboy who braved an inferno to lead an elderly woman to safety. He survived, but suffered serious burns.

You know these stories. They are a commonplace in the news, though often buried in the back sections of the papers with a mere human interest tag. They mean much more than that, and they occur far too frequently to be glossed over as a fluke. One recent report mentioned 35 local heroes who had saved as many lives or more. These were heroes assembled by one organization in a medium-sized city for one year. There must have been others, even there.

Greater love hath no man.... Risking or laying down one's life to save another is heroism laid bare. It is a purely selfless and beneficent act. There is no more striking example of our unique human contact with an Eternal Good. And none against which our supposed status as clever apes looks more foolish. Are there any beasts that affirm values higher than life by willingly making the supreme sacrifice? The anti-heroes are unduly fond of demanding a scientific explanation for everything. Very well, let them explain heroism.

According to all good "Galilean" science, the hero's deed is impossible. The whole weight of Darwinian evolutionary theory insists that we are no more than products of a blind struggle for existence, and that the sum of our behavior is explainable as, and only as, survival strategy. The epiphe-nomenalist contortions that begin with this formula are wondrous to behold. We either have to deny all spiritual values, or somehow batter them into a Darwinian script, along with beauty, reason, imagination, humor, literature, art and any number of other deucedly awkward human qualities, and thought itself. The hero makes things worse. He follows an "anti-survival" strategy, obviously just the opposite of what evolutionary theory predicts. This is not a small matter. In science, the exception does not prove the rule; it disproves the theory. To my mind it is simply inconceivable to reduce heroism to an attribute of natural selection. It is the epitome of extranatural behavior, and we find it nowhere else in Nature.

Doubtless the pained evolutionist will rush forward here to hypothesize (the scientific term for guess) that natural selection has conditioned us with an instinct (the scientific term for animal behavior we do not understand) to preserve our species: hence an impulse to aid one another in distress. It doesn't work. He has already hypothesized a stronger instinct for self-preservation. How to choose? If "at a pinch" we merely yield to the stronger impulse, we save ourselves and let the victim die. Heroes disprove this every day. If in fact we choose, then the faculty we use to do so cannot itself be an instinct or evolutionary conditioning. It has to be a higher faculty capable of moral decision. Even supposing we had a strong impulse to risk our lives for others, it is a wholly different matter whether we *ought to obey it* in preference to other impulses. The moral question cannot be avoided. This all comes back to the same thing. We cannot possibly deduce the hero's moral courage from the amoral, determinist "dance of the atoms" hypothesized in the natural world. Heroism is not a "natural event." The universe itself is not a natural event unless it summoned itself into existence out of the void—a most unscientific miracle. We can't have it both ways. If Galileo's theories prevail, values are nonsense. Conversely, if we have a spiritual nature and have reference to a real moral law, then we are in some manner cast "in the image" of our Creator. According to the hero, we are responsible to God.

Other lines of inquiry prove equally fruitless. There is no sense of the champion in "ordinary" heroism, so we cannot account for it—as if that were easy!—by citing patriotism or battle-trained courage. Reason does not explain it. Reason, given half a moment, tells us to call the fire department. Try any anti-heroic theory, and heroism remains stubbornly extra-natural. The fascinating thing is that we *do* try any and every theory—that we twist so long and hard to avoid the obvious truth that the hero acts in conscience. Why is it so important to anti-hero thinking to downplay or deny human conscience?

The last hope for the anti-hero is that heroes themselves can shed a different light on this. And indeed, our intrepid on-the-scene reporters rarely miss a chance to ask them why they did it. You'll find that their answers, understandably, are almost always vague and self-effacing: "Well, I had to do something" or "That kid woulda died" or "Shucks, I'm no hero, anybody would have done the same." (Mr. Skutnik offered just such a disclaimer.) That doesn't tell us much, at first glance. But think about it. Surely it is very odd that heroes accept so unquestioningly the ultimate moral responsibility?

I'm increasingly convinced that there is much more to the story. Consider the inarticulateness, the sameness of the "I just knew" testimonies, the almost unseemly modesty. I get a picture that something, well, eerie occurs in the crises. Heroes seem to experience some instantaneous and total awareness that "this is it." They "just knew." That is not at all like a rational assessment of a critical situation, which anybody can describe, but more like the voice of conscience, in a megadose. There seem to be no words to it, no message, no threats, no arguments, but rather an overwhelming knowledge of "some thing to be neither more nor less nor other than *done,*" in

George MacDonald's phrase. Whatever this strange awareness may be, it is no respecter of organized religion, as it seems to occur in people of any faith or none.

We'll have to do the best we can with a sense that can barely be described, much less vouchsafed. Yet I think it is a clue. What strikes me is that the same sort of experience has been mentioned elsewhere, in entirely different contexts. C. S. Lewis, as a young atheist wrestling with God, recorded a "moment of wholly free choice." Even so gifted a writer as Lewis could only vaguely describe the experience, though it was intense and affected him deeply: "Without words and (I think) almost without images, a fact about myself was somehow presented to me. I became aware...." Lewis, this once, sounds strikingly like the tongue-tied hero. It is tempting to speculate that God takes a direct hand in the moment of crisis: that it is Rightness itself that is "somehow presented to" the hero. What would a communication from God be like, if not this: something we know perfectly but cannot put into words afterwards; something outside regular channels, as it were?

I do not pretend to have the answer. Yet we do at least know that heroism is an extraordinary act of goodness, performed by "ordinary" persons from whom we do not expect it. Lewis wrote elsewhere, "There is nothing indulgent about the Moral Law. It is hard as nails. It tells you to do the straight thing, and it does not seem to care how painful, or dangerous, or difficult it is to do." Heroism is precisely this, obedience to Moral Law despite all pain or peril. In this sense, the hero experiences Morality directly: he obeys God's will. Did he have any choice? Lewis thought so, but faced the question frankly: "I felt myself being, there and then, given a free choice. I could open the door or keep it shut ... no threat or promise was attached.... The choice appeared to be momentous, but it was also strangely unemotional. I was moved by no desires or fears.... I say, 'I chose,' yet it did not really seem possible to do the opposite.... You could argue that I was not a free agent, but I am inclined to think that this came nearer to being a perfectly free act than most ... perhaps a man is most free when, instead of producing motives, he could only say, 'I am what I do'" *(Surprised by Joy)*.

Well, no. What is scientific law but a pale and subjective grasp of some tiny part of God's actions? All scientific findings have the nature of brute fact, entirely meaningless in themselves. We cannot interpret them, nor even assume they are more than a statistical fluke valid in this corner of creation, unless we have already acknowledged God's sovereignty over the cosmos. It is no accident that modern science arose from a specifically Christian cosmology. Dante put it elegantly: "All things preserve a mutual order, and this it is that maketh the Universe like unto God." Science, far from having any divine qualities—omniscience, omnipotence, immortality—will survive only as long as it implicitly acknowledges God's order.

Personal responsibility is the ultimate bugaboo of the anti-heroes. To mention our duty to obey God is shockingly bad manners in anti-hero sanctuaries, which include no few supposedly Christian churches. The anti-heroes will take any pains to deny duty, hence transcendent purpose, in human life. They construct great theories of a dead, uncaring universe to be free of responsibility: where there is no possibility of infinite personal disaster; where we can just be carefree beasts, and death ends all—a universe with an exit sign. But is that how it really is? They construct whole behavioral sciences to blame our every difficulty on "social conditions" or a bad environment or a hateful class: anything but sin; and an infallible signature of their dogma is to call for government remedies to all problems: anything but individual responsibility and right conduct. But is that how it really is? They construct positivist philosophies—based on the incredible idea that only empirical sciences can produce valid knowledge—to deny all human spiritual nature beyond the reach of scientific instruments. Reason itself is beyond science. Therefore (ahem), reason cannot produce valid knowledge, and it follows (ahem) that the findings of empirical science, and the doctrines of positivism, can be valid only if illogical. This is the sort of pickle we get into when we go to any extreme to deny responsibility. Worse, under positivism, the truth is always hostage to future scientific discovery, and thus can never be known. But is that the way it really is?

And at last, unconscious of the irony, the anti-heroes come to the presumption of dictating to God what kind of God they will have before them. Hegel's *Geist,* the Absolute, the Great Spirit, will do very nicely, thank you. Nifty abstractions can be safely fenced off at an infinite distance from the affairs of men. The unapproachable divine would have too much taste to meddle with its lowly creatures. It would never dream of snooping into our private business, nor of tampering with that magnificent creature, Nature, nor of making *demands* on us. It would allow us our personal space. Never, ever, would it say: "Be ye therefore perfect." But is that the way it is?

Not if heroes are heroes. Not if Mother Teresa loves babies or Pastor Bonhoeffer laughed at death or if "ordinary" people will risk their lives to save another of God's children. Autonomous Man is still in there pitching, but he is a cruel superstition: his flock is not happy and never will be. Anti-heroes deny everything but the self, and thereby deny all that can make the self unique and precious and happy. "The one principle of hell," said George MacDonald, "is, 'I am my own.'"

Heroes are all who obey God in small matters as well as great. Heroes are all who keep the commandments, nurture their family, and pay their way in life without complaint, no matter how burdensome the anti-heroes' taxes become (God asks only 10%, and that's voluntary). Few of us are called on to brave fire or flood, but everyday matters are quite enough to deal with in moral responsibility, God knows. Yet it is promised that no burden shall be too great.

Heroes are individuals. They come one by one, each in his unique way. The collective is, literally, unreal. We all belong to countless contrived collectives—member of this, member of that, member of society—but what does any boil down to except an aggregate of real and unique people? Does anybody spend full time exhibiting the characteristics of a member of a union or the PTO, or of being an American citizen? Have you ever spent one minute trying to act like a "member of society"? Of course not. Nobody ever has. Yet any number of anti-hero idiots make handsome livings pretending to divine the workings of society and claiming to speak for you, its certified member. If we are to achieve that noble abstraction called a good society, who, pray, will inhabit it save the human material we have now? How can it be "good" unless *we* are good? The only path to a better future is the old one: each of us trying to better ourselves and to present society with "one improved member."

In short, we have to be heroes ourselves, and live by the words, "Thy will be done." After that everything is fun. Turn off the TV and read a book. Play with your children. Start a garden. Write an overdue love letter to your mother and father. Snub a politician. Down with abstract models, down with power, down with Big. Life and love are person to person. Love thy neighbor: even politicians. Get out of yourself and live.

Chapter I
The Failing Light

The Sea of Faith
Was once, too, at the full, and round earth's shore
Lay like the folds of a bright girdle furled.
But now I only hear
Its melancholy, long, withdrawing roar,
Retreating, to the breath
Of the night wind, down the vast edges drear
And naked shingles of the world.
> —Matthew Arnold (*Dover Beach*)

Er nennt's Vernunft, und braucht's allein
Nur tierischer als jede Tier zu sein.*
> —The Devil, in Goethe's *Faust*

Every man becomes the image of the God he adores. He whose worship is directed to a dead thing becomes a dead thing. He who loves corruption rots. He who loves a shadow becomes, himself, a shadow.

> —Thomas Merton

---

*Man calls it reason and uses it simply to be more beastly than any beast.

We live in deepening shadow.

For a century, the seers among us have sensed a faltering of faith in the West. From Spengler to Solzhenitsyn, they have warned us with one voice of decline and the gathering dark. To Weaver, ours is the gloom of a deep abyss from which men no longer have a way to raise themselves. To Muggeridge, the "twilight of a spent civilization." To Nock, the onset of a new dark age.

As the shadow deepens, seemingly only those consumed by their own shady allegiances or by after-hours diversions remain unconcerned. In different ways, more thoughtful persons at every level express unease, bewilderment or fear. Where the learned may speak of "alienation" or a "psychological epidemic" or a "loss of values," the unschooled might with equal insight say, "It has all got too big," or simply, "Something is wrong, very wrong." Some would say life is no longer in right proportion, that it does not seem whole. Others see a lack of serenity, direction or human dignity. Yet others rail at immorality and depreciation of the value of life. The poet asks, have men forgotten what it is to be human? A Russian peasant, quoted by Solzhenitsyn, said only, "Men have forgotten God." They all mean the same thing. They all speak of the shadow. They all share the feeling that something terribly important has gone out of our lives, that somewhere, we know not just how, we made a wrong turning, and now cannot find our way home. Our old certitudes about our place in the order of things have crumbled. Are we being unmade as men? What are we, and what is our home?

These are cries of the soul. They flow to us less from observed experience than from feelings of loss and yearning. We learn nothing of them from the blare of the day's news. In papers or the glow of the tube, the pop oracles do not answer, or answer falsely. There we find but a welter of discrete "events" without meaning. Today there have been such-and-such crimes, tax increases, disasters, terrorist acts—cut away to a commercial showing luscious young Californians at the beach, in radiant health, ecstatically chugging a soft drink. All is well. All goes according to plan. Man does not live by bread alone, but by a balanced diet, an effective deodorant, sex, the acquisition of things, and more things, and more sex. You only go around once in life, so ya gotta reach for all the gusto you can. It doesn't matter what you believe as long as you believe something. Every day in every way, one gets a little richer, a little more assertive, a little more consciousness-raised, and, if this were not enough, average life expectancies are increasing. Yes, all goes exceedingly well. Hear, pilgrim, the CPI stabilized, the GNP is rising, and the DJIA jumped 20.625 today in moderately heavy trading. Who could ask for anything more? Such is the unending slaver of our oracles, and we soak it all in. We believe batting averages, the Fed's monetary aggregates, opinion polls, and the government's index of leading economic indicators. We do not believe the prophets.

This is what we ask of life. This is what we spend our dollars for. Why, then, are so many of us troubled? (Cut away to a man in strange dress, bearded, his face creased by sorrow. Aleksandr Solzhenitsyn is addressing the graduating class at Harvard: "The West kept advancing socially in accordance with its proclaimed intentions. And all of a sudden it found itself in its present state of weakness. This means that the mistake must be at the root, at the very basis of human thinking in the past centuries. . . . " The audience is restive.)

Of course many are not troubled. Some, especially among the young, having neither known any other life nor learned of any in their studies, see nothing amiss. But there are also those, older and less naïve, who see the shadow as light, and welcome it, and serve it. These persons, to a man, know more about the evils of the world than anyone else. They are the conscience and compassion of humanity, and know it, and tell us so. They find evil everywhere. They find evil even the good Lord failed to suspect, and their anger against it is ceaseless and righteous. They rail about everything that does not go according to the plan: about every real or potential inequality, every departure from perfect justice. They thunder against the rich and meliorate the hardships of the poor, the down-trodden, the dregs of society. They hold exploitive classes and nations to shame; they battle greed, fraud, pollution, under-taxation, superstition, and narrow-mindedness. Their great-est wrath is against the world's nuclear arsenals, our own most of all, which could destroy Life As We Know It many times over. Verily, they have long made their concerns America's political agenda, in minute detail, and have labored tirelessly and expensively to perfect us. Yet our problems worsen. It is maddening!

The gathering dark mocks its servants. (Solzhenitsyn continues: "I refer to the prevailing Western view of the world which was first born during the Renaissance and found its political expression from the period of the Enlightenment. It became the basis for government and social science and could be defined as rationalistic humanism or humanistic au-tonomy: the proclaimed and enforced autonomy of man from any higher force above him. It could also be called anthropo-centricity, with man seen as the center of everything that exists.... The Middle Ages had come to a natural end by exhaustion, becoming an intolerable despotic repression of man's physical nature in favor of the spiritual one. Then, however, we turned our backs upon the Spirit and embraced all that is material with excessive and unwarranted zeal. This new way of thinking, which imposed on us its guidance, did not admit the existence of intrinsic evil in man, nor did it see any higher task than the attainment of happiness on earth.")

The pursuit of happiness has been made fully open to us. Vast legal machinery protects it. Commentators extol it, civic groups defend it, great industries serve it with goods to meet every taste, desire and budget. Income redistribution gives all a chance for their share of happiness. Yet we are troubled. We have comforts and pleasures to satiety, but we are not happy. Something is still missing. Is it that we have forgotten our own selves? That must be it, many say; we have paid too much attention to frills and externals, and failed to nurture the one thing that matters, the Self, me, old number one. So we internalize like crazy and patronize the man counsellors of Fulfilled Selfhood. We slim down, get our act together, and yes, feel really good about ourselves. But the thought comes to us, perhaps even during quality time: Is this all there is? (Richard Weaver writes: "As one views modern man in his innumerable exhibitions of irresponsibility and defiance, one may discern, if he has the courage to see what he sees—which, as Charles Peguy reminds us, is the higher courage—a prodigious egotism.... The sin of egotism always takes the form of withdrawal. When personal advantage becomes paramount, the individual passes out of...the spiritual community, where men are related on the plane of sentiment and sympathy....")

We are trapped on a roller coaster of enthusiasms and dashed hopes. We rush from one fix to the next, following the latest fashions in self-fulfillment. We try pills, sensation, immersion in causes, carnality, the stylish guru, counseling, searching in widening circles for we know not what, always searching. We listen to anyone who promises to relieve our emptiness. The oracles assure us all's well, the professionals help us adjust, the shaman's incantations soothe us, and even the world-savers want only a few more decades and a few more trillions to get everything just so. Present realities are clear to us, and all the auguries bode well. We want so little: a bit of material comfort, freedom from onerous duty and suffering. That is not asking too much, is it? Yet, we moderns are haunted. Somehow we know a crisis is coming for us, as it did to a defector described by Whittaker Chambers: "One night he heard screams." (The new way of thinking, Solzhenitsyn sums up, "based modern Western civilization on the dangerous trend to worship man and his material needs. Everything beyond physical well-being and accumulation of material goods, all other human requirements and characteristics of a subtle and higher nature, were left outside the area of attention of state and social systems, as if human life did not have any superior sense. That provided access for evil, of which in our days there is a free and constant flow.... We are experiencing the consequences of mistakes which had not been noticed at the beginning of the journey. We have placed too much hope in social and political reforms, only to find that we were being deprived of our most precious possession: our spiritual life.")

Do we not hear screams already? A new specter stalks us, coming ever closer. Men willing to die mow down innocent strangers with grenades and machine guns in airports and restaurants and public squares. In a century that has institutionalized violence and inhumanity, that has shed more blameless blood than all before it, we fear most this new random carnage. In a time somehow inured to ideological murder and genocidal race and class war, we are brought up short by the terrorist. We do not understand him: why does he kill without apparent cause or purpose? We do not, because we long ago abandoned our belief in the evil in men. We have averted our eyes and made excuses for evil acts. We have hidden behind statistics, lulling ourselves to think that after ten murders, or a thousand, or ten million, the next is no longer a tragedy and a rending of human brotherhood. We have deceived ourselves to think that the great crimes happen "over there" somewhere, and would never touch us here. Through many years of moral negligence we have ourselves paved the road the terrorist travels. How can we even rebuke him from our own relativistic standards? It is he who rebukes us, believing us morally diseased and unfit to exist. However vile his prescription, however blind he is to the great remaining reservoirs of American decency, his diagnosis does not lack a degree of truth. The time may soon come when we hear the screams in our shopping malls and on our sunny beaches. (Chambers, who both turned to and broke with communism out of despair at the loss of Western faith, pinpointed our dilemma some thirty years ago: "[This] age is impaled on its most maiming experience, namely, that a man can be simply or savagely—above all, pointlessly—wiped out, regardless of what he is, means, hopes, dreams, or might become. This reality cuts across our minds like a wound whose edges crave to heal, but cannot. Thus, one of the great sins, perhaps *the* great sin, is to say: It will heal; it has healed; there is no wound; there is something more important than this wound. There is nothing more important than this wound. If we cannot get beyond it, to find meaning which includes it, the age can solve nothing for itself.")

There is no doubting the reality. Men are pointlessly wiped out every day. The wound cannot heal, nor can we even tend it, in our confusion. We have been cunningly taught that there is no force for evil in this world; trained from the cradle to make fun of the concept of the Devil. How could we serve evil better than by disbelieving it? What greater favor can we do for willful men than blinding ourselves towards their malice? We sense a growing evil, suffer it, perhaps practice it, reassuring ourselves it is not there. But it is.

The darkness falling on our Western world is of evil intent. It is as real as the AIDS virus, and far deadlier. The shadow blots, not the sun, but the light of the inner human world: the realm of thought and imagination and knowledge, of mind and spirit. It is a set of ideas that designs to shutter vision and constrict our knowledge, ultimately confining human thought within an airless, small, conceptual prison. The shadow poses as a philosophic system, but preaches the opposite of philosophy, a hatred of wisdom. It hides behind many doctrines and "isms" with but one meaning: a rebellion against God. Its "philosophic" definitions and ideas and dicta are but the weaponry of its purpose: it wields them in a total assault on the religious foundations and moral order of the West. It enlists apostates, fellow Westerners including no few Americans, to lull our defenses with the common speech, striking from within. It proclaims the subhuman status of men in order to boast the divinity of Man. It invokes the might of the collective to put individual persons in doubt of their souls. It flatters our vanities and feeds our lust, to enslave us. It incessantly portrays us as so many innocent beasts of the field, without a higher nature, responsibility, or transcendent purpose. It bends its very artifice and wile to extinguish our spirit. It reveals its purpose in the focus of its fury: against the extraordinary claim of Him, upon whose Word alone our civilization will live or die: "I am the Light."

I call this force and its works anti-heroism. Knowingly or not, we meet it every passing day. Many serve it, little knowing what they do. My hope is that this book will help us realize what we are dealing with. For none of us can be exempt from the commitment it imposes. Either we choose the Light or perforce join the clamor of the world, sowing the Dark. It is not a choice between different life-styles, or even between opposing philosophic conceptions of life, but between life and death. The world being built by anti-heroism exists for hatred of the human creature. It can never be peopled by men. It is death to enter.

Yes, the forces of anti-heroism pull us into darkness. Whether its shadow is a passing eclipse or the twilight of our hopes, no one can now say. What is certain is that we must indeed "get beyond it, to find meaning which includes it," if ever again we are to walk carefree under the sun.

Chapter II
Estrangement in a Strange Land

Culture...is properly described...as having its origin in the
love of perfection; it is a *study of perfection*."
—Matthew Arnold

"Now, then, is the moment for culture to be of service, culture
which believes in making reason and the will of God prevail,
believes in perfection...."
—Matthew Arnold

It may be, observed, that when a great change impends, the
minds of men will be fitted to it. If so, one examining
American culture today, with unjaded eyes, will find much
reason to despair our future. On every side we see the
unchecked spread of false values and decadence. Wherever we
look we see a dehumanizing impulse that has cheapened the
worth and dignity of life to the vanishing point. And we know
these reveal contagion in our underlying moral beliefs. Yet
our headlong decline evokes only a murmur of alarm and little

outrage. It is as if we were being fitted for—our own annihilation.

"...it is difficult to resist the conclusion," says Muggeridge, "that Western man, having wearied of the struggle to be himself, has decided to abolish himself." He calls the contagion, with considerable justice, the "Great Liberal Death Wish." Whatever we call it, no one doubts we have terrible weapons to finish the job with our usual, swift efficiency. But few notice we do it just as surely—if slower and more painfully—through starving the spirit. Man is the one creature on earth who cannot survive by satisfying his animal appetites. Yet on the evidence, we seem concerned with little else.

Look about you. If you have drunk too deeply of the spirit of the times; if you are comfortable with cultural trends, then look again, with the eyes of a loving parent. To see more clearly, you need only ask yourself if the cultural world is all you could hope and dream for your child. Is it? Look at our schools, our political system, our media, our celebrity "role models"—will these produce what Americans hardly thirty years ago thought they should be, "a type of man who sums up in his character a quality of understanding, of humility, of truth, of humor, of pregnant ideas, of universal sympathy and friendship and love"?

In a generation's time we have inverted the ideals of all previous generations of Americans. We do not even understand their words or wishes. In these few years a tide of anti-heroism, centuries in the making, reached its flood and inundated us. Many of us of no advanced age have watched it with adult eyes, and yet do not know what we have seen. Thirty years ago we had no drug problem. Marijuana, cocaine and the rest were relatively unknown. Crime rates were far lower and women could safely walk the streets in most areas. Abortions were rare, illegal, and to most, unthinkable. Taxes were less than a tenth what we pay now. First-class mail cost 3¢ and was delivered promptly. Coins were made of silver. Nobody worried about inflation. The "Deficit" was not an issue; the government still had occasional surpluses. The few sleazy porn parlors around could not legally show a woman topless. Nowadays, to find something morally safe for your child to read, you head for a special "family" bookstore. And you probably drive by half a dozen "adult bookstores" peddling every kind of filth the mind can imagine. You see such now on the outskirts of even small towns, not long ago bulwarks of sane and sensible life.

I am not idealizing, much less conjuring up a happy childhood or fictions about the "good old days." Life always has its problems. The change since has been staggering. If we look back somewhat further, say to the early years of the century, the change would seem far more dramatic. In those "horse-and-buggy" days we like to laugh at, life was indeed different. The cultural level was much superior to ours: popular magazines carried essays and poetry, and all towns of any size cultivated fine music and drama. Federal spending was a thousandth of what it is now. There was no bureaucracy or welfare caste or regulatory nightmare, and there were no federal taxes at all, None. Have a laugh about *that* come April 15th. Folks played sports instead of watching them, and made music instead of tuning in. They may have had fewer material possessions than we, but enjoyed them more, and felt richer and more blessed than we. Small wonder that, on any occasion or none, they'd say this was the best dang country in the world.

We hardly ever hear that today. It isn't so clear anymore, with America sinking into anti-heroism.

It gives me no joy to review present cultural indexes, to see how nearly we have squandered our estate. Heaven knows, I am no America basher—that unctuous breed who positively relishes our every failing and distress, whose words salt and poison our wounds. (You know them: finger-pointers, cranks, sourpusses, tortured aesthetes, uglies, marchers, who demand that the world pay for their personal failure. Thoreau knew them: "If anything ails a man," he said, "so that he does not perform his functions if he have a pain in his bowel even, he forthwith sets about to reform the world." They are a large part of the problem at hand.) In truth, with the passing years, I love more than ever this fair land, its quiet homes, its untamed libertarian energy. Much of it remains unspoiled, and in many ways a finer, heroic spirit still moves us. Yet it must be admitted that we have changed and suffered great loss. This is most plainly seen in cultural decline, mirroring our faltering faith. Not until we isolate the pathogen can we attempt a cure. Otherwise, like a victim of fever, we will only slip deeper into lassitude, uncaring as the disease steals our waning strength.

Our affliction is specific. It is not after all, as though, after two thousand years of contrary teaching, we have suddenly decided that sin is just the thing for more abundant life. The change was fostered and urged by a particular, anti-heroic view of reality. This view has historical origins in the West that can be traced. It is most readily understood (and derives its power) as a religion of Man, preaching a purely materialist interpretation of reality. We shall, I hope, learn a great deal about anti-heroism in this study. For the moment, with little falsification, we can generalize its doctrines as the opposites of traditional Christian belief. Where the Christian is taught that the meek shall inherit the earth, for instance, the anti-hero teaches Darwinism and conquest by the strong. Where the Christian is instructed to eschew the things of the world and to surrender life in order to find it, the anti-hero is solely concerned with the world. Seek life and treasure here, he says, yet he shall keep neither.

Anti-heroism leaves clear fingerprints wherever it touches our culture (and in this discussion I mean that term broadly, not only the fine arts but all our joint dealings). Among those we should watch for are assaults on, inversions of, weaseling about, and rationales for evading, traditional religious beliefs and a fixed, transcendent standard of Good. The anti-hero does not believe in a personal God or in any spiritual purpose of men, and he finds numberless ways to say we are so many corks on the water, with no responsibility, individuality or value to our lives. Listen to all the television newscasters for a day, a week, a year. You will never hear them say the one straightforward thing: that today's horror was *wrong,* an evil act. Every other conceivable explanation will be trundled out, lest we admit evil. Society was to blame. The terrorists were trying to dramatize their protest. The criminal came from a bad neighborhood. Only a psychotic would hack his mother into small pieces to collect the insurance.

Certain doctrines are equally revealing signatures of anti-heroism. Militant egalitarianism, for one: that obsessive urge all about us to deny all individuality and reduce everyone to "social units" of statistically identical condition. Wages are to be equalized, school classes leveled to the rate of the slowest child, the successful or rich humbled. Materialism, in the philosophic sense, for another. This is the claim that the things of this world are all there are, and it pretends to forget who is the "prince of the world." A collectivist bent is certain anti-heroism. It is, indeed, a sign of the immaturity at the heart of anti-heroic tenets. The anti-hero, like the adolescent, is the perpetual sucker for "group formation," and attributes mystical qualities to the group. "Peer pressure" and the voice of the mob reduce his guilty feelings about his acts. Like a child he thinks history began at his birth, and he cultivates a scorn for the past. Like a child he is sulky about accepting responsibility and dreams up ways to blame anybody, blame the whole world, for his own shortcomings.

The anti-heroic siege of Western values is comprehensive, and we could discuss it at almost any length. Let me merely mention a few other qualities to watch for, with details to follow in later treatment. Look for an almost clinical aversion to suffering. The modern thinks the least discomfort is the curse of the fates and proof aplenty that there is no God, never suspecting that suffering is our greatest teacher. Look for an equal obsession with comfort, possessions and, most of all, sex. These are as close to happiness as the anti-hero can get, with sex the holy of holies. No imaginable coupling is to be overlooked, much less forbidden and no orifice neglected. Never mind that children are abused or lethal diseases spread. Buggery and pedophilia must be counted among the new "rights" the anti-hero seems to discover every day (at the expense of the old ones). Watch for the urge to lay bare all things, a tearing away of all veils of decency, an obscene (in the old sense) desires to see all in its seamy, "natural," reality. Watch for the related "comradely" or Jacobin denial of manners, forms, tact, ritual, piety, ceremony: the inversion of civilized community. Watch for new expressions of the immoral formula, "the end justifies the means." Listen for aversion to science as the determinant of all truth, as if truth were bound to the material world which is all that science can investigate. Listen to the tireless moralizing by those who mind everybody's business but their own and will not speak of real good or evil. When you hear or see these things, you have found anti-heroes in their chosen calling of destroying the West.

Post-Christian Flocks

In his Inaugural Lecture at Magdalene College, Cambridge, in 1954, *De Descriptione Temporum*, C. S. Lewis ventured his view that, "whereas all history was for our ancestors divided into two periods, the pre-Christian and the Christian, for us it falls into three—the pre-Christian, the Christian, and what may reasonably be called the post-Christian." He went on, "... it appears to me that the second change is even more radical than the first. Christians and Pagans had much more in common with each other than either has with a post-Christian. The gap between those who worship different gods is not so wide as that between those who worship and those who do not."

At that time, few would have questioned the predominantly Christian character of American culture. (In saying so, of course, I intend no slight to adherents of other great religious faiths or their contributions.) We are, according to Justice Douglas's famous dictum, a religious people whose institutions presuppose a Supreme Being. From the colonial period until the recent past, the Christian faith was undoubtedly the greatest influence on our public arrangements and patterns of life. In terms of sheer numbers, the Christian community remains much the largest. But today we must question whether its influence still predominates; whether, indeed, we have made the radical transition to a post-Christian culture.

To be sure, church attendance remains high and television ministries command a large following. But not all is rosy behind the numbers. A "liberalizing" trend has long been evident, especially in "mainline" protestant denominations, now also in the Roman Catholic church. This amounts to a "post-Christian" invasion of Christianity itself, expressed by an unscriptural and decidedly anti-heroic focus on political and social issues and "the things of this world."* As a result, many an ostensibly Christian pastor is in the vanguard of anti-heroism, preaching the gospel of materialism. We see such startling anomalies as Protestant clergymen funding revolutionary terrorist groups, and Catholics advocating "liberation theology" and attempting "dialogues" with Marxism–Leninism. Congregations in significant numbers are now run by and for "those who do not worship." At the very least this is abdication of the Christian mission. In truth, it is often subversion and abnegation of the faith, depleting its strength and leaving its flock leaderless and helpless to ward off the

---

*The question is not new. An anti-heroic "worldly" role for the church was advocated at least a century ago—and vigorously rejected by the orthodox as the antithesis of the faith. The historian Stephen Tonsor relates: "As early as 1911 Ernst Troeltsch in his magisterial work, *The Social Teaching of Christian Churches,* argued emphatically that "in the whole range of early Christian literature—missionary and devotional—both within and without the New Testament, there is no hint of any formulation of the 'Social' question; the central problem is always purely religious, dealing with such questions as the salvation of the soul, monotheism, life after death, purity of worship, the right kind of congregational organization, the application of Christian ideals to daily life and the need for severe self-discipline in the interests of personal holiness...."

anti-heroic assault from without. Other signs of disaffection or unrest in the Christian community have been much remarked, from such phenomena as "Jesus freaks" and rock masses, to the spinoff of befuddled and bizarre cults. It is clear that spiritual hungers are not being satisfied.

Edmund Fuller examining these matters, was led to "a brutally hard fact. Notwithstanding the visible presence and influence in our society of traditional religious belief and worship, we face an increasingly dark side of American culture....In many aspects our society is severely demoralized. It is also strongly materialistic." This much is plain even to anti-heroes, who seem to thrive on preaching a materialist philosophy, while denouncing its results wherever found—roughly, everywhere but in themselves and their preachments. Fuller merely repeated an old, proven lesson of history in warning that high culture can neither be built nor maintained except on a religious basis.

The collapse of Western belief under the blows of the modernist, secular thought has been widely noted in the form of "alienation" or "malaise." The modern so afflicted has been too dehumanized to fight it off. Abraham Maslow, one of our most well-known psychologists, saw this in his clinical work: "my healthy subjects," he said, "taught me to see as profoundly sick, abnormal or weak what I had always taken for granted as humanly normal; namely that too many people do not make up their own minds.... They are pawns to be moved by others rather than self-moving, self-determining individuals. Therefore they are apt to feel helpless, weak, and totally determined; they are prey for predators, flabby whiners...." They are, in a word, the victims of long taught and here successful anti-heroic doctrines that the human is precisely helpless and his fate is determined by "forces." The anti-hero has said just this for a century and more, but does not believe it: he is the predator and propagandist, seeking control over men, seeking to destroy religious belief and self-sufficiency to remodel men for his New Order.

Carl Jung also saw the modern malaise in his work and was blunter about it: "I have treated many hundreds of patients, the larger number being Protestants, a smaller number of Jews and not more than five or six believing Catholics. Among all my patients in the second half of life [that is, over age 35], there has not been one whose problem in the last resort was not that *of finding a religious outlook on life.* It is safe to say that every one of them fell ill because he had lost that which the living religions of every age had given their followers and none of them has really been healed who did not regain his religious outlook" (emphasis added).

For further evidence of such demoralization, we never have to look far. All concede we are suffering an epidemic of drug abuse that slipped out of the slums of the shadow to claim even grade-school children for its victims. Drugs permeate the "rock" culture, itself anti-heroic, and the world of highly paid professional athletes who are heroes to young people. But drug abuse is pure escapism, a contrivance not to get a "high," as parlance has it, but to sink to the hedonistic low of raw sensation. Drugs are a flawless reflection of anti-heroism, a denial of life and a statement that there's nothing more to us than satisfying animal feelings. If, as the anti-hero contends, we are but purposeless beasts in a materialist cosmos, what conceivable argument can there be against another snort? It feels good, and that is all that is supposed to matter nowadays. By no coincidence, drug abuse is most prevalent in those anti-heroic utopias of the flesh, the Scandinavias and Californias. In the form of alcohol abuse, it is rampant in all the "workers' paradises."

Relatedly, we note the shocking increase of suicide (the second leading cause of death) among teenagers. Youngsters are, as ever, the most vulnerable to drink in the anti-heroic spirit of the times; and without experience or grounds for reflection, the most apt to succumb. They are the first and easiest casualties of the anti-hero and his spiritually empty world. These sad, sad children leave notes to say that their lives were without meaning or purpose, and thus better cut short. They have understood only too well, as children do, the real messages of the age. We never hold our "opinion molders" to account for these tragic and needless deaths, but we should.

Young people used to get their values from their family and their church. Today both of those are targeted for destruction by anti-heroism. The principal influences on children are the media, notably television, and public schools— both bastions of anti-heroic indoctrination.

The media are what we know most about, so I need mention least. Turn on the radio and you will find it overwhelmed with the jungle throb and infected themes of rock. Read the papers—as perhaps you have been obliged to, as a parent, to help your child stay informed—and obscenity is the rule. That is, obscenity in the old sense of putting our grief or suffering or shame up to public view. In the interests of titillating readers or creating publicity or celebrity, the modern journalist stoops to anything and actually encourages, evokes, and "makes a virtue of desecration," as Weaver put it. The old rule, from the Greeks to the last century, was to avert our eyes from human tragedy and shame, lest human civilization be torn. The new and anti-heroic is to expose all to view, to show a gamey "reality" it is the purpose of civilization to refine. Propriety was abandoned and privacy invaded, lest they inhibit the modern's demand for total sensation. Cultivated manners, forms, morals and ceremonies meet the same fate, anathematized as "undemocratic."

Touring this country a century ago, Matthew Arnold noted that "if one were searching for the best means to efface and kill in a whole nation the discipline of self-respect, the feeling for what is elevated, he could do no better than take the American newspapers." Today he would not waste his breath: discipline and "what is elevated" have long since vanished, even as ideals. In their place is a sorry array of political mumbo jumbo, usually managed mundane, to the same purpose, even when it does not resort (as it often does) to outright propaganda.

For all this written large, just turn on the television— which we do, on average, for something over forty hours per week. There we glaze our eyes, and minds with the now proverbial sex and violence, car chases, and unending inanities. We drink in the "what is" of life in great draughts, neither asking for anything uplifting nor caring that we cannot find "what should be" in network programming. Nowhere is the same stunted, anti-heroic view of life more shamelessly expounded than by network newcasts with their wearisome liberal slant. Yet what do these smiling, meretricious preachers offer that is not standard throughout the day's fare? Some of them, at least, think they are being strictly neutral in presenting an anti-heroic view, and they may have a point; it is the norm. For a full measure of Lewis's post-Christian men "who do not worship," just watch the soaps, whose characters never go to church except to get married (and remarried every week or so thereafter). About the only way to see anything resembling worship on TV is to stay up late and watch old movies.

The anti-heroic view saturating television is largely that of producers in New York and Los Angeles. Yet it is unfair and incorrect to suppose that they are intent on degrading us. They are in business, obliged to serve up the kind of programming we, as customers, want. Otherwise they will be replaced, as in any other business, by those who more accurately cater to our wishes. I don't doubt that there are some in the trade who gag on their own handiwork, and would rather give us *King Lear* than *Dynasty*. But it doesn't sell, and they must please us or suffer the losses themselves. In the end, we consumers dictate the programming. We see ourselves truly reflected in it, and the image we see is vulgar, hedonistic and tasteless. We see our own anti-heroism.

Failing Grade for Schools

The other great transmission belt of anti-heroism, directly to the young, and through them more generally, is public education. Nothing hits home harder than this to me, as an educator. I see its product every day, even though the young people in my charge are, in the main, the sturdiest survivors of public schools—the ones who, through family or religious influence, have fought their way clear.

The problem with our schools is not want of effort or money; we have long been lavish in those regards. We falter in having forgotten what education is. Nock argued more than fifty years ago that education had vanished entirely from America. Muggeridge snorts that "education" today is the great liberal poohbah, a "gigantic fraud" at public expense which seems almost intended to bring down civilization. The whole point of education was to pass along civilized and moral values from one generation to the next. What is now "taught" in public schools is the opposite—a smattering of facts and "subjects" as scrupulously free of values as the anti-hero can manage. And make no mistake, anti-heroes regard the schools as their own private preserve and demand monopolistic indoctrination in their own view. Anything other than uniform standards would be "undemocratic," you see, and they create huge bureaucracies to determine the standards.

The anti-heroes have been most successful in stripping all religious content out of public education with a ludicrous interpretation of the First Amendment, which was intended to guarantee tolerance and free expression of religion. Today a schoolchild can join a communist club, or promote homosexual activity on school grounds, but cannot say a prayer or read the Bible there. Thus is realized a long-standing goal of the humanists, unbelievers who preach a "religion" of Man and exterminate all real religious professions by the power of law. A recent, prize-winning essay for the American Humanist Association targeted the schools with the conviction that "the battle for humankind's future must be waged and won in the public school classroom by teachers who correctly perceive their role as the *proselytizers of a new faith*." Those we have in hordes already. You have probably met them: "teachers" who teach that every question of right and wrong is "judgmental," even as they indoctrinate valuelessness. In their care, according to Secretary of Education William Bennett,

40% of today's 14-year-old girls will be pregnant before they are 20, half illegitimately; and the suicide rate keeps setting new records.

At the level of higher education, it is those who have sucked in anti-heroism most assiduously—the "best and the brightest," if you want to believe anti-heroic conceits—who go on to the so-called prestige universities, public or private. Where they will study under the hippie-yippie counter-culture rebels of twenty years ago, now tenured professors, and pay dearly for it, as befits the children of yuppies. And there they will learn to be more effective anti-heroes. Whether they get anything resembling an education out of it is another matter. At this writing, the big deal in education is to be able to build shacks on the campus green to "protest injustice." It will be something equally idiotic tomorrow.

Government at all levels is the purveyor of most education, and usually the worst. Degraded, anti-heroic curricula serve its purposes well and expand its power. Students trained in conformity and "adjustment" grow up to be compliant and docile taxpayers, neither mentally nor morally able to offer any resistance to growing state interventions. The State itself is the principal instrument of anti-heroism. The bloating of the federal government over the past fifty years is the most visible symptom of the anti-heroic penetration of American life. Having nothing to "render unto God," anti-heroes must perforce render all to Caesar. They are, to a man, all junkies of statism. In the absence of divine authority over men, the State of necessity becomes the final authority, taking on a quasi-divine—but far from benevolent—character. The apotheosis of the State to godhood is explicit in totalitarian regimes, which war against all other religious observance ("Thou shalt have no other gods before me"). But all anti-heroic influence tends to the same end, the total State.

America was founded on exactly the opposite principle— another lesson taught falsely or omitted altogether in public school textbooks. The Founders agreed that government was at best a necessary evil, to be limited to a few specified functions by "the chains of the Constitution," and never to be trusted. The goal was maximal liberty and minimal state interference, a view presupposing that men are self-controlling, moral beings. The colonists had fought for their independence from onerous taxes and "a swarm" of the king's officers, with the slogans "Don't Tread on Me" and "Life, Liberty and Property." They meant to secure their liberties for all posterity with a limited, internally checked form of government and with the Constitution.

All this is gone, upended by anti-heroism in a virtual revolution. The greatest political changes, most agree, occurred in the Roosevelt years, beginning in 1933. But the real revolution began much earlier with the ascendancy of anti-heroic ideas, often imported from Europe. In the new view it is the individual person who is not to be trusted and the State that can do no wrong. It is as if we inverted Jefferson's maxim: "That government is best which governs most"—no matter how bumbling, wasteful, boneheaded, bureaucratic, frustrating, bossy and expensive its actions. The traditional relationships between the people and the State have been reversed. Where once government was conceived as the servant of the people, serving with their consent and at their sufferance, it has now become the master, and citizens are called "subjects." Cooperative society gives way to coercive rule. Equal opportunity for all in liberty surrenders to a massive maze of stolen legal privilege in the form of tax breaks, subsidies, tariffs, protectionism, legal monopolies and so on. From a system rewarding diligence, prudence and thrift, we turn to one of "income redistribution," penalizing effort and rewarding the most indolent, useless and unproductive among us (bureaucrats very much included). Said the breathless ideologue of a century ago, when the State had absorbed all social energy, it would wither away. His legacy is the superstate that is the most characteristic mark of the twentieth century. It is the individual who has withered away. We have become so many units for government statistics, so many income-producers to be taxed, so many subjects in bureaucratic dossiers.

Accompanying this massive reversal of the American experiment in liberty has been a great politicization of our thinking and an almost beserk reference to "democracy." We are inundated with politics. Hardly a news items appears that is not couched in political overtones. It is the same story. Having, at anti-heroic urging, discarded any higher truth or authority over men, we necessarily turn all matters into political questions, to be settled by the councils and tribunals of men—preferably by counting heads. This elevates mere process to an absolute—another anti-heroic superstition. Follow the correct (democratic) procedure or formula, and never mind whether truth is served or the results are good. What follows is, in fact, very often atrocious: Hitler was elected, after all. But the anti-hero always has a high-sounding argument at hand, and he uses it constantly to justify his attacks on America's heritage and to conceal his loyalty to her enemies. But it is a cheat. His theories deny a genuine morality. He borrows his high-sounding arguments from the older Christian order in self-interest: to destroy it and replace it with anti-heroism. He doesn't care a fig that it's a cheat, either; his rule is any means to the end. The rest of us would do well to heed what anti-heroes really urge, and never mind the fancy arguments.

Unwanted People

One sad example is abortion. How, in this instance, can the anti-hero, or more often anti-heroine, make a virtue of killing her unborn baby? First, she has to euphemize like crazy. Call it a foetus, never a baby. Call the act "terminating a pregnancy," not abortion, much less murder. Declare the foetus is not alive (it is). Declare it is not "Viable" (so what?). Declare that the child would be "unwanted" or "defective" (so what?). These are all transparent excuses. We do not—yet—go around killing people because they are unwanted or defective. The Nazis did, the Soviets still do, and we will too, as anti-heroic ideas are accepted; but for now we resist. So-called "mercy killings" are still prosecuted as murder, a vestige of the old, heroic order. The advocate of abortion still needs a high-sounding argument, and finds it in "choice" and her "right" to control her own body. That the baby is no part of her body, and that, in fact, the mother did not control her body, are neither here nor there. The abortion advocate is "pro-choice." Choice is a thing we are born with, demand and relish. It is our innate freedom. It sets us apart from the beasts. No rigorous anti-hero believes that choice really exists; all is determined. Yet they all argue for choice—process—as the high road for their real aim, killing babies they don't want to take responsibility for.

A liberal, said some bitter wag, is one who deplores the killing of baby harp seals and defends the killing of baby humans with equal vigor. It is a dreadful but direct comment on the death wish at the heart of anti-heroism. Spare those cute little seals, but snuff your own inconvenient baby—that's your choice. It is a choice between evil and good, and we have no "right" to choose evil: that we do not see. It is a "choice" carrying the statement, it is morally permissible to kill humans, and indeed, the most defenseless and innocent among us, the unborn children. That we do not see either. In the end it reflects the pure anti-heroic view, the earthbound hatred of humanity saying there is no God, there is no wrong, and all humans are worthless. That abortion is a question at all marks a triumph of anti-heroism. Since the fateful *Roe* vs. *Wade* decision in 1973, legalizing abortion and indeed making it available at the expense of taxpayers who loathe the practice, there have been, at the time of this writing, an estimated 16,000,000 abortions—a slaughter of innocents dwarfing our war casualties and traffic deaths combined, not to mention the toll in Hitler's Holocaust. By the time you read this, those figures may seem paltry: we kill about 4,000 more of our children every day. What is most inconceivable to me about this is the appearance of women who do not, as women always have, long for a baby at their breast or the promise of grandchildren to dandle at their knee. They must have hearts of stone, these modern anti-heroines, preferring their own convenience, killing their unborn, instead of offering a mother's love to a child.

Not unrelatedly, the anti-heroic makes itself felt in a supposed alarm over "overpopulation." The earth cannot support so many of us, according to this view. Which happens to be exactly wrong. We have had an immense increase in world population since that drear preacher, Thomas Malthus, first expressed it at the end of the eighteenth century. In freedom it is production that has outstripped reproduction, not the other way around as Malthus had it, for the simple reason that free men earn their way in life. Each new life is, or can be, an economic asset, not a detriment, for America or the world. Free borders, and the unrestricted movement of labor and capital, are thus basic to a civilized order, and were in fact enjoyed by all the advanced countries in the West earlier in this century. The anti-hero, as hostile to freedom as to unwashed human life, finds innumerable reasons to oppose any increase in population, whether from birth or immigration. We can't have them, the arguments go, because they are a drain on finite resources, they are the wrong race, they are cheap labor, they are a burden. They are nothing of the sort. This hostility really reflects an obsession with material possessions and a selfish (and mistaken) fear that if others come along, there won't be enough "things" to go around. It is also racist, an unsuspected but pure application of anti-heroism. In the end, the anti-heroes erect Berlin Walls around their utopias, pretending to keep out the envious, but in reality fencing in their slaves.

Here, too, we meet again that citified, stifling view of life that seems to breed anti-heroism twice as fast as any other. The modern city marks a cultural failure of sorts. The city-dweller is mobile and rootless; he hardly knows his neighbor. No neighborhood or community can form to induce good behavior. Miscreants are not rebuked through acquaintance or community sanction; contributors are not rewarded by neighborhood pride. The effect is atomism, everyone for himself.

The result is a callous disregard for the rights and privacy of those unknown people nearby. Acquaintance and stability soften and civilize our relationships. It is one thing to cuss out an anonymous driver for a mistake, quite another to start to do so and find we are addressing a neighbor we've known for thirty years: then we catch ourselves, remember our manners, and become more forgiving. It is precisely this person-to-person civility that has become unobtainable in the cities. This might be overcome with an intensely cultivated moral atmosphere, but anti-heroism evokes just the opposite. And so the cities become jungles, atomized, governable if at all by raw force. The failures in this regard have been so glaring I need not mention them further.

As Jefferson tried to warn us, the more government undertakes, the less it can perform its basic functions of keeping order, dispensing justice, and providing for the common defense. All of these are at present in disrepair. The anti-heroes are so busy inventing new "rights" that we forget the old and fundamental rights of life, liberty and property, with which the new conflict. You cannot, for instance, declare a right to abortion at government expense without contravening both the baby's right to life and the taxpayer's right to keep what he earns. Such declarations are, to my mind, a none-too-subtle attack on our genuine rights. We spend more money on law enforcement every year, and the crime rate unfailingly goes up. We spend more money on education every year and the test scores unfailingly go down. What's going on here—other than the obvious fact that the government is the most bumbling performer we could turn to for either function? I think ideas have consequences. The real deterrent to crime is moral law. We are to love our neighbor.

We do not harm him: it is forbidden. We do not steal his property because it is in every sense his, the product of his effort, and in no way ours. No man of self-respect would touch what does not belong to him.

Anti-heroism (as usual) promotes the opposite view, and as such is a stimulus for rising criminality. If, for instance, we are informed by the example of the IRS that no man has a right to his earnings, then what is wrong with stealing? If there is no right and wrong, no just God, as the anti-hero says, then nothing may be called "crime" either. When the strong prey on the weak, it should be applauded (and often is) as survival of the fittest. When such philosophies are in vogue, it won't be long before the burglar helps himself to your silverware and the rapist batters your daughter, without a twinge of conscience. Anti-heroic thinking creates crime. Our old, lost heroic order suppressed it by insisting, at least, that wrong is *wrong*.

Before we take leave of the rude, anti-heroic intrusions of government, we must note its greatest effrontery: its trampling of the whole concept of justice. According to three thousand years of Greek, Judaic, Roman and Christian teaching, justice means "to each his due," equally before the law. About a hundred years ago at Harvard Law School, then as now in the vanguard of anti-heroism, the good professors decided that what was important was winning the case, not justice. And there began an avalanche of injustice.

It has long since become routine for lawyers to use delays and legal trickery to gain acquittal for crooks they know full well are guilty. This practice is defended not only as permissible but "ethical": in the name of providing the "best possible" defense. But the tactics employed can be ethically questionable or worse, and the end served is the defeat of justice. This process has been abetted by a long series of court decisions establishing a wide array of ultra-finicky procedural "rights" for the accused. Let the police or prosecutor make the slightest error, and all the evidence in an otherwise open-and-shut case can be thrown out, and a criminal freed. Thus justice is subverted by the "winning is everything" doctrine, an anti-heroic formula. Under it criminal activity becomes more profitable and crime rates climb.

But that's just the start. Having bitten the apple, the legal profession and "public interest" groups have in recent years engineered what has been called the "tort revolution." What it amounts to is a system of legal theft. It was aimed at the rich (naturally), but will soon affect all. Its implications are not fully realized at this writing, but it is a disaster in the making which, I fear, will strike soon.

The nature of the beast is this. A tort, in law, is an injury. If, say, a workman is injured on the job through his employer's negligence, or a patient is harmed by his doctor's carelessness, the party so injured can sue to recover damages. This is the common law, and it is just. If you hurt somebody or his property through negligence, you should recompense him. "Malpractice" by a physician is the best known example. What the "tort revolution" achieved, in an astonishingly short period, was to overrule the question of culpability in law. In other words, the defendant need not be shown to be negligent to have his socks sued off. Moreover, the law was widened to make almost anybody, even churches, liable to lawsuits, and fattened to include triple "punitive" damages, and to include the flimsiest cases based on workplaces or products sold decades ago. The new rule is, if you get injured, no matter that it is entirely your own fault and nobody else's, somebody else can be forced to pay—a ton. This naturally invites a flood of litigation, with numerous extraordinary out-of-court settlements to avoid even richer jury awards. Litigiousness has become the national pastime. Lawyers, who can collect huge contingency fees (that is, a large piece of the action), have not exactly been vocal in protest. Some now advertise on television what used to be called ambulance chasing.

The target of this assault is "deep pockets." Justice is not even to be considered. To take an example less extreme than we think, the idiot who cleans his ear with an old can opener and draws blood, can sue the manufacturer—including personal suit against anybody in the corporate structure—for "pain" and "mental anguish" not to mention treble damages. Real cases: a gymnast missed his one-and-a-half rollout in a trampoline, hurt himself on landing, and sued the manufacturer of the mat. He was awarded $14.7 million in the initial case. Or there was a fellow who stacked up too many Corning Ware dishes in his closet. One fell and he suffered a "serious gash." He was awarded $804,000, because the company "failed to warn the owner that the dishes might fall and shatter if stacked five deep...." There are altogether too many other stories of the sort. We need merely note the underlying, classically anti-heroic premises: the denial of personal responsibility (which amounts to a denial of human personhood: we will meet it often), the same old "any means to an end" formula, and the old Marxist prejudice against commerce or success.

Because of recent piecemeal reform legislation, this "tort crisis" seems over now according to many observers, but it continues to hit home. Businesses offering goods or services that can conceivably be held to be "risky"—which is just about everything—are themselves at serious legal risk. Their insurance companies have to jack up liability rates to cover tort settlements. Small businesses are still being forced into failure or bankruptcy because they cannot afford insurance. Hard hit are ski resorts and skating rinks (customers fall down), family-owned bars (customers get themselves a snootful and hurt somebody), and obstetrics (babies born brain-damaged through nobody's fault often get large awards to pay for their medical care). Net result: goods and services we need for our livelihood and sometimes for our survival (vaccines and new drugs are under siege) get prohibitively expensive or dry up entirely. One out of eight obstetricians is already out of business. What are expectant mothers to do? Nearby obstetrical care is no longer available to many. Through manipulation of our legal system, the anti-heroes deal us another deadly blow.

None of this would have been possible had we maintained the most elementary concept of personal responsibility—that is, our ancient, heroic and correct view that a human being is much more than a natural automaton. Interestingly, we see again that those whom anti-heroes regard as evil—businessmen—are given a fully human status: their evil is purposeful, and they are to be held responsible for it (and then some). The rest of us are consigned by legal theory to be unpersons, irresponsible beasts, helpless to use gym mats or stack Corning Ware correctly.

The Impoverishment of Nations

Hostility to free markets is a general and clear signature of anti-heroism. This, in part, reflects the lingering effects of

Marx's primitive "economic theories"—if they may be so dignified. These were so rude as to be demonstrably false before the ink was dry, and embarrassed even socialists. (Some future student will find Marx's flighty assumptions, abstractions and tortuous arguments the very model of anti-heroic thinking—the sort of thing that led Marx to insist wages must fall to subsistence levels smack in the middle of a century of rapidly rising wages.) However absurd the theory, all its prejudicial conclusions were retained and are still widely expressed in hatred for, and attacks on, a free economic order ("capitalism").

In another sense, Marxist theory did not and does not matter. Its real purpose was to turn envy into righteousness and to justify the immemorial resentments of weaklings and failures toward more successful men. In envy, Marx's followers already clung to the ancient fallacy that "wealth" was static, not constantly created. It follows from this blunder—exploded by Adam Smith a century earlier, in *Wealth of Nations* (1776)—that to acquire wealth you had to *steal* it from somebody else. All they wanted was an excuse to unleash their envy and hatred with moral righteousness, and Marx gave it to them: "capitalism is theft." With this they could claim justice while revenging themselves on their "bourgeois oppressors" with merciless class war and extermination. No demonstration in this century has been more overwhelming than the folly and brutality of this thinking, and the moral as well as economic superiority of free markets. Yet the anti-hero nurses his old fallacies and false righteousness to vent his grudges against "the rich." Deep down he says, "It's not my fault I am not more successful. It's theirs, it's the system's, it's the world's." Deeming himself to be sensitive and superior, he reasons that if the world does not recognize it, the world is not good enough for him. He will punish it. If the system doesn't put him at the top of the heap, nobody else can be, either. He will level it. If he is not financially successful, he will turn up his nose at "grubby materialistic commerce." If he inherits wealth, he is commonly filled with guilt, and often uses his money to advance "the cause." He gravitates naturally to bureaucratic or tenured academic positions, where advancement is by seniority and success is not measured in dollars. There he can nurse his brooding grudges and form cliques with others of like mind, to get mutual support and to rail against the injustice of it all. From this cesspool of voodoo economics, whiny self-justifications, anti-heroic posturing and venomous envies springs the modern's loathing for free markets in a free society. America, symbol of freedom and success, is for that very reason the quintessence of evil in the eyes of the anti-heroic intellectual—here as well as abroad. We do not understand anti-heroism adequately until we see its roots in envy and its motivation in revenge.

Nobel laureate Milton Friedman has remarked that "all interventions [in the market] are counterproductive." This is true, and once it might have alerted us to the cost of political meddling: it could harm our standard of living. This is no longer enough. The ascendancy of anti-heroism, especially in the last two decades, has lulled us to believe that our vaunted standard of living is all there is, and that a perpetually rising Gross National Product is our promise of heaven on earth. In this we forget our higher purposes in life, and make ourselves accomplices in our own execution. The anti-hero knows, if only instinctively, what we are forgetting, that the marketplace has more and higher purposes than money grubbing.

Markets reflect our spiritual values as well as our free economic choices. They are a bulwark of life, liberty and what Weaver called "the last metaphysical right," property. If in nothing else, we can at least see that economic freedom gives us the surplus we need for charity and philanthropy, for caring for the needy, for building synagogues and churches. We err greatly in separating things into neat little categories: commerce here, charity there. As Ludwig von Mises showed, they are all part of an interlocking system of free choice. Recent scholarship by George Gilder and others has established the moral and altruistic basis of entrepreneurial capitalism. Lord Acton used to be fond of saying that the tenets of modern economics could all be found in the Gospel. We have always been able to *see* the difference: not only the obvious economic superiority but the moral health on this side of the Iron Curtain. What we can add now is impeccable and rock-solid economic theory why it works so. We have not been deceived that ours is the better system in all senses.

The anti-hero is especially crafty in persuading us that money, not morality, is all there is to markets. That opens every door to his attack. Heavens! He does not want to kill the goose, no sir. He just wants to regulate the market, tame it, tax it, suppress "greed," prevent "fraud," stop pollution, correct market inefficiencies, and blah blah. We've all heard it. And in his sway we think, he's just fine-tuning; let the experts keep the GNP rising, do the planning, improve our standard of living. But he is destroying our markets, our freedom and, what matters more, our moral capacities. The economy is not a "thing"; it is ourselves exercising our free and moral choices. Markets—"people power"—are strong and resilient, but cannot withstand indefinitely an anti-heroic siege that brings grafters and politicians into the service of anti-heroic ideologues, do-gooders and "public interest" busybodies. We have lost a sizable fraction of our freedom and rights to this weird coalition, and notwithstanding a few successes with deregulation of late, stand to lose much more—or all. There's nothing between us and Soviet-style bread lines except restoration of the heroic, religious basis of life.

William F. Rickenbacker reminds us that "the Christian revelation is explicitly economic in a way that is impossible in the Oriental type of religion that urges total withdrawal from the material world." It is equally incompatible with the pseudo-religion of man, the anti-heroism that reduces everything to the material and mundane—to money, putting it crudely. Our traditional, and now faltering light, he adds, is the "very special aspect of Christian revelation that makes of economics a partner in a spiritual enterprise. We are not instructed to turn our backs on the world. We are instructed to populate it, have dominion over it, stand ready to deny it for Christ, but not to make a career of denying it.... The central Christian observance is a supper."

We must, in short, keep our balance between the worldly and spiritual sides of our nature. The former, carried to its extreme, its *reductio ad absurdum,* by anti-heroism, produces what I think is the ultimate, ignoramus temerity of the modern world: central economic planning. It sounds so cool and scientific and rational that we are easily seduced by the idea. But what it amounts to is the imposition by force of the notions of a few government whizzes in place of and overruling the infinitely better informed choices of all of us in the market, each of us informed by our own circumstances and ever-changing scale of virtues and preferences. The presumption that the central planner can do better for us than millions of us can do for ourselves, is monstrous. Our "unplanned" open market is the reason our stores overflow with luxuries while workers stand in line for necessities in anti-heroic utopias.

I have explored this at some length elsewhere,* so need not pursue it here. However, I would like to echo one point by the biologist Lewis Thomas, that we don't understand any living thing, not even the simplest. With what incredible gall, then, are we to claim to "plan" the doings of that most complex creature, moral man? In this regard, "I have an earnest proposal to make," said Thomas. "I suggest that we defer further action until we have acquired a really complete set of information concerning at least one living thing. Then, at least, we shall be able to claim that we know what we are doing." For that simple organism, anyway. "The delay might take a decade; let us say a decade. We, and the other nations, might set it as an objective of international, collaborative science to achieve a complete understanding of a single form of life.... As to the subject, I propose a simple one, easily solved within ten years. It is the protozoan *Myxotrichia paradoxa,* which inhabits the inner reaches of the digestive tract of Australian termites." The idea, of course, went nowhere, and we still know little about *M. paradoxa.* But the anti-hero, in conscienceless cruelty, goes on advocating or creating "five-year plans" to dictate the lives of all.

America by the Throat by George Roche, Chapter VI (Hillsdale, MI: The Hillsdale College Press, 1985).

Unnatural Arts

There are many other indices of anti-heroic encroachment into America's moral heritage which are revealed in our present culture. We could mention little symptoms: the use of the word "subject" for citizen that I mentioned, or the use of A.D. at the end of a date instead of at the beginning to say, "In the year of our Lord...." Or, more seriously, the steady conversion of Christianity's most holy day, Easter, into a Christmas-type holiday for fun (egg hunts) and possessions (basket stuffers). Or yet again, at very deep levels. The existence of suffering in this life is by all odds the strongest argument for atheism. We all know some suffering. The good may die young. Even innocent children may be snatched from our arms by death. How can this be? Why would God permit it? It takes a mature understanding of life to find even the beginnings of an answer. We may, in time, see that in God's eye death is no tragedy. We may, with wisdom, learn that God's noumenal gift of choice risks failure, defeat or suffering in return for the chance of personhood and triumph. We may reach Muggeridge's view that "the only thing that's taught one anything is suffering; not success, not happiness, not anything like that. The only thing that really teaches what life's about—the joy of understanding, the joy of coming in contact with what it really signifies—is suffering, is affliction." But all this wanes in our anti-heroic age. "Nothing," said Chambers, "is more characteristic of this age than its obsession with an avoidance of suffering. Nothing dooms it more certainly to that condition which is not childlike but an infantilism which is an incapacity for growth that implies an end." Here again we see an advancing childishness in our thought and institutions, disdaining discipline and responsibility. Let anyone today try to tell a union boss that labor is a divine ordinance!

To G. K. Chesterton, this is the "sterilizing spirit in modern pleasure. Everywhere there is the persistent and insane attempt to obtain pleasure without paying for it. Thus, in politics, the modern Jingoes practically say, 'Let us have the pleasures of conquerors without the pains of soldiers: let us sit on sofas and be a hardy race.'" There can be nothing nobler for anti-heroic beasts than plusher comforts and avoidance of pain. "Yet," says the modern Greek writer Arianna Stassinopoulos, "the doctrine of our world, 'Forsake your inner truth and live this tortuous life ending in a meaningless death, and you shall receive nothing in this world or the other,' is listened to and obeyed." It is a virulent immaturity that decrees that life begins at birth (if one is so lucky as to escape the abortionist) and ends seventy years later (if one is so lucky as to escape cost-conscious euthanasia), forever, with a fist clenched toward the God who is not there. We see the age of infantiles in those who make a career out of forsaking God and lamenting that they are godforsaken.

The inroads of anti-heroism are, perhaps, most conspicuously revealed in the essence of culture, literature and the fine arts. The simplest, most accurate statement of our arts is that we no longer have any. Virtually all the best of our theatrical repertoire, our art, our music, our ballet, our architecture, our sculpture, our literature, is a century old and often far older. We see and hear and understand less and less of it. Our cultural drought may even be discerned in the prices of classical paintings and art objects, which just keep rising because, as Will Rogers said of real estate, "they ain't making any more of it." Souls starved for beauty have no choice but to seek out older works. Why is this? Or perhaps the question should be, what is it we try to express with our sterile "arts" today that is so different from the expression of Western masters in past centuries?

Look around you: Sculpture welded in junkyards. "Art" created by dribbling or splotching paint on canvas, or by making geometric patterns with drafting tools, or claimed for "realist" works portraying jut-jawed brawny proletarians or soup cans. Atonal or discordant "modern" music, or the 119-decibel shriek of rockers. Books full of pulp porn and empty of inspiration, churned out to evoke sensation. Poetry relieved of all discipline, a mere blurt of words in blank or free verse. Essays abandoned altogether. We make no art. We make daubs and junk and boxy buildings and screeches. Even the pornography we produce by the ton is unartistic and hideous. Art, as much or more than anything else, is a mirror of what we think of the world and life. Ours reveals nothing more plainly than that we think reality is foul or chaotic, and that we detest our existence. Our works are "nightmares of a materialist society," as Muggeridge put it. Their total abandonment to Self bespeaks their refined anti-heroism, a hatred of humanity and life.

To be sure, artists in our time tend more to anti-heroic views than most of us, and this helps account for the outpouring of trash in the name of art. But that is not a fully satisfactory explanation. Critics praise the stuff, and somebody must buy it. It is obviously accepted in fairly wide circles. More damning is the absence of any recent art in the heroic mode.

A friend who knows these things better than I once defined music for me as "that which makes you want to dance." Given the ghastly sounds that bombard us in this music-starved age, we may need a more rigorous definition. Perhaps we could define music as sounds where you can actually tell when the musician makes a mistake. Detecting blunders anywhere in our "fine arts" is practically impossible. Say you have before you a classically geometrical Mondrian, except the curator spilled ketchup on it. The critics not only could not tell the difference, they would exult over the bold manipulation of materials to create this intensely meaningful smudge in the regularity of life. If you think I am exaggerating, remember that some years ago at a New York auction, bidding reached many thousands of dollars on a famous abstract painting before someone noticed that it was being displayed upside-down. Actors in some of our high drama could switch to Tagalog or Urdu with nobody the wiser. Or let the guitarist hit a horrible clinker and the next day we will be reading about the "new wave" in rock. In a word, we not only do not have any serious culture; we can't even tell that we do not. Anything goes, and almost everything does. Any and all manner of tripe is presented to us by intense aesthetes as Art with a capital A. (Gilbert and Sullivan, please call your office.) Do we not find it passing strange that we have to argue whether a piece is beautiful, or whether it *is* art? It is the formless, standardless, anti-heroic lust for "experience" that makes art undefinable. Ultimately, all art is moral in nature, and only moral criteria give it standards and definition. You find no morality in the anti-hero's handiwork.

Most of our "literature" is unworthy of the name and hardly worth discussing. But I might note another of those little details that can reveal so much (about education as well as literature in this case). Writers in the past used to make frequent allusions to the whole range of classical literature, even dotting their work with untranslated passages of Latin and Greek. They could assume their readers were familiar with it, and that it was held by all to be worthwhile. Nobody now makes much reference to either classical or recent literature. The former is unstudied or out of style, the latter incomprehensible, unfamiliar or useless. About the only references universally understood today are snippets from television commercials.

Interestingly, the heroic survives unbowed, if not un-bloodied, in some specialties, notably Westerns and science fiction. These too are under anti-heroic siege, but their writers are a sturdy breed, not so easily hornswoggled. Author Marc Simmons fired back in an address to a Western writers' convention. I'd like to quote it at some length because it shows clearly the war between the heroic and the anti-heroic:

> Last year the critics at [our convention] as much as said that Western writing is a failure because it refuses to follow the socialist line—that line which contends that the cowboy was a phony and is a creation of Hollywood, that the American pioneer was wholly predatory, and that Indians were all noble and caring of the environment.
>
> Our detractors tell us that unless we debunk the West with pens dipped in gall, unless we rewrite the past to conform with current notions of social justice, unless we renounce indivi-dualism and pledge allegiance to the bogus doctrines of the day... they will persist in labeling us as sellouts and they will persist in trying to discredit what we write.
>
> The reigning fashion in literature today—both East and West—is that known as *naturalism.* Its chief aim is to picture the man in the street *as he is,* giving emphasis to the seamy side of life and to the trivial and petty part of human nature.

There is little or nothing to uplift the spirit in naturalistic writing, for in the professed interest of clinically recording human behavior, authors of this school accept as an article of faith that we are all *hollow men*—ineffectual, uncertain, insecure, anxiety-ridden, confused.

More than that, these authors believe that human affairs are inexorably governed by outside forces over which we have no control. In other words, each man and woman is like a cork tossing down a mountain stream, pushed this way and that by a capricious current.

The individual, so the argument goes, has no say or choice in the direction he travels; essentially he is helpless, ruled by deterministic forces in our society and environment.

A hundred years ago, Americans would have laughed.... (original emphasis).

Mr. Simmons has given us a classic picture of the anti-hero and his stamp on the whole of our culture. Note well that the anti-hero does not believe that *he* is "determined." That is so much camouflage for his very purposeful war against our American heritage and our traditional beliefs and culture. He assails us with "bogus doctrines" or name-calling or mockery or anything else at hand. His words and arts are accusations, aimed not at our failings but at the best within us. In the world he creates there is to be no joy and beauty, because, he, not God, creates it. We have only to ponder the ugly, bleak, drear homogeneity of his dark vision to pray for his lost soul. His art paints the hellhole in store for us, should he prevail.

"Modernism," says Daniel Bell, "has been a rage against order.... The emphasis is on the self, and the unceasing search for experience. If Terence once said, 'nothing human is alien to me,' the Modernist could say with equal fervor, 'Nothing inhuman is alien to me.' Rationalism is seen as devitalizing; the surge to creativity is propelled by an exploration of the demonic. . . . The crucial insistence is that experience is to have no boundaries to its cravings, that there be 'nothing sacred.' " Truly, here is the exact statement of cultural anti-heroism: "nothing sacred." God raised us from the dust; rebellious man announces he will return us to the dust and its ancient owner. This is the New Order. This is why we make no art and sing no songs of joy.

In times past, with heroic conceptions, the West produced much of the finest art the world has ever seen. There was then no "art for art's sake": another expression of self. The artists of the West made gifts for their Creator and hymns to praise Him. One cannot offer God less than the best and most beautiful within; and one's joy, so inspired and freely given, returns to the world and all men as true art, unsought in itself, glowing in its adoration. From an outward, objective, heroic vision of life came Michaelangelo and Cellini, Raphael and Rembrandt, Shakespeare, Milton and Goethe, Herrick, Pope and Schiller, Bach and Mozart and a hundred others whose creations lift our souls.

Before we debark from this tour of cultural degeneracy, we should look at one last anti-heroic imprint on our way of life—indeed, the most pervasive and obvious. This one happens to be the principal bait the anti-hero can hold out to a relatively healthy but non-intellectual majority. (Intellectuals themselves are exceedingly easy prey for each others' moony theories.) It is the lure of sheer animal appetite, and as such, identifies itself at once a key feature of anti-heroism. I refer, of course, to sex.

I don't have to tell anyone we are awash in sex. I don't have to tell you where to find it. The stumper nowadays is to find some islet in our culture that is not saturated with sex. It has invaded the schools. We have had nude drama, topless classical recitals by lady musicians, even topless sermons by lady preachers. That's just the tame stuff, as we all know. We have gone through what we call "the sexual revolution," and declared ourselves the victors. Yet the same impulse was instantly obvious to such observers as Canon Bell before Hugh Hefner came along, and before it was legal to publish so much as a topless photo. Now we get stag films at the drive-ins and even in schools. What a dreary lot it is, too: not only anti-heroic in theory but in execution: cheap, crude, devoid of all artistry, gross, every hint of the erotic replaced by the graphic. The "winners" of the sexual revolution have managed to make even sex unsexy. That is the way it works everywhere in a World Without Heroes. We grab for the bait, for achievement and status unearned, for possessions without labor, for power without humility, for mastery without discipline, for sexual raptures on the cheap without responsibility, and for happiness without giving or love. Each time our grasping hand closes on the emptiness that lies behind our every lust and every anti-heroic promise. We tear away the very veils of civilization for the satisfaction of self, and find only dust and the void. The veils, we forgot, were what lifted us above raw sensation and the dirt.

Muggeridge had the keen insight that, "Sex is the only mysticism materialism offers, and so to sex the pursuers of happiness address themselves with an avidity and dedication seldom, if ever surpassed. Who among posterity will ever be able to reconstruct the resultant scene? Who for that matter can convey it today? The vast, obsessive outpouring of erotica in every shape and form; in book and film and play and entertainment, in body and word and deed, so that there is no escape for anyone. The lame and the halt, the doddering and the infirm, equally called upon somehow to squeeze out of their frail flesh the requisite response. It is the flesh that quickeneth, the spirit that profiteth nothing...." Here, child, is the meaningless murmur of your age: "As for the farm-yard—what a gilded sty has been devised! What ambrosial fodder! What performed rutting, melodious orgasmic grunts, downy straw and succulent swill! If the purpose of life is, indeed, to pursue happiness here and now, on this earth, then, clearly, it can only be realized in terms of what this earth provides—that is, of goods and toys, of egotistic success or celebrity, of diversions like speed and travel and narcotic fantasies; above all, of sexual pleasure and excitement which alone offers an additional illusory sense of transcendent satisfaction...." If the formula doesn't work this time, try again, try harder. Go for it. Grab all the gusto you can. Ignore the consequences. Never mind that what you get for your trouble is trouble: the explosion of divorce, illegitimacy, abortion, parentless children and teenage suicides; of mental illness and crime; of visible decadence. Gloss over all loss: the songs unsung and joys unfelt, prayers unsaid and Sabbaths never observed, the steady erosion of family bonds, security, stability and higher human purpose. Clutch for your straw, your moment of sterilized recreational bliss. If it feels good, it must be right; the oracles all say so.

The saddest sight in our cultural mirror is not how far we have strayed from American ideals or how deep we have sunk into cultural degeneracy. It is our habit of seeking ever more sensation and sinking ever lower. The anti-heroic hucksters are sly. They lure us with their worldly shoddies, the sex and baubles and glitter, asking only our souls. A giveaway. Men don't have souls anyway, they say; it's all free! But their wares never satisfy and the promised happiness is farther than ever from each. We are becoming junkies in our hopeless chase, reaching ever more desperately for the next fix. Nothing else matters, does it? Not where we have been, where we are going, what we should be. We must have another fix, and so begin to march in lockstep, urged on by the drumbeat of the jungle, toward the abysm. Chesterton could have been speaking of us in remarking, "Men seek stranger sins or more startling obscenities as stimulants to their jaded sense. They seek after mad Oriental religions for the same reason. They try to stab their nerves to life, if it were with the knives of the priests of Baal. They are walking in their sleep and try to wake themselves up with nightmares."

On Hope and Healing

It takes nothing more than waking up to end a nightmare. Our bad dream will end as soon as we see what it is. I believe that it is already ending, and that the worst is behind us. But we are barely past the crest of the anti-heroic tide. There is much peril before us, and much to do.

Let me put it in plain old American: we have got ourselves into one heap of trouble. We have been bamboozled and swindled blind by a bunch of European pointy-heads peddling a crock of 98-octane hogwallow. I can promise you in advance they are pitching pure bull, but beware: it is strong stuff and as mean as any notion that ever entered the minds of men. The deep-thinkers have been working on it for half a thousand years. All that time they have strengthened their web, threading it with deep-sounding arguments and subtleties, and baiting it with dark mysteries and elusive delights. Already they've snared half the world with it, including a lot of our own leaders and teachers. So, watch out: these guys are pros. But what they're hustling is snake oil and poison, or worse.

What we are up against, in short, is an alien philosophy. It wraps itself in the robes of religion, because men respond to that. But it is an anti-religion: the opposite of all Judeo-Christian belief. It pretends to come upon us like a mysterious incurable infection, but that's more of its hogwallow. We can and will trace its origins and effects, and expose it as the evil work of men. We will thrust the anti-hero into the bright light of day, where all his wiles will look as ridiculous as they are.

Hey, this is America. Wake up—it's a bright new morning, and we have things to do! Maybe first of all, get rid of those bunco artists bringing us down. A bunch of smooth operators they are, web-weavers who make us drowsy and unresisting with talk, talk, talk until we slip into stupor and dark dreams, and are gone. Oh, they are good at it.

But we are better. Rise and shine! We don't have to take any flimflam from anybody. America was never like they say. We have never acted like so many ants to be stepped on or colonized by bullies. It was not by acting like "pawns of fate" that we tamed a continent and conquered space, time and the skies. We got where we are with equal measures of moral rules and plain practical sense. We Americans have always known something the world sometimes forgets: that the right tree bears the good fruit. We can judge anything by results. If our machine doesn't work, we know we botched the design. If we put water in the gas tank, we know that's why our car doesn't run. The same for the philosophic schemes of men. If the results don't live up to the promise; if we are not happier and morally healthier for them, we *know* beyond any doubt they are wrong. Somebody screwed up.

Yes, we still have a choice. Anti-heroism has no irresistible claim on us. We can dump the whole reeking works over the cliff with no more than a decision to do so. Its claim to make a full and true accounting of the whole cosmos is just ludicrous. It is literal madness. It is our best scientists who tell us how little we know of even the material world science can study. It is our wiser philosophers who remind us how little we have unraveled of the mysteries of life. Who, but the anti-hero, is so presumptuous and proud as to press a claim for governorship of the whole cosmos when we cannot govern nations or even ourselves?

Let's use our American sense. It is anti-heroism that flunks the test of truth. If it could have made us happier and better, it would have long before now. Instead it makes us miserable. If it were true, it would always have been true. There could never have been any dispute about our way of life at all, nor any arguments against it to beguile us today. We would always have been what the anti-hero says we are now, mere beasts of the field, more intelligent than the others perhaps, but literally unable to do or see more than beasts can do or see. We would never have had any great literature or art. There would never have been such a thing as America. The nature of reality has not changed. We have changed, because we have been suckered by evil lies. And we can change right back again by seeing through the lies and saying no to them.

We did this to ourselves. There's nobody else to blame if we get conned. I ask what could be the last rational question: Is this what we *want?* We can, at will, have the time-tested health of the heroic view; we can have the Word, which has guided us and never left us, and to which by no means all of us have turned a deaf ear. Or we can sink deeper into the come-lately grunts of the world, whose Master could not be more obvious from the mess we are in. The one thing no man can do is stand aside. We each must choose our God, the light or the dark.

Chapter III
The Origins of Modern Unbelief

Like Macbeth, Western man made an evil decision, which has become the efficient and final cause of other evil decisions.... The defeat of logical realism in the great mediaeval debate was the crucial event in the history of Western culture; from this flowed those acts which now issue in modern decadence.
—Richard Weaver

We were born in a dark age out of due time (for us). But there is this comfort: otherwise we should not *know*, or so much love, what we do love. I imagine the fish out of water is the only fish to have an inkling of water.
—J. R. R. Tolkien
(Letter to Christopher Tolkien)

A "new way of thinking" that has penetrated and pervaded our whole culture over several centuries is difficult for us to imagine, and even more difficult to detach ourselves from—as we must, if we are to find our wrong turning. It becomes the common currency of our thought: transparent to the many because it is too close and familiar to see; apparent only to the few, like Solzhenitsyn and Weaver, who have mastered the perspectives of other ages and places. In the grip of the new we lose—without even sensing our loss—what we need "most of all," according to C. S. Lewis: an "intimate knowledge of the past." For we must have "something to set against the present, to remind us that the basic assumptions have been quite different in different periods and that much which seems certain to the uneducated is merely temporary fashion... the scholar has lived in many times and is therefore in some degree immune from the great cataract of nonsense that pours from the press and the microphones of his age."

The modern has no such immunity. It is, indeed, part of his "new thinking" that the past was dark and backward, or at best, of no interest to our modern arrangements. The story of historical change from theological beliefs of old to scientific, rational, pragmatic thinking today, is often told, and always told as progress. Our journey, it is said, was from superstition to enlightenment to emancipation. Steeped thus in the doctrines of progress and evolution, the modern sees us riding the crest of human advancement, with each point in time better than those before, each year better than the last. He thinks the jeer, "you can't turn back the clock," will put dissenters—he calls them reactionaries—in their place. It only lately begins to dawn on him, and only in the rudest way, that a future under a nuclear cloud is sharply at odds with his theories of automatic progress. But this dilemma eludes his solution; ignoring contradiction is also part of his instruction by the "new thinking."

The modern is thus a "provincial in time," bound to the present more firmly than ever the peasant was bound to his land. Says Weaver, "A creature designed to look before and after finds that to do the latter has gone out of fashion and that to do the former is becoming impossible." In his "presentism," he is the fish with no inkling of water, forced to swim with the current. Tolkien's lament at being "born out of due time" is meaningless to him; what other time is there? Even less can he penetrate the acute sentiment of Eliseo Vivas that it is a mark of decency to be ashamed of having been born in the twentieth century.

This orientation is enough, in itself, to mark the "new thinking" as anti-heroic. An order scornful of its roots will swiftly lose sight of its future. It can retain no sense of where it is going, nor set its compass, nor measure its advance, without remembering where it has been. The same scorn will deafen it to the wiser counsels of the past. Its thinking thereby becomes progressively more ingrown, its own counsels more halting and confused, its motion rudderless. Just such a sense of aimlessness has long been remarked in America, and is now felt by many.

But that is not the half of our dilemma. Those who toil to dismantle the West, the anti-heroes, the Innovators, as Lewis termed them, intend and induce our confusions. Destruction of our history is essential to their "new thinking." Well do the Innovators know that men without a past are forever children, easily manipulated and enslaved. Well do they see that the broader perspectives of a civilized history are the principal obstacle to their ambitions, the one unflinching witness and moral rebuke to their will. They move against it with all their craft. They deliberately deface our heritage and profane our shrines. They derogate traditional ways of thinking and religious beliefs, meaning to seal us into an endless present where men can no longer conceive their humanness and purpose. Every avenue of escape is under their attack at the conceptual level, much as Orwell so chillingly portrayed it in *1984.* Not idly do totalitarians—on both sides of the Iron Curtain—control information and rewrite history day by day to serve the ideological ends of Big Brother. An uncontrolled press offers no immunity. Our media are, on the contrary, more effective exponents of anti-heroism because their stance is voluntary. (Orwell modeled his "Ministry of Truth" on the BBC.) Our homegrown Innovators have found it is *very* easy to burn books, and without a hint of public protest. They simply "revise" them, on the complaint that the role of women, minorities or whatever "victim" group is politically fashionable has been downplayed by history. After the revision—surprise!—the political fashion remains and the history is gone. For instance, it is now impossible to find a public school textbook that gives an accurate account of the formative role of Christianity in American history. It is almost impossible to find one that mentions religion at all. Even such concepts as husband, wife and family have been carefully removed. Children in our public schools are taught a pure grade of anti-heroism. The Innovators keep trying to bring private schools under their control as well, so far with less success.

It is at this terrible disadvantage of "presentism" that we must confront the anti-heroic infection in our lives. There is no cure for it within our accustomed "new way of thinking": if we go on trying to see ourselves in the usual way, we will not see at all. And if we do not escape, it will be harder for our children to do so after their indoctrination in anti-heroism at school. The cure is in the perspectives of the eternal—in a truth that transcends time. Only with the concept of a timeless truth can we rise above the delusion that all things are to be measured by their place in time. We have to sweep away the trashy modern superstition that history is on some sort of grand, unstoppable march to human betterment. That picture was painted by pseudo-philosophers long dead and dead wrong. In its thrall, we automatically assume that "new" is better. The ceaseless anti-heroic murmur for "change" is a statement that everything past is evil, and *any* change is better. This is not only idiocy but moral defection. Does anybody really believe Germany was the better for Hitler? Change for the worse, both personal and social, is more the rule than the exception. Humans are born backsliders. It is difficult to better oneself, easy to succumb to temptation and slip into bad habits. The "new is better" doctrine is simply camouflage to excuse all our failings and immoral behavior. Evil does not gradually become good with the passage of time. Yet that is what we believe. We virtually welcome evil, in our present debasement, *because* it exists today where it did not yesterday. That is what we sink to when we judge doctrines on a scale of time and not by whether they are true and good.

With the concept of an eternal truth, we can understand Weaver's charge that "to establish the fact of decadence is the most pressing duty of our time...." Once that same story—of the Western transition from a religious to a secular basis—is seen as decline instead of "progress," all the pretensions of the whole modernist enterprise drop away, and we see ourselves at last in a stark, clear light. We see, too, that our descent has been great, down what we now call a "slippery slope," to the brink of the abyss. But for the first time in living memory we will find real hope, and direction, and purpose. The way will again be open to find redemptive meaning in life that we seek in vain from our own era. To admit that we made a wrong turning is only the first, but the most important, step in the journey home.

Weaver pinpoints the error in a mediaeval debate fully six centuries ago. Those times seem so remote from us, and the issues involved so obscure, that few now have any idea what was at stake. Moreover, tracing the spread of philosophic ideas over centuries is hardly everybody's cup of tea. Yet we owe it to ourselves to trace the gradual change in Western thinking, however briefly—if only to assure ourselves that a fateful turning was made long ago, that it was historical and traceable, and that it vents its full force on us now in the twentieth century. It will also help to understand that, given time, a very clever creature called man can, with a snowballing array of prideful speculations, scientific errors and self-serving rationales, persuade himself that night is day and evil is good. (For the serious student of these matters, Weaver's own brilliant exposition, *Ideas Have Consequences,* is a must.)

Before that long-ago debate, we understood ourselves to be creatures of a dual nature—as it were, part beast, part angel. We had been cast by God in His image, yet fell into sin in the rebellious wish to be "as gods" ourselves. Thus we became estranged from our Creator, forever torn between the downward pull of our materialistic, self-indulgent, animal appetites, and our elevation in spirit—the unslaked thirst again to be the good and obedient children of the Eternal Good, from Whom separation is death. The anti-hero, at his guileful best, will by no means deride this familiar story, but rather portray it as a charming myth sprung of man's innate but rather adolescent fear of death. Now that we have come of age, he will add, it is time to put all that aside and claim our destiny as autonomous, mature men. He will leave out that part of the story which told us death had been conquered, and he will not tell you that death is his own prescription. Where the old teaching was to renounce life and the things of this world for life everlasting, the anti-heroic is to renounce your soul and you can have neither your trinkets nor life.

In those six centuries, then, we have come from what even Solzhenitsyn recognized to be an excessive emphasis on our spiritual nature to a totally animalistic view of life. We are but beasts sprung from natural process; there is no God; there is no authority other than our own; there is no right or wrong; there is no imperative except the survival of the species, achieved by the strong preying on the weak. Indulge your every animal appetite, o modern man! This is the drumbeat of our "progressive" culture, its throb everywhere loosing the jungle instincts in us.

How could this total turnaround happen? With the power of ideas. When William of Occam—does one in a hundred of us now remember him?—claimed so long ago that universals have no real existence, he set in motion the whole chain of ideas that now denies us our souls. A "universal," to philosophy, is our conceptual categorization of a thing. Is there, for example, such a thing as Apple? We know the things so categorized—the sweet-tart crunchy fruits we so enjoy. But does Apple itself have a real existence? Occam said no, won the debate, and put Western civilization into reverse gear. It is very easy to sympathize with his point that the Apple concept is merely a convenience to the human mind, without external reality. It is very difficult to see where he erred. There is, after all, no Apple-god out there.

The mistake was incredibly subtle. To deny "Apple" is, in the end, to deny the reality of human concepts. It is to deny the workings of the human mind, and accept only the data of sensory experience—the careful study of which we have refined to call science, and with which we have transformed the world: all-too-conveniently forgetting that experience does not interpret itself, and that science is a dependent of human intelligence and our power to classify the data with universal concepts. With the idea of Apple or Tree or Genetic Coding, if you please. Yet with all of our science, we could not so much as identify an apple without the prior concept of Apple.

After that we are on the road to hell without the faintest idea why. There comes the claim, centuries ago, we do not remember, that only data of the senses, run through the scientific mill, are "valid" human knowledge (scientism). There follows the claim that only material phenomena are to be considered as determinants of our life force (positivism). Then follow all the death-seeking claims that a metaphysical view of life is unreal, that thought is not even thought, that we are all whirled about by a carousel of insensate "forces" (logical positivism and all known socialist stupidities), help-less and purposeless beasts.

It is the wondrous curiosity of our times that only those who serve evil act as humans. Denying any purpose to life to the rest of us, they act with purpose. After all, it is only with malicious intent that we can oppose the godhood of the State and the designs of Big Brother. Yet to act with intention is the refutation of the whole modern world, which depicts us as helpless pawns of deterministic "events" beyond our control. We are born free. We set our own compass in life. If we were the helpless, hopeless, prisoners of fate we are represented to be, there could never have been the beautiful thing called America. The anti-heroes hate America. Everything about America is wrong, they say, and should be "changed." You have heard that about every passing day of your life, have you not? America, in their eyes, is a mass of problems and an evil conception. Because there is so much of the real America left, it all stands in the way of a revised, properly Sovietized America.

So there we stand. The merchandizers of the modern and the anti-heroic, themselves (we hope) believers of their own propaganda, offer us a view of ourselves and our purposes as purely bestial. They do not know that they are recreating a barbarism older than written history. That barbarism is, indeed, clear to anyone who still believes in right and wrong.

The way out, and the only way, is the chosen rejection of the "new way of thinking." But according to older wisdom, we can always choose what we think, can't we? So, let's look at some of the conceptual contrivances that set the anti-hero apart in what he is pleased to call thought.

"If I am asked, as a purely intellectual question, why I believe in Christianity," G. K. Chesterton wrote early in this century, "I can only answer, 'For the same reason that an intelligent agnostic disbelieves in Christianity.' I believe it quite rationally upon the evidence. But the evidence in my case, as in that of the intelligent agnostic, is not really in this or that alleged demonstration; it is in an enormous accumulation of small but unanimous facts." It is this evidence, this accumulation of facts, that now concerns us. Chesterton, in this instance, was not writing a Christian apologetic, nor am I here. My subject is this world, not the next. Irreconcilable philosophies are at war in the West, and the battle between them is being fought here and now, with immense consequences for our future.

Interestingly, the questions have changed little since Chesterton addressed them nearly eighty years ago. But the evidence has changed; and so has the tide of battle. It has been many years since religious belief could safely be scorned as "unscientific" and embarrassingly naïve; and many more years since the educated fully expected the conflict to end in unconditional surrender by religion. But it was science that changed in those years: toward a new cosmology eerily suggestive of the old creation story. And religious faith has grown much stronger, surely impelled to some degree by the collapse of secular prescriptions in a bloodied and uneasy world. The conflict in the West is no longer the one-sided affair it seemed to be at the turn of the century; but it still rages. Certainly belief (or disbelief) in Christianity remains the pivotal question in secular matters as well as religious, for all of Western civilization was built on Christian foundations. Ultimately, therefore, the validity of one view or the other toward this question will determine not only the course of civilization, but whether we will even have one. Hence our concern here with the evidence, the accumulation of facts.

For four centuries, Western man has been cut loose from his moorings in a church-centered order. For two, an anti-heroic world view, an agnostic humanism, has been ascendant in the West. In its effect, this new world view may—without finger-pointing—be usefully likened to the growth of a cancer in a human body. (This is not to cast the anti-hero in the role of the "heavy"; we may curse the fates or blame our own bad habits for contracting the disease, but we can hardly blame the cancer for being what it is.) The point of the analogy is this. Like a cancer, anti-heroism is, as it were, sprung from Christian flesh; it is parasitic, borrowing both its reference to right and wrong and its secular structure from Christianity; and it is utterly antithetical to its host, the West of traditional Christianity: one or the other must die. This is, then, Total War. Indeed, we may carry the analogy one step further. As a cancer kills itself along with its victim, as the human cells go mad, so the anti-heroic view is so bent on the destruction of the Christian religion that it will destroy itself and bring down the world if it must in the effort. For the anti-hero, this is war without mercy. It was thus in Chesterton's time too: "This," he said, "is the last and most astounding fact about this faith; that its enemies will use any weapon against it, the swords that cut off their own fingers, and the firebrands that burn their own homes. Men who begin to fight the Church for the sake of freedom and humanity end by flinging away freedom and humanity if only they may fight the Church. This is no exaggeration: I could fill a book with instances of it." Toward the end of the century and its experience, we could fill many more.

Hostility to religion, and revelatory Christianity in particular, by the intellectual classes, is unique to the modern era. Never before have the better educated failed to uphold a religious basis for life; and never have less educated men been so deprived of moral leadership. I deem this among the most crucial questions of our time. Why has "modern man," the anti-hero, ceased to believe in traditional Judeo-Christian teachings, and even in God? Was it through the superior insights and knowledge of modern times, or was it error?

To answer these questions, we examine here a sampling of the charges the anti-hero brings against Christianity. The list of charges is long, but we need not cover it all. A few examples can pin down the frames of mind involved, and I leave it to your own "sense of the fitness of things" to decide which is right. Afterwards, we will similarly examine the positive beliefs of the modern anti-hero that purport to replace the old verities.

"Miracles are Impossible"

We do not think much about miracles any more, and that is a victory for the anti-heroic view. Yet we should. A miracle is God's action in time, in space, in nature. It tells us not only that God exists, but that he is the personal God of Christian concept, alive, creative, all-powerful and caring. Conversely, if miracles are not possible, either there is no God, or else He is abstract Spirit, infinitely removed and in effect powerless, hence safely ignored in the affairs of men. In either of these cases, the whole of Christianity is quickly and handily dispatched. A strong, dogmatic disbelief in miracles is a certain signature of the anti-hero.

Unquestionably central to Christian belief is the "Great Miracle," comprising the divine Incarnation and the Resurrection, Christ rising from the dead, miraculously restored in body as well as spirit. But equally central is that these miracles occurred *in history*—seen, investigated, recorded and attested by many who were willing to die to make their witness of them. These miracles—or whatever the events were—struck the Roman Empire in the full summer of its power with tidal force; such that even so belligerent and grouchy an anti-believer as H. G. Wells would later proclaim them "irresistibly, the center of history." For the faithful, except that Christ died on the cross and rose again (I Cor. *xv:*3-19), all Christian belief is "vain," a false witness before God, and those professing it are "of all men most miserable." A true disproof of miracles, one must concede, would therefore be a total refutation of Christianity; and for our purposes, by extension, a deathblow to Western civilization.

In return, the anti-hero especially must concede that whether these miracles occurred as alleged is a question of fact, not faith. Dogmatic statements prove nothing. A disproof of miracles cannot be valid unless it is on a factual (and in this case historical) basis. Anti-heroes love to boast that they look at the evidence, whereas believers accept miracles because of their faith: which is the exact opposite of the truth. It is believers who do the investigating and decide each case on the evidence; and anti-heroes who make a blanket rejection of all miracles with the dogma of a godless cosmos. How, for example, does the anti-hero reply to the historical case for the Great Miracle? Not with facts, but with a generalization which presumes to know the whole truth about the universe; a *gnosis;* a formula (formulas being another sure signature—and incurable addiction—of the anti-hero). He simply proclaims them "impossible." Neat. Directly to the point; and every bit as useful as any other eighteenth-century formula.

This one is easily traced to the famed *Essay* on miracles by the philosopher David Hume (1712–1776). Hume, renowned as a skeptic and empiricist, was in many respects the prototypal modern anti-hero. His system ruled out any knowledge not based on sensory experience (the scientism implicit in Occam's nominalism is stated frankly by Hume), and treated the scientific tool of probability as a philosophic device. With these methods, he pronounced the impossibility of miracles.

Hume derived probabilities from collective human experience, then applied—what else?—another formula as an assumption: the more a thing happens, the more likely it is to recur; and conversely. (False, and don't bet on it in Las Vegas.) Miracles, he said, are unique and wholly improbable interventions by supernature into nature. (How could he possibly know? Some say they are common.) Therefore, as the least likely of all events, miracles are a violation of the laws of probability. (No, and it is not possible to calculate the odds of a miracle anyway.) More: they violated the "firm and unalterable" laws of nature; our experience against miracles is "uniform." Case closed—just like that! Obviously if the laws of nature cannot be broken, and if miracles are assumed to break the laws of nature, then miracles are "impossible," or so remotely improbable that any other explanation of them, however bizarre, is more "likely." (We've had plenty of those since Hume.)

Hume's argument has been called circular, but really doesn't rise to the level of argument at all. It is mere assertion. He simply asked the same question in two different ways, as C. S. Lewis observed: "Do miracles occur"? and "Is the course of Nature absolutely uniform?" Then, by asserting the latter to be true, he "concluded" that the former was false. GIGO in computer parlance: garbage in, garbage out. The real question—whether the miracles did, in fact, occur as Christianity and history attest—was never discussed; and Hume had no answer. One may justly take this as evidence there is no refutation. If Hume had had a good factual case, he wouldn't have had to resort to such legerdemain. In truth, the historicity of the events has survived constant attack for two millennia, and is stronger than ever in modern scholarship.

Nevertheless, the intellectuals of that time were hungry to disbelieve, and embraced Hume's nonsense as Revealed Truth (just as their brethren, a century later, would embrace Darwin). Hume's formula has been muddying thought—and scholarship—ever since. That is: anything assertedly less improbable than the assertedly most improbable event, a miracle, is to be believed; rather than admit the miracle. It is illuminating to see what these supposedly hard-headed skeptics will believe, in order not to believe in miracles. Among the "explanations" of miracles offered and taken in all seriousness are these, described by Lewis: "Collective hallucination, hypnotism of unconsenting spectators, widespread instantaneous conspiracy in lying by persons not otherwise known to be liars and not likely to gain from the lie—all these are known to be very improbable events: so improbable that, *except for the special purpose of excluding a miracle,* they are never suggested. But they are preferred to the admission of a miracle" (emphasis added).

One other feature of the Humean argument should be noted. It takes for granted that a miracle would "violate" the laws of nature. This has not been established, and it need not be so. Scientific laws say nothing about the *origin* of "events" in nature. (Unless the universe is completely determined, with every event determined by a prior cause, in a seamless web all the way back to Big Bang, or wherever it all started. But if this were so, we could never have developed a science to find out about it; or to put it another way, scientific findings would themselves be determined rather than scientific, and we would have no reason to believe them.) All scientific laws describe process. They take the form, "If thus, then so": in such-and-such conditions, such-and-such will happen. Scientists—Eddington, for one—have argued that the human mind introduces events into nature. (In fact, you changed the shape of the entire universe when you chose to pick up this book.) Such an act does not violate nature's laws, but introduces something new into the process which thereafter, instantly, becomes subject to the laws. (If you drop the book, it will fall.) As men can change nature with their mind and will, so surely God in the Christian concept could do so, without "violating" the laws of His own creation. He did, after all, by this account, create the very laws the anti-hero tries to hold inviolable by God.

Needless to say, allegations of miracles did not end in biblical times, and efforts to explain them away are not improving in quality. There were, for instance, many miracles documented in the Middle Ages, but the anti-hero pooh-poohs them—the Mediaevals were so superstitious, you see. Ask how they were superstitious, and the reply is because they believed in miracles. Circular arguments don't help; and neither does ignorance of history. The Middle Ages were not superstitious, and especially not compared to our own times. One confusion ought to be cleared up here. A Christian is not *required* to believe in contemporary miracles by his creed. Nor is there anything mystical involved. A miracle, then or now, is accepted (or rejected) on human evidence, viewed with plain common sense. The only dogma which demands a statement about miracles is the anti-hero's own, which must deny them absolutely. In other words, dismissing miracles because their alleger (or investigator) is a Christian is wholly unjustifiable. And dismissing them by portraying the Mediaeval Schoolmen as ignorant, gullible bumpkins starts to get hilarious.

As many or more miracles are alleged in our times, times which certainly do not share in the supposed superstitions of the Middle Ages. And these (e.g., the miraculous cures claimed at Lourdes) are often subject to grueling scientific and medical investigations, which disallow all but a handful of the claims. But what are we to make of the very few that pass every test and defy scientific explanation? Current fashion among the skeptics seems to be simply denying that a miracle *is* a miracle. The disbeliever glibly asserts that the supposed miracle was just a natural event that we don't happen to understand yet, but will some day, when our science improves. Now, this may or may not prove to be true; but as yet it is no answer. What it does reveal is the philosophic stance of the speaker—and the surprising residual strength of naturalism, long after science abandoned it and philosophy dismissed it. The implicit assumption is that the miracle *must* be a natural event, because nature is "all there is." Even now is echoed the sad faith of nineteenth-century man in the "incurable routine of the cosmos." Seventy years after Einstein showed us a new and wholly different and mysterious universe, faith in Newton's dead cosmos is strong. With it, hand in glove, is the old deification of Science (complete with a capital S): the childlike faith that men's laboratory research will, in time, know everything, and make us masters of all nature. But omni-science and omnipotence belong to God, not man. And there is nothing innately impossible about miracles in Einsteinian cosmology.

I'd like to recall one other case. Earlier, I speculated that miracles may be an everyday occurrence, citing the unexpected and very mysterious heroism of "ordinary" people who sacrifice or risk their lives to save others. Whatever else these commonplace events may be, they are not "natural." They are the exact opposite of Darwinian "survival strategy," and thus a flat contradiction of the most hallowed tenets of evolutionary science. (The evolutionists who wish to tell me that one day science will have an answer to this are, in the same breath, saying that their present theories of evolution are false—and I'll wager they would, to a man, choke before uttering such heresy.) "Ordinary" heroism, moreover, is an act of the highest morality, supreme obedience to God's will ("Greater love hath no man...."). Morality is equally inexplicable to naturalist philosophies, and for that matter, to science. And yet more, there commonly occurs in these acts that baffling, immediate knowledge by the hero of what he must do—some sort of knowing wholly different from rational analysis, which the hero cannot put into words afterwards, and cannot bring himself to take credit for. I may well be mistaken in suggesting that this instant knowing may be a direct communication from God, by channels we do not know. But I can't think of any other way to account for it, and so far as I know, nobody else has offered any explanation at all. We do have extensive testimony that this tongue-tied sense of visitation by God has been experienced by many, in many different situations, for whom the experience was felt to be the most moving or pivotal in their lives. On the evidence, I think these cases do involve acts of God, and I will be interested to see what factual reasons the anti-hero can find for denying it.

What holds no water is the anti-hero's voluble, but never scientifically verified, assertion that all of this is out of bounds—simply because "miracles are impossible." That is dogmatism speaking, not evidence. Let he who will unseat the historical and present cases for miracles, do so if he can, with better evidence. But until a factual rebuttal is ventured for us to consider, and none is, we can be very comfortable with the vast accumulated evidence in favor of miracles. In the meantime, traditional Christianity comes through without a scratch. The anti-hero will have to dream up some entirely different reason for pitching out Western institutions and society.

"Man is merely another animal species distinguished from others—if that—only by superior intelligence."

This next charge by the anti-hero is very odd, more a mockery of Christian teaching than a refutation. If we are but brutes, we are, presumably, stripped of our souls, and our religious beliefs would not make sense. Our pretensions to a spiritual life, much less life eternal, would be foolish; and indeed, they have long been made to seem foolish by the anti-hero. But if he is right, how did humankind ever form the concept of spirit in the first place? Nature is amoral. There is not a hint of the otherworldly in the workings of nature or the behavior of beasts. There is nothing around us from which to conceive a spiritual basis for life. We literally could not imagine such a thing, for even imagination must have something, some hint, to start with. A world with only beasts can have no gods, and this is what the anti-hero says the world is. Yet in our world, one of the beasts worships.

Odder, the anti-hero asserts our status as mere beasts in the name of a breathtaking vision of a new world order and a glorious future for humanity. Alas, there will be no humanity to enjoy it. Our new beasthood takes away, not our souls alone, but everything about us that is uniquely human. We lose—are losing—our literature and poetry and art, our laughter and our tears, our ceremonies and celebrations, and ultimately, all hope. We are becoming what we are said to be: unmen; beasts. Some may find these thoughts hyperbole. I wish they were. Precisely as the anti-hero's charge has spread through the West, we have been ravaged by a tragic dehumanization. A glance at our literature or culture or art will show how far we have sunk from the heights of Western creativity. The idea also takes the form of a denial of men's moral agency, a repudiation of personal responsibility. Beasts have no responsibility. This notion saturates behaviorism and centralist politics. We find it in the claim that alcoholism is an illness, that poverty is caused by slums, that criminality is the product of a bad environment, that all manner of human problems are "society's" fault: anything is to blame but our own misbehavior. Of these matters, we have more to say elsewhere. Meanwhile, let no one feign surprise that a broad denial of our humanity is reducing us to beasts. I think it is meant to. At least the anti-heroes, with admirable consistency, make no pretense to being human themselves. Although they often call themselves humanists, they are full of contempt for the human values and ideals that help us rise above our animal nature. All this is idle sentimentality; their concern, they say, is strictly with the truth. And they marshal whole sciences to give more currency to their charge. But is it not peculiar that a beast claims to honor Truth?

That we are animals, everyone has always known. It needs no philosophic explanation. What needs explaining, if I may put it so, is that we are the only animal that *knows* it is an animal. Other species show no awareness of this. They all give every appearance of accepting what they are without question; certainly none publishes treatises or holds seminars on its animal status. Surely we must be grateful to those men and women who, for no reason apparent in natural selection, search the rock and sift the soil to find bits of bone to prove we are related to birds and fish and primates. We know because we found out. The Galapagos finches have exactly no interest in these matters.

Man is a very *strange* animal. Everyone knows that, too. Not that there is anything particularly queer about our physical equipment; this is all quite reasonable. But gorillas have hands as we do, yet use them for very little, and never to play the piano or skip stones or whittle or write letters. Dolphins have bigger brains than we do, but you seldom hear them discoursing on nuclear physics. Chihuahuas are more hairless than we, but have never thought to wear clothes. People everywhere wear artificial coverings, and so far as we can tell, have done so since they became people, even where protection against the elements is not needed. Why *do* we wear clothes? There is nothing like this in nature. But our kind, like no other, has a sense of wrongness about itself, and we feel shame about it, and cover our nakedness. Man alone weeps for cause, and "is shaken with the beautiful madness called laughter," as Chesterton put it, "as if he had caught sight of some secret in the very shape of the universe hidden from universe itself." Man alone can tame other species; or perhaps I should say, humanize them, for man is the only wild animal: all others conform to the behavior pattern of their kind. It amuses him, and he thinks nothing of it, but any other species would think—if it could think—that this capacity was fabulous. It would suppose us to be gods (or at times demons, but no less extranatural on that account). Chesterton observed, "... the more we really look at man as an animal, the less he will look like one.... It is not natural to see man as a natural product. It is not common sense to call man a common object of the country or the seashore. It is not seeing straight to see him as an animal. It is not sane."

What is this mysterious quality about humankind that sets us so far apart from other animals? Why are we alone consumed with an insatiable curiosity about our status on this earth? With what uniquely human equipment do we hypothesize a truth about our existence and seek to harmonize our experience with this truth? These are the questions that have always been at the heart of philosophic inquiry. The anti-hero, in effect, dismisses them all with one mighty axe stroke: There are no qualitative differences. We are just smarter than other beasts. We can be no more than sentient animals, and one cannot be entirely sure of our sentience, either. Whether our thought be real or apparent, it is in any case no more than the end product of a long struggle for survival.

This, I submit, is the only truly new doctrine of the anti-hero. Never before have men regarded themselves as merely animals. Not just Christians but pagans, ancient or modern, polytheist or pantheist, have always thought otherwise; and have given a flood of testimony through the ages about the spiritual side of man. Even atheists asserted the unique humanness of humans with vigor until the rise of anti-heroic thought. This new doctrine reveals a great chasm in human thinking that divides us from all past wisdom. But then, nothing less than the discovery of some great new truth, or the baring of some dark, deep longing in our nature, could have spurred the immense effort over the past century or two, by reasonable and intelligent people, to prove that—we aren't people. Which was it that impelled this prodigious labor, a shining new truth, or all-out rebellion against God? This we must know; for if the anti-hero is wrong, if he has thrust us into a war against the still living God, our works will be bitter indeed. And just this is the singular fact of our time. In the high noon of the teaching that men are mere brutes, men have never been more brutal toward one another. This is evidence, is it not? And evidence bought at fearful cost. More innocent blood has been spilled in our century than in all time before us. The brotherhood of man is torn every passing day by warfare and terrorism without mercy. Nor is it any coincidence that much of the violence was, and is, perpetrated by believers in the anti-heroic doctrine. Those who think themselves beasts see nothing amiss in behaving bestially. Yet all this was supposed to be on behalf of a new and better order for, well, beastkind that has nowhere appeared, and if the traditional wisdom of mankind is right, never will.

It is not difficult to see where modernist thought went wrong. It runs aground on the fundamental contradiction at the heart of all naturalist philosophies. You cannot conclude that "the universe is all there is," and that men therefore are mere beasts, without reasoning. But reason itself is a great mystery. It is not to be found in the mindless physical world. We cannot derive reason from unreason. If our reason is valid, it must have been given us by some ultimate Reason outside this world: by God. But then, the universe cannot be "all there is," but rather, God's creation. If our reason is not valid, then we haven't any basis for believing the conclusion that the universe is all there is. Either way, the doctrine is proven false. Somehow, in thinking about the universe, the anti-hero forgot that he was engaged in one of its greatest puzzles—a beast thinking about the universe. His doctrine accounts for only that which needs no explaining, our animal status. It fails to account for precisely those strange qualities about us that are the starting point of philosophy: our Reason, our Free Will, our adherence to a Moral Law that is not of this world. Instead, the anti-hero tries to explain all this *away*—and with another dratted formula!

It doesn't work. It keeps smashing into the basic contradictions. We can no more deduce free will or morality from nature than we can our reason. They are purely extra-natural qualities. We must use our will to study the world. If we conclude that the world is of a character that does not allow free will, we destroy our credentials for saying so. We seek knowledge as a good. If we conclude ourselves amoral beasts in an amoral world, we have destroyed our own findings. If we dismiss our thought as the meaningless secretion of the brain organ as asserted by epiphenomenalism—and this is the most rigorous formulation of what beasthood in a mindless universe really means—we dismiss everything built with thought, including this one. There is no escape from this trap. The real question is, how did we get into it?

I think it goes back to that remarkable fourteenth-century debate among the Schoolmen over nominalism. We rightly deem William of Occam the winner. But it is far from clear that he was *right*. In denying the reality of universals, ultimately he denied the reality of Truth itself. It is not too strained a simplification to say that men *did* abandon truth in time, and replaced it with scientism—excluding, by definition, all knowledge except that derived by empirical science. Scientism is the heart and soul of anti-heroism. But science has no instruments or meters or tools to measure heart and soul. It cannot analyze our souls with gas chromatography. It cannot weigh our spirit. It is stone blind to all the mysterious qualities of men that make us men. It is only if we look at ourselves with the eyes of men that we see ourselves as more than beasts. It is impossible to do with scientific methods. So it happens that when the anti-hero denies the reality of metaphysical knowledge, of knowledge that cannot be confirmed by science, he denies our humanity itself. With this reasoning, the anti-hero turns men into brutes. The rest is ghastly history. Science, wielded by moral men, is a most admirable tool. But it is a limited tool. When we attempt to make it an absolute, when we try to make it the source of all knowledge, when we make it a god, we make ourselves demons.

"Primeval religions arose in ignorance and fear, and therefore give a false picture of life."

Let us consider briefly this one last charge by the anti-hero, a sweeping denial of Christian or any other religious belief. From the previous discussion we can see very quickly how this fits into the anti-hero's frame of mind.

It seems to me singularly difficult to compress much more ignorance and prejudice into a proposition than this one. When you try to look at the evidence for it, you find there is practically none. We know little more than superficial detail about prehistoric men, for the simple reason that they did not keep records. How do we conclude that he lived in darkness and fear? All peoples have had a tradition that the earth was much kinder in the distant past; and all have a tradition of a Fall. Such legends as we have of dark religion or human sacrifice portray them as a new and horrifying thing. Neither can religious belief be considered primitive. It requires great refinement of mind and a considerable knowledge of the natural world. Christianity itself is anything but simple. Life is not simple, and Christian teaching addresses its deepest mysteries. One would have to be wholly ignorant of Christian doctrines (and the anti-hero often is) to deem them obsolete or simplistic.

The anti-hero likes to think of himself as enlightened and modern, which is fine; but it certainly does not justify his general prejudice against anything that is old or (in his view) "superstitious." His own non-religious view sinks on the contradiction in naturalism, and can itself be called a superstition. Certainly, his quasi-worship of such strange gods as Nature and Evolution and Historical Determinism is the mark of a primitive.

Once again, the anti-hero's charge is far more sweeping than the evidence will allow, and that is really all one need say about it.

The common thread in the several charges brought against the West by the anti-hero is that they see one side of human life, the earthly, animal side. They disallow our higher nature, our spirit, our soul, our claim to be creatures of God made in some manner in His image. Looking at life only through the limited lens of science, denying intellection, introspection, or revelation as a valid source of knowledge, denying even the reality of Truth, they give us a picture of life that is simply untrue. We are not mere beasts and we do not act as if we were. The universe is not a dead machine but a vital, ordered, beautiful work of art. The anti-heroes, for all their claims, are men, and live by the ways of men. No sooner do they deny goodness in the cosmos than they exhort their flock to build a better order for mankind. Yet their claims are false and devisive, and leave the mass of men at a loss to know what to believe. The pretensions of religion are mocked, but science gives us no moral leadership; and gradually we sink to less human, less civilized, less moral state. We have not built a new order, but destroyed an order that was good.

But there is always evidence we can consider, and facts we can accumulate, to reach the truth. The anti-hero simply gets his facts wrong. It was just the same in Chesterton's time: "The agnostic...is a non-believer for a multitude of reasons; but they are all untrue reasons. He doubts because the Middle Ages were barbaric, but they weren't; because Darwinism is demonstrated, but it isn't; because miracles do not happen, but they do; because monks were lazy, but they were very industrious; because nuns are unhappy, but they are particularly cheerful; because Christian art was sad and pale, but it was picked out in peculiarly bright colours and gay with gold; because modern science is moving away from the supernatural, but it isn't, it is moving towards the supernatural with the rapidity of a railway train."

We do ourselves the greatest disservice by consenting to the anti-hero's charges against the West, without having all the facts at hand.

Chapter IV
The Curious Faiths of Anti-Heroism

It is required
You do awake your faith. Then all stand still;
On: those that think it is unlawful business
I am about, let them depart.
—Shakespeare, *Winter's Tale*

While the mute creation downward bend
Their sight, and to their earthly mother tend,
Man looks aloft and with expectant eyes
Beholds his own hereditary skies.
—Ovid

In recent years, a god called "the Me" claimed so many con-
verts that the 1970s became known as "the Me generation."
Professor Robert Nisbet included the mystical tenet of the Me
in his *History of the Idea of Progress:* "All that matters is
what lies within the Me, its pains and its release from pains."

The Me's apostles soon filled the paperback racks with exhortations for one to discover the Real Me and set it free. For those poor souls in a fallen relationship with the Me, secular redemption was promised through exercise and jogging, better nutrition, transactional analysis, group encounters and the like; and in the event of any failure whatever, counseling, always counseling. Robert Capon explored this subject in detail and it is indeed food for thought.

If so unpromising a god as unrelieved narcissism, the Me, can form the basis for a mass religion, it is indeed wisely said that everyone must believe in some god. By "god," I mean whatever preemptive Authority we set over the mystery of our being. The Authority, of course, can be virtually anything, secular or divine, from the Me, or the sun, or cocaine, to the Tao of the East, the one God of Islam, and the Holy and Undivided Trinity of Christianity. To a son of the Enlightenment, the god of all men is Man, our collective being transcending the individual, and thus apotheosized. Men may die, but Man will live forever, under the care of the heavenly host: Science, Progress, Enlightenment, Evolution, Revolution, and all the angels on high. Man, made priest of creation through Nature's selection, shall rule the very cosmos. Men "shall be as gods."

This is most curious. We see we are, as it were, god-ridden or god-fueled. The most resolute efforts by Rational Atheist Societies and Militant Atheist Leagues succeed only in producing weird new faiths of their own. It appears literally impossible for us to believe in nothing. Without an absolute standard of Good, we have no way to discern between better and worse; our life loses all direction; we can't think at all. Our minds just don't work that way. Yet if we are, as the anti-hero insists, purely natural creatures in a purely natural universe, how could a god concept have possibly arisen at all? Nothing like this is observable in nature, nor could it ever in a purely material cosmos. When we look at nature with the eyes of beasts, we see only nature. Only when we look at her with the eyes of men, with reverence and wonder and intelligence, do we see spirit. And we all do see the workings of the divine. The god concept is common to us all, and nags us all unmercifully. Where did it come from, if not from our Creator? How else could it be that our minds will not function without a god figure? Surely it is clear we carry within us a divine spark, else we could not conceive these matters, much less long to be "as gods." One is reminded of the first moment we did see ourselves with the eyes of men, as related in the creation story in *Genesis*. There occurs one of the most striking passages in mythology—and as we'll see, I do not use that word to mean "false." (We may think of *Genesis* as fanciful, but next to all other creation myths it is as prosaic as a newspaper report.) When Adam and Eve had eaten the forbidden fruit, "the eyes of them both were opened, *and they knew that they were naked.*" Their first act "as gods" was to get dressed—imagine! All peoples of all times have worn clothes, and it is one of those maddening details about this strange beast, man, that defies materialist theories. Here, allegorically, at the beginning of our career in the god business, what we saw was our fall and our shame. No evolution myth can give us half so good an account of ourselves.

And that is a prime clue to our nature, this everlasting temptation "to be as gods, knowing good and evil." Is it not just this that impels the anti-hero to dethrone God and deify himself? As we saw in the last chapter, anti-heroism centers in rebellion against all religion, and against Christianity particularly. Yet anti-heroes, as all other men, must have god concepts. The philosophical inquirer will always find it rewarding to ask what god a man will believe in, if he won't believe in the Creator. It is ever instructive to see what the anti-hero *will* believe, in order to disbelieve in God. We therefore ask here: with what god does the anti-hero displace the Almighty? To what faith or faiths does he cling?

The investigator would find many. There is a pantheism, made to look new and modern when it is as old as man, dressed in the conceit that it is more spiritual and refined than the old faiths, when it is merely so dilute and empty as to be no faith at all. There is what Professor Voegelin terms gnosticism, which in simplest terms is the reduction of complex reality to *gnosis,* formulas, with neither reverence nor understanding: a permanent lure for the anti-heroic mind. But it is a trap, egotism posing as knowledge, and its fruits are bitter. There is "alienism," in Joseph Sobran's coinage, a sort of holy rejection of the normal and enduring foundations of civilization, a rejection of the center in favor of the abnormal, the outsiders, the minorities and supposed victims. And many more. As before, we need not examine all the curious faiths of the anti-hero. A close look at a few will do. But it may be said: wherever the doctrine that "religion is irrelevant," or worse, is voiced or implied, you have found the influence of anti-heroic faith.

Naturalism

The view that Nature is "the whole show" and "all there is" is as old as mankind. The polytheism of the ancients was a form of naturalism, for the gods were not believed to exist outside

Nature and creators of the world. In modern times, infused with the findings of a growing science in the West, naturalism has become immensely influential in all our lives. All anti-heroes cleave strongly to naturalism, whether through a scientistic basis or as an unexamined premise about the nature of reality.

Let us attempt a definition. Nature, in this view, is the interlocking system of the physical universe. The Natural is what comes forth or goes on of its own accord, spontaneously, unasked. All finite events are part of the system, and nothing exists outside of Nature. Nature is thus the Ultimate Fact, the self-existent thing, on which all phenomena depend and of which all phenomena are a part. In our own century, the physical universe has been given a highly specific shape and size by Einstein's equations, and beyond it is nothing—not infinite empty space but literal nothingness. Everything in space and time is part of Nature.

The contrapositive view may be called supernaturalism: the belief that the Ultimate Fact upon which all depends is in some manner above and beyond Nature, out of space and time, and is the Creator of the universe. This view is likewise as old as mankind. But let us limit it here to the Western view of God, other forms of supernaturalism being irrelevant to this discussion.

The argument, today as of old, is which is right: the naturalist or the supernaturalist? This may seem far removed from practical concerns, but there could hardly be any more important concern—or any more down to earth. To abridge a famous remark by Chesterton, "There are some people, and I am one of them, who ... think the question is not whether the theory of the cosmos affects matters, but whether, in the long run, anything else affects them." For, of course, if we believe life is a purely natural event determined by a purely natural cosmos, our institutions and customs and personal lives will be shaped by that view, and will be totally unlike life built on belief in God. Indeed, the whole story of the past century or two is the remolding of Western life under the growing reach of naturalism.

The naturalist view is completely determinist. That is, all "events" interlock, and all are the result of previous events, in an unbroken chain of cause-and-effect going back to the beginning of things. Thus no serious naturalist believes in human free will. If our will were more than an illusion, we would actually be introducing "new" events, without previous cause, into Nature's system (and without her say-so). This would put us outside the system, dictating to Nature instead of obeying her, so it is not possible under naturalism. This means you literally have no choice about reading this book at this moment; your doing so was, as it were, determined by the stars. Nor have I any choice in what I'm writing, being, as it were, merely a stenographer for what is dictated by the dance of the atoms. Consequently, if I were to write that all naturalists were ugly useless cockroaches, the naturalist would have to agree that Nature herself forced me to say so. But would it mean anything? Of course not. For the same reason, the statements naturalists seem to make in apparent defense of naturalism are illusions, written by Nature, without meaning. Yet they seem to believe their own babble. Why?

Kindred difficulties—which is to say, impossible contradictions—await us if we look at the naturalist view of thought and morality. The rigorous naturalist claims that human reason is also an illusion, and thought a meaningless secretion of the brain gland. Any other interpretation would allow human reason, again impermissibly, to overrule Nature and change the system from outside it. Or to put it another way, we all accept and use the rule that no thought or reasoning is valid if it is the result of irrational causes. We automatically disallow the drunk's claim, no matter how closely reasoned, that he is under attack by pink elephants. The same principle applies to all thought, to reason itself. Human life arises from irrational causes, the physical universe. If, through natural selection, we develop what we think is thought and reason, it is nonetheless an illusion, the result of irrational movement by atoms in our brains.

The central claim of naturalism is that Nature is the whole show, and that there is no God outside her intruding. Human claims to spiritual nature thus suffer the same fate our claims to reason. Nature is amoral; men are part of nature; we can have no moral nature. The same universal law that we use for reasoning is equally applicable to moral behavior: we automatically disallow any moral claim that can be traced to self-interest or amoral causes. Because amoral Nature is the cause of all events, all human morality is disallowed; it is deemed another illusion. There are no such things as good and evil, right and wrong; any contrary opinion is leftover superstition from a pre-scientific age.

Step by rigorous step, the naturalist thus denies our human qualities, but each time ignoring the contradictions that leave the theory of naturalism in ruins. Contriving the theory required a great deal of thought and the finest scientific reasoning: only to conclude that thought and reason are meaningless. If the conclusion is correct, the theory is nonsense and no one need believe it. If the conclusion is false, it is just that, false, the theory is again nonsense. To unblinded eyes, the naturalist chose the career that led him to conclude that choice is impossible. Why, then, should his apparent choice make any difference to anybody? Finally, he denies all morality in one breath, and exhorts us all to become naturalists in his next—for the good of mankind.

Naturalism, looked at philosophically rather than through the truncated thought of science, is an insult to the intelligence. I do not see how its theorists, even if their minds are epiphenomenal, can stand building a world view on two-words blatant contradictions. As I. A. Richards put it, "We cannot have it both ways, and no sneers at the limitations of logic... amend the dilemma." Confront the theorist and he will gently agree that naturalism is a web of illusions, that his work and thought are illusions, that the theory is not true and makes no claim to be. He may add something to the effect that our will and reason and thought, so-called, were some sort of evolutionary development useful to survival as a species, though still illusory. But that won't do either; it took a lot more than meaningless thought to dream up Darwinism. There really is no arguing with people who claim to have proved no proofs are possible. Yet the next day the naturalist, human after all, will be back in the pulpit urging his views on us or writing another book that Nature is the whole show.

For instance, a few years ago Hamilton, Trivers et al. launched something called kin theory, stating that instances of "cooperative" or "altruistic" (how would scientists form such a concept?) behavior are genetically determined, according to the nearness of transmissible genes. Roughly stated, we are more likely to do something nice for our children than for our second-cousin's children, and not at all likely to be nice to a neighbor's dog. Now, I don't know the gentlemen and have no idea whether they are naturalists of the sort we have been discussing. However, this is the sort of theory naturalists love to seize on and apply to human behavior with little or no evidence (the study in question concerned insects). If the theory applies to us, it means that Lenny Skutnik would almost surely not have dived into the Potomac to rescue a stranger; but he did. Surely it must mean that no human would ever risk his life to rescue a drowning cat; but they do. The error of naturalism lies in equating insects with people, on ignoring the rule, "one law for men, another for things." Or again, Harvard sociobiologist Edward Wilson affirmed (*On Human Nature,* 1979) that "life and mind have a physical basis," and that the "minimum claims" of evolutionary theory are that the behavioral and social sciences have to be "consistent" with the laws of physical science, and "linked in chains of causal explanation." Wherewith we learn that, "The emotional control centers in the hypothalmas and limbric systems of the brain flood our consciousness with all the emotions" used by "ethical philosophers" in perceiving "standards of good and evil." Mind is "an epiphenomenon of the brain," secreting the meaningless illusion of thought. Bravo! Dr. Wilson, on a classic presentation of naturalism. My hypothalmus and limbric systems this very moment are flooding my epiphenomenon with the delightful, albeit meaningless, thought that thought is meaningless. It would be mischievous to wonder whether, if thought is so useless, Harvard oughtn't throw open its admissions to all students? Or just close shop? (Pardon me, my limbric system made me say that.)

After we see the fundamental fallacy of naturalism, there is nothing more to be said to its adherents, and only one more thing to be said of the theory. Namely, it is a blunder of unbelievable cost at the center of the great tragedy of our era. In denying our humanity, it has made us brutes. In denying God and all moral authority, it has delivered us into the coercive power of the unlimited parasitic state. In rejecting a moral order, it has torn the restraints off mass war, off political genocide and persecution, and off crime. Under its malign influence, the values of life, liberty, property and family have been under constant assault and gravely damaged. In a word, naturalism is a weapon in the hands of the anti-hero intent on bringing down all civilization.

You see, it really does matter, and matter very much, how we think about the cosmos.

New Myths for Old

Albert Jay Nock once remarked that he would almost pin his hopes for the hereafter on a chance to talk with Socrates, Rabelais and Jefferson. Given the chance, I think I'd choose to eavesdrop on a conversation between Hugo Dyson, J. R. R. Tolkien and C. S. Lewis at Magdalen College, Oxford, September 19, 1931. All three of these brilliant scholars felt that something remarkable occurred that evening, and were moved to write about it later. Tolkien didn't leave until 3:00 a.m. Dyson and Lewis, still pumped up, walked and talked till dawn broke. The conversation was a turning point for Lewis, and in this one may say that it has changed the world. Lewis, once an outspoken atheist, had only shortly before become "the most reluctant convert in all England." But he had gone no further than theism, merely intellectual acceptance of an Absolute Being. But as he wrote his close lifetime friend, Arthur Greeves, a few days later, "... I have just passed on from believing in God to definitely believing in Christ—in Christianity.... My long night talk with Dyson and Tolkien had a good deal to do with it." Thereafter and for the rest of his life, Lewis was, of course, an outstanding Christian apologist, perhaps the greatest of our time. Something remarkable surely *did* occur that evening.

The subject that so excited their interest is not one we would be likely to guess. It is one the anti-hero would greet with a yawn or dismiss with rationalist scorn. If we ourselves pay scant heed to it, that marks another victory for the anti-hero. But if the conversation at Magadalen is any measure, we may be missing something important or even profound. The subject was mythology: that tattered, much-debunked, remnant of truth robed in the imagination and fables and poetry of the ancient world.

To the modern mind, demythologization perhaps marks the triumph of science over "superstition." But myths were common to all people, and remain so to all but the enlightened Westerner. Can we be so sure they did not have reference to a deep yearning in our own nature? And can we be certain we have not replaced them with new gods, new superstitions, and a new mythology in our own style that we do not see as such? It seems to me little better than an anti-hero conceit that all that "old stuff" was nonsense, and that we are ever so much smarter than our ancestors. It is surely unfair to label as "myth" something we mean to call false.

It is by no means my point that we all ought to rush out and buy a copy of *Bulfinch's Mythology*; and even less that we should *believe* the old stories. Even the ancients did not believe them in the same sense that, say, the monotheist believes in God. My point, rather, is to find out what they were all about, and what they tell us about ourselves. For this, our hearing must be respectful: we learn nothing by scoffing. We also want to know why the anti-hero is so insistently skeptical of myths. Could he somehow feel threatened by old yarns of giants and feathered snakes and Olympian beings? This would indeed be curious. Yet I did a little checking, and found that the anti-hero view of mythology has made it into the dictionary. In Webster's Second Unabridged (c. 1930), "mythical" still meant simply "based on myth." In the Third Edition (c. 1960), the synonym given for mythical is "fictitious," and among the definitions is "... ignorantly or willingly without facts or in defiance of facts." Myth has become a lie, and an almost malicious, reactionary lie at that.

And that is the odd thing. Why would anyone labor to prove that myths aren't *true?* Myths are flights of fancy, daydreams, fairy tales. They were never meant to be taken literally. Only poets can make them, and they can only be appreciated artistically. Some are good, some childish, some funny, and some approach profound art (as in Greek trage-dies). They show every degree of skill, of mind, and of imagination that humans possess. But always they are art, the songs of poets and mystics, to be enjoyed in symbol and wonder; to be understood, if at all, by not trying to understand them. A myth loses all its delight the moment some academic spoilsport says, "This is what it means." The anti-hero not only says this, but adds that the myth is a lie.

Arianna Stassinopoulos, one of the most gifted young minds of our time, warns us that the anti-hero's "war against imagination is complete. Yet imagination is man's most princely faculty—the one that most sharply distinguishes him from other creatures. It is imagination which gives meaning and value to our experience, which both discerns mystery and brings comprehension and order to the world." "It may," she adds, "seem absurd to 'the modern mind,' but a great part of political history is purely symbolic. The Bastille, when it was taken, was not a horrible prison—it was hardly a prison at all. (It was found to contain only seven old men who were annoyed at being disturbed.) But it was a symbol and its destruction was the breaking of a stone image." Hence to judge the incident by its almost ludicrous facts would be to destroy one of our better modern myths, "the storming of the Bastille."

What we learn from myths is not that there are giants with one eye, or that the cow jumped over the moon, or that the Bastille held seven old men. We learn that men are poets and mystics moved by the mysteries of life and the divine powers of nature. We learn that we who are human yearn to share in the mysteries about us, yearn to add meaning to mystery by personalizing it, yearn to finish the tales. Always our myths bespeak our wonder that nature is, precisely, unnatural, a thing touched somehow by divinity. Should the story tell us, said Chesterton, that when we pluck a certain flower a princess in a castle across the sea will die, a thing impossible seems almost inevitable; our imagination accepts it before cold reason can say nay. Scientific literalism may sneer that this defies the laws of nature, but cannot explain why our heart leaps and our blood pounds. In truth, the nature we are part of is larger and far more beautiful than is seen by the anti-hero literalist. Pity the sad soul who must regard a tale in "scientific" terms, for this is the only way it can be completely misunderstood. Adds Chesterton, "... he who has no sympathy with myths has no sympathy with men."

The one thing we cannot say about myths is that they are lies. The anti-hero, thinking himself enlightened by saying this, denies his own humanity. Myths are men's stories, a common heritage of all peoples. They have always been—until the rise of the anti-hero—a reflection of something very deep in our nature, and a common source, in symbolic language, of the transcendant truths that bind us in human society. Who, except in a truly natural, wonderless world, would say that a tale is nonsense and that dreams cannot come true? But if we inhabited such a world, men themselves would have been wonderless things, unable ever to spin myths. And here we see what this odd dispute about mythology is really about. Mythology has always had religious overtones, reflecting the quest of man's soul for its rightful home. This the anti-hero must ruthlessly suppress. There is no scrap of room in his lonely cosmos for anything unnatural or divine. No hint of the miraculous or even the imaginative may intrude. But the anti-hero's "scientific" literalism gives us a world far too prosaic for our spirit, our imagination, our humanness—and we hate it. We are forever unhappy in it. It gives us nothing but earthbound appetites when we long to soar above ourselves. All our great myths knew better than this, and gave us wings for the starlit skies.

The argument is thus between the would-be rationalist and the poet who likens a skylark's flight to a rose in thick foliage. The prosaic mind can claim that there is no comparison between them, and in a sick way this is true, or rather half-true. But is it all we want of life that a skylark may be no more to us than a bird, species *Alauda arvensis?* This is what Dyson, Tolkien and Lewis were arguing about: the truth of myth and metaphor. Let us advert again to their memorable conversation.

Tolkien—author of the best-known, most loved fairy tales of our time (*The Hobbit* and *The Lord of the Rings* trilogy)—wrote a poem about the experience, titled "Mythopoeia." Only a few lines of it have been published. But he did say of it elsewhere, "I once wrote to a man [Lewis] who described myth and fairy-stories as 'lies'; though to do him justice he was kind enough and confused enough to call fairy-story making 'breathing a lie through silver.'" Lewis lost the debate, knew how badly he had lost, and would in time write wonderful myths both for children (*The Chronicles of Narnia*) and for adults (*The Space Trilogy*). In his next letter to Greeves, Lewis explained: "Now what Dyson and Tolkien showed me was this: that if I met the idea of a sacrifice in a pagan story I didn't mind it at all; again, that if I met the idea of a god sacrificing himself to himself.... I liked it very much and was mysteriously moved by it.... provided I met it anywhere *except* in the Gospels. The reason was that in pagan stories I was prepared to feel the myth as profound and suggestive of meanings beyond my grasp even though I could not say in cold prose 'what it meant.'" (Clearly, Lewis had still been in the grip of the rejection of Christianity that is central to anti-heroism.) He continued, "Now the story of Christ is simply a true myth: a myth working on us in the same way as the others, but with this tremendous difference that *it really happened:* and one must be content to accept it in the same way, remembering that it is God's myth where the others are men's myths: i.e., the pagan stories are God expressing

Himself though the minds of poets, using such images as he found there, while Christianity is God expressing Himself through what we call 'real things.' "

Whether or not one agrees with Lewis here, it is clear that his rejection of mythology had not been "rationalist" at all, but dogmatic. It is essential to the anti-hero's belief that all religion be meaningless, and that Christianity in particular be untrue. That is why the anti-hero labors to call fairy stories lies. With this he devises another dratted formula, itself logically impeccable, but too conveniently forgetting that syllogisms have no necessary relation to reality (e.g., only unicorns have scruples; Socrates has scruples; therefore, Socrates is a unicorn). In this case, the formula is: all myths are untrue; Christianity is a myth; therefore—well, you get the picture. Thus one may, with perfect accuracy, speak of "the Christian myth," only to have the lazy mind dismiss Christianity as untrue. That mind has been suckered by the false premise planted by anti-heroes that myths are "untrue." One might add that the Christian, referring to historical events as "mythic," is using a narrow and formal meaning of the word, wholly unlike the broad and unappreciative usage of the anti-hero. No one, including the Greeks, ever thought that Ceres and Zeus and Athena were historical figures. One may claim that the story of Christ did not happen, or was other than alleged; but not that it was "mythical" and *therefore* untrue.

The other side of our story is that the anti-hero, human despite his own protestations, is a prolific spinner of myths himself. Given his stunted and bloodless view of life, his myths are usually pretty awful, but there is no doubting the breed. Real Deities, announced in Capital Letters, parade around and do all manner of weird things among themselves, or to Man. In the myth of Historical Determinism, the goddess History moves forward in stages, carrying us to ever higher states of society, until we embrace the heavenly Socialism in the end. History's sister, Economy, likewise determines that Capitalism (an evil god indeed) will be overcome by Socialism in time. There are swarms of deities in the anti-hero's pantheon, all perfect and quite impervious to human frailty. The Presidency, Democracy, the Working Class, Higher Education, the Environment, Girl Scouts— there are no end of them, all immortal, all beyond sin. Hence, the Presidency survived Nixon and lives on. Economy was ravaged by Inflation, but will recover. Every human group or institution is personified as a deity ("the White House said today..."), and every tale told about them is a true myth, as real to modern listeners as the doing of Greek gods were to the Greeks. Except we have far more deities and tell far more myths about them than the ancients. The only reason we do not see all this as superstitious in the extreme is that we have discarded the art of making *good* myths, and rebuked the sense of reverence that wells deep within us. All we have left is a horde of wretched ideological myths, redoubled in number to make up for their almost total lack of art. We see again, in our petty appeals to the goddesses Ecology, Natural Selection, Improving Technology and all the rest, how profound were the warnings that if we will not believe in the True Myth, we will believe in anything. No more today than in the ancient world can the human mind get along without reaching for the divine.

Only one of the anti-hero's myths seems to me to have any beauty or depth to it; so perhaps it is the most central and deeply felt. No, not the myth of Revolution's struggle to create

Heaven on Earth: that one is appallingly ugly. The pretty one is Nature By Herself. It starts no more strangely than pagan tales of giants cleft in two or she-bears carrying the stars in a box *before* creation. "In the beginning, there was a large agglomeration of neutrons that Big Banged." It is the tale of expanding matter, adrift within literal nothingness, with stars dying and supernovae collapsing to give us the heavier elements that make life possible, leading to Man's annointment as priest of Nature Herself. It's all familiar, so we needn't recount the details, nor even deny that it may be true in detail. Besides, our delight in myth does not lie in true details. Who could not love this wild, menacing, life-giving, mysterious, hilarious goddess Nature; this changeless, ever-changing cascade of shapes and forms and lines and colors and perceptions, this torrent of kangaroos and volcanoes and rainbows and skylarks and giggling brooks and slimy things and sunsets and stars pinpricking the night? We fear her but adore her, Nature, this wild and wonderful thing, and cannot bear for her to be tamed, a mere created thing ruled by some god. One would be hard of heart not to rejoice in a myth so grand.

I grew up in the Colorado wild country, love it still, and hate to obtrude a prosaic thought into so charming a myth. But that's not how things are. The reality is even better. We have all of nature to love, but there is more. Look around you. Do you see *anything really* natural? The room, its furnishings, your clipped nails, this book in your hands, every word in which results from human choice—these are all triumphs of men's mind and will over nature in the raw. Indeed, every facet of civilization is unnatural. All this bespeaks a different-ness that we have ourselves introduced into a formerly pristine Nature. You and I certainly prefer these triumphs; else we would be outside shivering, perhaps dying, on what is, as I write, a bitter cold night. Would we think Nature so wonderful if we were crouched in the snow, naked as all other creatures, temperature below zero? If we are no more than children of Nature, we could not change her. But we do. No more striking showing of this exists than in the laboratories of our scientists, who can transmute the very elements, turn lead into gold with fission power, or even create *new* elements. We applaud ourselves for these achievements. But wild Nature offers no such gifts to her own.   The reality is that human mind and spirit and will are things not of Nature, but that have invaded her from within, partly for good, partly for ill. I must ask: would the wild and wonderful Nature of myth change one iota if we ourselves changed our concept of her origin? Is she any less marvelous if we suppose her to be a creature of God, obeying the Laws we fancy so much but attribute to her instead of to God—would she be any different by what we think? Of course not. The sun will rise in the East whether we think Nature a creature of God or self-sprung.

Yet, in another sense, nothing could matter more than what we think about Nature. The moment we start conceiving ourselves as her creatures alone, we start losing our human, unnatural, ability to take delight in this strange goddess. Purely natural things have no awe, no poetry, no joy, no myths. Insofar as we subsume ourselves into the Myth of Nature By Herself, we forfeit the human sense wherewith we could have adored Nature as the ancients did. I count that another tragedy of a World Without Heroes: that we lose even our naturalness along with our humanness.

The Sterilization of Public Square

The role of religion in public life has been debated and fought almost continuously since the Scopes Trial in 1925. Tiffs erupt periodically in the press, or in political debates. Not a Christmas passes but that a civil liberties group will sue to prevent some unenlightened community from putting a crèche in the public square. Every year, a few state legislatures will try to find a way around the Supreme Court's ban on prayer in public schools.

Amid the rumbles is the anti-hero's unwavering conviction that public affairs must be sterilized of all taint of religion. This is as much a policy question as a philosophical one, but it is worth a brief look here. At the root, of course, is the anti-hero's faith that all religion is meaningless. But at the policy level, a suspiciously human quality creeps in, for instance the moral thought that public schoolchildren should not be forcibly subjected to anything untrue. (Anti-heroes keep acting like moral beings despite themselves.) And with this, with an appeal to fair play, they can enlist the aid of their victims: anyone opposed to the total secularization of school curricula or of other aspects of public life.

We all agree, after all, that the State apparatus should be strictly neutral as between all sects and religions. This is in the Constitution; but so is a provision that the State may not impede freedom of worship in anyway. For most of our national history, no great problem was seen with minor religious observances in public affairs, so long as they were voluntary and did not appear to pose any threat of an official state church. But things changed drastically with a Supreme Court decision thirty years ago that put unreligion, atheism, under the freedom-of-religion guarantees of the Constitution. This meant that the State had to be neutral between religion and atheism—which is not possible. With this legal wedge and a demand for fairness, anti-heroes have pretty well driven religious observance of any sort out of public life, especially public schools. And they have lawyers on 24-hour call ready to sue should there be any further outbreak of worship. Under present law, schoolchildren cannot look at the Ten Commandments in school, or read the Bible ever as literature, or have a religious club after school (communist clubs are allowed), much less pray.

But the anti-heroes are cheating. They are forcibly imposing anti-religious values on most of the nation's schoolchildren, and in very large doses. Public school curricula, strongly influenced and often controlled by anti-heroic academics, are awash in naturalist explanations of life, and the denial of moral values. Courses in the sciences, especially the social sciences, are often taught as outrightly hostile to religion. The State, constitutionally required to be neutral, is anything but fair in practice. Somewhere in its bowels, it knows the anti-hero doctrines being taught expand its own power and prestige, and indeed, breed new generations of docile, subservient taxpayers to be bled for its own advantage.

In short, the large majority of parents who do not want their children subjected to anti-religious teaching are being bullied and abused by law, by the anti-hero minority. Most cannot afford to do much about it. After being taxed to pay for the public schools whose policies they object to, they haven't the resources to send their children to private schools. Yet the growth of private religious schools has been striking in recent decades. These are usually low-budget affairs, but often get far better scholastic results than their public counterparts. Of course, being private, they are free to offer any religious observance or instruction desired, without legal restrictions.

It is only in the public sector that forcible imposition of a "religious" view is causing a headache, and part of the problem is that the public sector is growing like a toadstool, making the headache worse. A revolt is brewing. Between the grating relativism taught and the sub-mediocre academic results achieved in public schools, it's no wonder. For the first time in our history the value of public schooling is being sharply called into question. Serious alternatives (such as the voucher system) are being considered to let parents choose the education they want for their children. For most of us, a way out can't come soon enough.

This is the anti-hero legacy to our schools.

It is important that we see it here, close to home. The influence of fancy, philosophical dogmas on great events far away can seem too distant and abstract for us to grasp. But our public schools are close and real and well-known to us, and we all see the damage done them by anti-heroism. I'll say again, it matters very much, and in our immediate affairs, how we think about the universe.

Reflections

"When the men of science have said all their say about the human mind and heart," wrote Nock, "how far they are from accounting for all their phenomena, or from answering the simple, vital questions that one asks them! What *is* the power by which a certain number and order of air vibrations is translated into processes of great emotional significance? If anyone can answer that question believe me, he is just the man I want to see."

And just the man the world wants to see. Science, for all its brilliance, is blind to the things that matter most to us, in our hearts and minds and souls. Its genius has been our downfall. For two centuries and more, men have placed their faith and hope in scientific advance, dazzled by its success and certitude. But to do so, we must put aside our very humanity, for that part of us is forever veiled to scientific inquiry. This is the mistake of the anti-hero, seeing the natural side of us that needed no explaining, and ignoring our spiritual side, nay, denying it with scorn. Let it not be said of his doctrine: "It can't all be wrong. It must have some truth to it, to make such an immense impact on the world. Where there's smoke, there's fire." It *is* all wrong, and its results show it. It got its power from the seeming perfection of natural science in times long gone, science now obsolete. But anti-heroism is not science, it is philosophy built on flawed perceptions of scientific findings, and on some false findings at that. It deals in ideas, not science, and its ideas must be judged by their truth.

In looking at the curious faiths of the anti-hero, we do not see ourselves. We do not see men. We do not see real people trying to live life on a human scale, and get along, and love one another, and care for our families.

We see, rather, grotesque beings, automatons spun by an uncaring goddess called Nature. We see a beast that thinks it thinks, but some of its "most advanced" thinkers say its thought is a meaningless illusion. We see a beast that acts as if it could act, but has no will to do so. We see a beast that aches in its soul to be good, but has no soul and inhabits a place that has no good. We see a beast that cries out in joy when an imaginary dragon is slain, and weeps real tears when an imaginary princess is felled by an imaginary flower; yet one having no imagination or spirit.

There is no such beast. We are human creatures of a loving God, who take joy in life and grow in His spirit, or not at all.

Chapter V
Sociobabble:
The Unmaking of the Word

And out of the ground the Lord God formed every beast of the field, and every fowl of the air; and brought them unto Adam to see what he would call them: and whatsoever Adam called every living creature, that was the name thereof.

—*Genesis* 2:19

All metaphysical community depends on the ability of men to understand one another.

—Richard Weaver

The corruption of man is followed by the corruptions of language.

—Emerson

This is a severe test of our synchronized organizational parallel reciprocal monitored time-phased capability.

—From a bureaucratic memo

In the war for the West, no more peculiar casualties have been recorded than those inflicted by Washoe, the world's most famous chimpanzee. Washoe has been taught to communicate in sign language. In the thrill of trying to communicate with another species, three psychologists, wagging signs in front of the poor animal, have had their fingers bitten off. If you're keeping score, count that World—3, Anti-Heroes—0.

The experiments with Washoe are part of a frantic effort in recent decades to "get through" to some other Intelligence, of any kind, anywhere. Apes of different kinds have been "adopted" and raised as human babies to receive intensive language training. The cries of whales have been analyzed by computers, and radio telescopes scan distant galaxies seeking intelligible signals. Despite premature and exaggerated claims, the success rate for all these efforts is exactly zero. Space probes to the moon and Mars found those bodies utterly lifeless (and few now recall the fears, and decontamination of the Apollo space capsules, lest some deadly microbe be brought back from the moon). No terrestial creature has been taught to use language. Even the sign language used by Washoe is now seen as simply a system of signs and responses to get rewards (bananas), empty of symbolic content. In other words, in the view of the semiotician Sebeok, animals have communication but not language.

Man alone uses symbolic language. This ability, perhaps more than any other, sets us apart from the natural world and all its creatures. It is, moreover, a stubbornly unnatural ability; without it we would be animal, not man: unable to think about ourselves, and unaware even that we were "animals." Nothing that is distinctively human is possible without true language. If in fact we were the aimless and fully "conditioned" beasts that anti-heroism holds us to be, it would be inconceivable for me to write these words, or for you to read them. My words are all, or mostly, symbols for which there is no corresponding reality in nature. There is, for instance, no entity in nature to give meaning to the word "animal." Rather, the word is a category comprising many diverse entities, and derives its meaning wholly from the classifying actions of the human mind. More bluntly, it is what we think that gives reality to the word. Thus, the anti-hero who declares us to be "animals" is employing a symbol, a universal, a word that can in no wise be either postulated or affirmed by empirical science. *By his own positivist rules,* he is using a concept that is strictly out of court: one he himself insists can neither have a real existence nor be a part of human knowledge. His declaration is a cheat, but anti-heroes seem to have no difficulty overlooking the contradictions in their dogmas. He can escape this trap only by abandoning his world model; for to use words, to symbolize ideas, is an event both unique and unaccountable in all known natural history. It is to step into the noumenal: into a world both larger and irrefragably "other." "In the beginning," say those still-astonishing words in the first verse of *St. John,* "was the Word."

The great rhetorician Richard Weaver writes: "At the beginning I should urge examining in all seriousness that ancient belief that a divine element is present in language. The feeling that to have power of language is to have control over things in deeply embedded in the human mind. We see this in the way men gifted in speech are feared or admired; we see it in the potency ascribed to incantations, interdictions and curses. We see it in the legal force given to oath or word. A man can bind himself in the face of contingencies by saying

Yea or Nay, which can only mean that words in common human practice express something transcending the moment." In this essence of language lies the meaning of Adam naming the animals, hence classifying and ordering them, the necessary first step in man's control over nature. We are, of course, still doing this in science. "As myth gives way to philosophy...the tendency to see a principle of divinity in language endures." *Logos* is expressly identified with God by *St. John,* imputing the rational design of the cosmos, "for without him was not anything made that was made." In the coming of Christ, "the Word was made flesh and dwelt among us." Says Weaver, "The allegory need give no difficulty; knowledge of the prime reality comes to man through the word; the word is a sort of deliverance from the shifting world of appearances. The central teaching of the New Testament is that those who accept the word acquire wisdom and at the same time some identification with the eternal...."

There is an obvious, almost overwhelming, metaphysical flavor to language, even without reference to a divine dimension to it. The word touches the deepest mysteries of our being and is our entry into the noumenal world beyond the illusions of the senses. Even so simple an action as making a promise or taking an oath involves moral agency, purpose and an act of free will in a predicted future. None of these fits a deterministic cosmos. Animals do not make promises, and it is extremely doubtful they have any sense of the future. Language is thus independent of space and time; it transcends all physical phenomena. We can easily talk about things that are neither spacially nor temporally present (dinosaurs, for example). Moreover, language is suprapersonal, uniting otherwise unique minds in a common bond of understanding.

Meanings are incorporated into it by collective decision only. No individual can use it successfully without reference to pre-established meanings, nor can he change it without the general consent of other users. No coinage will make it into the dictionary except by the assent of many who find the new word useful (I have a friend who is disgusted that his apt term for New York City, "BigApolis," wasn't accepted). The word and the free market are the only perfect democracies we have, and both impose strict order on their users. (And in both cases, one notes, the order is infinitely more reliable than supposedly "collective" decisions through any other mechanism—especially politics.)

Clearly, language reflects, in great detail, the prevailing world view of its users. Indeed, there could hardly be a more accurate mirror of our beliefs than our words and the way we use them. We may, therefore, most confidently read the collective mood through linguistic analysis. The late Richard Weaver examined thus the American soul in our times, with such force that one can scarcely approach the subject without giving him the credit; and I wish to acknowledge my own debt to him here. Many observers and scholars have contributed. All, in some way or another, remark upon a serious degeneration in American English marked by ignorant and slovenly usage. They also observe a large incursion on new terms, most notably from the jabberwocky of the social sciences, signifying belief in what I am calling the anti-heroic: the dehumanizing impulses of materialism. Defenders of a civilized order must view this invasion with alarm.

Of these matters we will have more to say. But first let us trace in outline the sources and motives of this attack. The metaphysical basis of language puts the word at once outside the borders of the anti-hero's "one world"—that crimped and imaginary domain of the senses verifiable by empirical science. But to the anti-hero, there can by definition be *nothing* beyond the natural; and so he wars on metaphysics. Language, which the anti-hero must use, along with everyone else, to make his point, rebukes his world model. What is he to do? Why, change language. And how? Very simple: by invoking his god, science. The metaphysical content of language must go; it is but the legacy of a superstitious past; it is "unscientific." Language, in short, is to be sanitized and purified until it contains only positive terms validatable by the experience of the senses. Just so, in Orwell's chilling *1984*, was language systematically stripped of all meanings that could interfere with the will to power, the will of Big Brother. The insight is keen. The little-mentioned but real purpose of "cleansing" language is social control. Totalitarian states routinely manipulate language and control information (Orwell wasn't predicting, he was observing). A dehumanized language, if successful, would create slavery more dreadful than chains, for the slave would be denied even the concept of freedom. Any inroads in our language by anti-heroic thought are ominous.

Another line of assault stems from the deep impulse of anti-heroism to deny human uniqueness. A proof that we are truly special and unique, qualitatively above the beasts, collapses all anti-heroic dogmas. The reductionist impulse thus takes heart in its interpretations of a long series of scientific discoveries. The findings of Copernicus and Galileo supposedly displaced man from his special place at the center of being (though the anti-hero would do well to read Copernicus's praise of God's wisdom upon showing the earth revolving around the sun). The positivist "sciences" of the last century, and particularly the theories of Marx, Darwin and Freud (all now in disrepair), lent credence to a purely naturalistic view of man. Yet take away our religious beliefs, our art, our culture, our science, still we remain unique: the one creature that uses symbolic language. We speak to each other as men, not beasts. Language may be the last citadel of the human mind, but it is the strongest. While we have the word, we remain unconquered.

Newspeak: A Quick Battleground Tour

Item. From a sociology paper: "The findings here mentioned are merely suggestive; and they are offered in no sense as proof of our hypothesis of folk–urban personality. The implementation of the analysis given here would demand a field project incorporating the type of methodological consciousness advocated above. Thus we need to utilize standard projective devices, but must be prepared to develop, in terms of situational demands, additional analytic instruments."

This passage, unfortunately, is only too typical of the breed, and indeed, far cleaner than most. Two questions spring to mind: Do the authors know what they are talking about? Probably not. And what does this mean? I struggled a good while trying to translate it. I finally got, "Our findings are tentative. To prove our point, we would have to do another project using the same methods, or try others if those fail." What the authors conceal in their oleaginous jargon is that they had nothing much to say.

Item. From a wire service story: "As the coffin was lifted and carried to the altar, more than 3,000 mourners sung (sic) the hymn, 'O God Our Health and Age Has Passed.' " One can only echo James Jackson Kilpatrick's reaction to this howler: "Yipes!"

Quick quiz. Can you fathom the meaning of these contemporary terms?! (1) compliance assistance officer; (2) unemancipated minor; (3) ARC; (4) DHing; (5) foodiegate; (6) lentilburger; (7) tax base erosion control.

Answers: (1) policeman; (2) teenager, in a federal description; (3) remarkably, this is an acronym built on top of *another* acronym; it means "AIDS-Related Condition," i.e., the symptoms observed before the onset of Acquired Immune Deficiency Syndrome; (4) an acronym for Designated Hitter turned into a verb ("Smith DHed for the Sox last week"); (5) as barbaric a metanalysis as one hopes ever to see: "gate," false suffix from Watergate, meaning scandal, and "foodie" (gag) referring to the commodity stolen—coined to name a case of fraud by a London chef; (6) you know what it is, but its history shows how fast we can go downhill: first came the hamburger, short for Hamburger steak" and having nothing to do with ham; add a slice of cheese, the meat disappears, "burger" comes to mean a sandwich, and we have a cheeseburger; after this, depending on how we stuff the bun, we get lentilburgers, nutburgers, sushiburgers or what have you. A dog food company has now added a false prefix as well, to create "Smorgasburger"; (7) a tax increase, of course, and shame if you didn't guess it. Any official term involving the word "tax" (including "tax cut" in almost every case) means a tax increase. That is how government works.

Another quick quiz: why do we put up with this cascade of ugly coinage and ignorant usage? One could add further examples indefinitely. Such chroniclers of the word as

Kilpatrick, William Safire and Leo Rosten never have to worry where their next barbarism is coming from. Why *do* we tolerate it? I wish I had a quick answer, or at least one more comforting than that we don't know any better.

Clear language begins with clear thought. We are all rightly suspicious of evasive, or weighted, or overcomplicated usage. We wonder, if that fellow has something to say, why doesn't he get on with it? Why the doubletalk? This is a wonderfully healthy reaction to every sort of pedantry and propaganda.

We react so, that is, if our own sense of style and grammar has not been dulled to the intrusions of bad or deceptive usage. Unfortunately, in our age of widening illiteracy, this is no longer the rule. A century of steadily worsening education has disarmed our capacity to sniff out spurious thought. When we fail to fend off minor misusage arising from ignorance, we leave ourselves open to the far more serious misrepresentations of the propagandist. Jacques Barzun observes, "The duty of Intellect being to analyze and keep distinct, its failure in the face of so much nonsense and confusion argues dwindling forces of resistance. . . . The condition is progressive. . . ." Resistance falters, moreover, as anti-heroic warfare against Western belief intensifies and attacks the very meaning of our words. The attackers, to their shame, employ a ruthless language of deception, ultimately for political reasons. Its aim is less to demoralize than to dehumanize us, and make us easy prey for the escape-proof New Order they intend to rule. Such language has metastasized through the academy and the press, and does its harm even when innocently employed by convention or fashion. Hearing it constantly, we are less and less able to discern its deceptions. Among the most "disturbing" tendencies of our time, Weaver declares, "is the easy divorce between words and the conceptual realities which our right minds know they must stand for."

It becomes thus our pressing duty to clarify and restore meanings, and to rearm ourselves against the ideological subversion of language. The propagandist has at his disposal dozens of devices for shading his language to fool us; but none that we need be unaware of. He too must convey his case with the word, however distorted. All language usage is open to view and analysis. With common sense and a little savvy, we can smoke out the bias, the smuggled assumptions, and other anti-heroic distortions that are steadily making Newspeak a reality. And we too can refer to that working blueprint for the conquest of language. The dutiful party member Syme put it this way in *1984:* "Don't you see that the whole aim of Newspeak is to narrow the range of thought? In the end we shall make thoughtcrime literally impossible, because there will be no words in which to express it."

Let's begin here by sampling the nature and extent of deceptions in political language. (In the subsequent section we will look more closely at specifics, and particularly at the headwaters of linguistic pollution, the so-called behavioral sciences.) For this we turn to some remarkable findings by a pair of our most perceptive writers, Tom Bethell and Joseph Sobran. Bethell employed a sophisticated tool in his work: a computerized information retrieval system with "access to individual words and phrases in a wide variety of newspapers, magazines and wire services," and also numerous Soviet bloc speeches. This system is admirably suited for empirical analysis of current political usage. One can retrieve the desired words or phrases, or even all instances where certain words appear close to each other, along with the full text of the original source material. With its aid, "I have been collecting words and phrases, and trying to elucidate the disguised premises and arguments that often underlie them," Bethell relates. "Set forth as a glossary, these words and phrases almost constitute a new political language."

For example, with *leader, autocrat, strongman, dictator* a "pattern...in favor of the communist bloc emerges." Namely, a communist head of state is almost always called "leader," the only innocuous term of the four. "Dictator" and "strongman," the most offensive, are reserved for heads of "right-wing regimes," itself a nasty term for "anti-communist." Another quality of governments headed by "dictators" and never "leaders" is that they are all friendly to the United States. They may have objectionable aspects, heaven knows, but none is "right-wing" as we use the term, and none even approaches the totalist rigidities of Soviet bloc dictatorships. Apart from a single, stray reference to Castro, Stalin—long dead—is the only communist "dictator." "Otherwise, current communist dictators are about as easy to find as unicorns in the woods," Bethell remarks.

Other findings. The term *cold war rhetoric* is used by the Soviets and the U.S. press to criticize—the U.S. In no case was it said of the Soviets, despite their unpleasant habit of threatening to incinerate other countries. Similarly, *provocative* is applied only to U.S. actions, never Soviet. Miraculously, only the U.S. is involved in the *arms race*. The massive Soviet arms buildup in recent years is apparently above criticism. When Bethell told the computer to check instances where the words "Reagan...bellicose" appeared close to each other, it "provided me with a hard day's reading." A like search for "Brezhnev . . . bellicose" came up empty. (Perhaps Brezhnev's war of aggression against Afghanistan was not bellicose.)

In case after case we find usage that is lopsidedly anti-American and is at least implicitly pro-communist. And this, remember, is the usage of our own press media. Discount the fact that this is a free country, and the media can criticize it as they please; and that the Soviet "press" is free only to criticize us; still the pattern remains disturbingly one-sided and gives a grossly false picture. America, despite its failings, is a grand and generous country; the Soviet Union is a murderous, totalitarian hellhole—to understate things. Wording that conceals and distorts this reality is a lie. The observer can find one bit of amusement in it, though, with an unpolitical German translation of "the leader." What term could better describe the reigning Soviet thug than "Der Fuehrer?"

Sobran offers us the correct incantation for a successful revolution. Declare for Moscow at once: "As soon as you announce your Marxism, a predictable series of things begins to happen. First, you will get support from Marxism's corporate headquarters in Moscow. An international advertising campaign will begin. . . ." He adds, "It is vital to your Marxist credentials that you denounce the United States. As soon as you do this, help will also arrive from America." At this point, everyone will join the incantation. The problems in your country will be diagnosed as *poverty, corruption, political repression, censorship.* The reigning *regime,* no doubt "right-wing," will be an *oligarchy.* (Inevitably a few ultra-wealthy families will own practically all the land.) Your movement to *liberate* your country and institute *land reform* will be *indigenous.* It will be supported by *progressive forces.*

Resisting it will be likened to *looking for communists under every bed.* There you are, nothing to it! Murder a few small-town mayors, blow up power lines, radio stations and newspaper offices, and you can soon be getting multimillion-dollar aid from the U.S. Congress. If all this sounds depressingly familiar, it is because the same terminology is trundled out for every totalitarian assault on the West. What's worse, it is employed as readily by the liberals and "progressives" of the free world as by the aggressors—a sorry measure of the anti-heroic penetration of our language. Somehow, after so many years of this, the genocidal dictatorship that follows every successful "revolution" remains "unexpected," and those among us who employed these Big Lie techniques never see their own hands as bloody.

Elsewhere, by exploring the current taboo words, Sobran gives us further insight into the beliefs of our times. For instance, echoing trends we have seen again and again, the term *international communist conspiracy* has disappeared, and the *free world* is almost gone. *Tyrants* have become "leaders." *Leftists* have become *activists,* and the only communists left are *avowed* (evidently the underground variety is to remain hidden).

In not unrelated trains of thought, *God* and *Jesus Christ* "are of course unmentionable" (except in blasphemies). Fornication means becoming *sexually active,* and I am reminded of a memorable newspaper headline: "Mom ponders approach to sexually active son." An unborn baby has been reduced to a *foetus,* and killing it is as easy as *terminating the pregnancy.* (But no, we can't speak of *aborting* it; that makes abortion sound too much like abortion.) Homosexuality can no longer be *perversion* or *sodomy.* Indeed, after

ruining the perfectly good word *gay,* the *homosexual* is now at
the insistence of those concerned restored to the acceptable
vocabulary. As a hangover of the militant 60s, the innocuous
"Negro" is displaced by *black.*

Most of this, not all, reflects deceitful usage, and all of it
reflects the anti-heroic view. In some cases we can, of course,
simply as a matter of good manners, accept the terms those
involved prefer. But, to restore clear meanings, we must
nevertheless insist on straightforward terms. Contemplating
euphemisms, Chesterton reminded us that anti-heroes "introduce their horrible heresies under new and carefully
complimentary names." Murder, for instance, for which "the
social justification...has already begun," might, he volun-
teered cheerfully, be termed Social Subtraction, or Life Control
or Free Death. But beware of every euphemism. Every one "is
used in favor of bad morals. When somebody wishes to wage a
social war against what all normal people have regarded as a
social decency, the first thing he does is to find some artificial
term that shall sound relatively decent." Which is how killing
babies comes to be called terminating pregnancies.

The use of dysphemisms or pejoratives offers a kindred
insight. The "devil words" of the day nearly all seem to
originate in the purest egalitarianism: *sexism, racism, discrimination, prejudice, bigotry....* All this, too, is unrelievedly
anti-heroic, and the arguments in its favor are as thin as the
frosting on diet pills. Every human being, of every race, creed,
Preference, gender, self-description or state of mind is, after
all, unique. Comparisons between us are apples to oranges to
pomegranates. No hint of superiority or inferiority is implied
by the absolutely truthful statement that boys are different
from girls (which I happen to find more interesting than

those that follow), and that girls are different from other girls, and boys from boys, and blacks from blacks, and whites from whites. All this is certainty by every measure humans possess, not least empirical and genetic sciences, so what is confounding about it? Every human being is one of a kind. When we rank our abstract "equality" too high, we can neither knock nor lust after the different qualities of others, and about two-thirds of the fun of being human is gone, just like that. The anti-heroes are such killjoys.

Let me conclude this discussion with a last warning that no misusage of words, however innocent it may seem, can be indiscriminately accepted. Perhaps the least suspicious term I have mentioned was that double acronym, ARC. It is efficient usage—six words for the price of three letters—and there is a good case for that. Nevertheless, acronyms are not necessarily to be trusted, and here is testimony to that point by an expert, George Orwell: "Even in the early decades of the twentieth century, telescoped words and phrases had been one of the characteristic features of political language; and it had been noticed that the tendency to use abbreviations of this kind was most marked in totalitarian countries and totalitarian organizations. Examples were such words as Nazi, Gestapo, Comintern, Inprecor, Agitprop." What in fact was discovered by totalitarian propagandists was that the shortened term drew the sting of the reality. Comintern sounds a whole lot better than communist International. Nazi, in its ascendance, was far more palatable than the "National Socialist" it stands for. If we rarely use the word today, you can thank Stalin, who knew what it stood for. Fearing competition with his own brand of socialism, he banned the use of "Nazi" and ordered the use of "fascist" instead. Stalin had a long arm. This usage is still in effect and is still observed here in America thirty years after Stalin's death. Is that not the epitome of all the deceitful language we have discussed?

Scientism vs. The Word

Language incorporates a collective assent to the meanings of words, often going back centuries. This suprapersonal quality makes it strongly resistant to change. The degradation of language that we observe in our time is therefore a sort of tidal movement begun long ago, and one that reflects some fundamental and widely shared debasement of belief. We must, then, find and unravel those errors of bygone philosophy that pollute language today, as a first step toward restoring the word. This done, we will be able to oppose all derivative usage, whether mendacious or merely ignorant. (The full remedy requires a return to classical education, in which is preserved and husbanded the word of a hundred generations.)

What errors do we look for, and where? We have clues. A change in belief so basic as to corrupt language must necessarily be religious in character, or more precisely, anti-religious. We must seek a radical alteration in the common world view, some new ground for reality. And as such a transition stamps language with the imprint of its new god as surely as it undermines the world of the old, we may seek it in language itself. Here Weaver gives us another clue, noting that "it is the nature of conscious life to revolve around some concept of value. So true is this that when the concept is withdrawn, or when it is forced into competition with another concept, the human being suffers an almost intolerable sense of being lost. He has to know where he is in the ideological cosmos in order to coordinate his activities. Probably the greatest cruelty which can be inflicted on psychic man is this deprivation of a sense of tendency. Accordingly every age, including those of rudest cultivation, sets up some kind of sign post...some idea abstracted from religion or historical speculation, and made to inhere in a few sensible and immediate examples."

This "signpost" and its examples are functions of the word. In times of waning religious belief like ours, there invariably emerge "god terms" that convey the essence of the new world view, and by which men reorder their values. That is, whatever the rising system of belief may be, we must all, through words, have reference to the highest and lesser goods; and similarly, through "devil terms," to perceived evils. With this in mind, we look for words that are the prime movers, the validators of knowledge, the arbiters of disputed authority: the terms with which we identify truth and morality. Among them, the word with the greatest rhetorical force to compel belief; the one that validates, subordinates and empowers all lesser terms, reveals the new *zeitgeist*, the new deity of the times. I submit that for us, the reigning god term is *science*.

I will go further: no other term even approaches science as the determiner of what we believe to be reality. Let me demonstrate. If you are reaching for a term that expresses complete certainty, you would say: "This is *scientific fact*." And if your assertion is correct, you have won. No other word or phrase has the rhetorical clout to gainsay you. One could not even protest that what you say is contrary to "the word of God." In the popular mind, science, not God, is invested with omniscience. You can argue with the word of God, but not with scientific fact. "Science," surely is the new deity: symbolically imbued with the charismatic or even mystical authority of godhood. Someday, through science, we will have complete control over nature: it is *omnipotent*. In time, science will have all the answers: it is *omniscient*. The scientific method is self-correcting: science is *infallible*. No knowledge can be valid unless it is scientific: science is the *creator*. All the attributes of divinity are present in these very common formulations.

The new deity is constantly invoked to certify the truth: "Science says..." or "Science now knows that..." and similarly. Its status of authority is obvious in these, but less so is the hypostatization of the word: the transformation of a conceptual entity into a concrete reality. This, too, marks the invoking of a deity. Science has somehow become a being, a rational spirit. Now, this is nonsense. Science is not some mystical being that can speak and pronounce judgments; it is not even an organized body of scientists. Beneath this abstracted deity are simply the accumulated knowledge and ongoing investigations in a broad but not unlimited field of study. Scientists have different theories, use different methods, and are all quite human. If there is any spiritual mystery in this, it eludes me. "The whole force of the word [science]," says Weaver, "nevertheless depends upon a bland assumption that all scientists meet periodically in synod and there decide and publish what science believes." Conversely, the authority of the word collapses when science is not conceived as a sort of divine entity. Consider, Weaver continues, "the changed quality of the utterance when it is amended to read 'A majority of scientists say'; or 'Many scientists believe'; or 'Some scientific experiments have indicated.' The change will not do.

There has to be a creature called 'science'...." Imagine with what glee the modernist would ridicule such a creature if he found it lurking in the thought of those "superstitious" Mediaevals!

The irony cuts much deeper. A primary attraction and surely a great merit of science is its *value-free* methodology to assure the *disinterested* pursuit of knowledge. This is intended to eliminate the biases, interests and errors the flesh is heir to, and it works well enough to exalt the scientific as the most (or in one view, the only) reliable knowledge of the material world. Who would have guessed that, through its brilliant success, this method of increasing our knowledge would itself be deified: a source of religious fervor and at times fanaticism? And deified, moreover, with the very attributes of God in the old Christian model: all-powerful, creative, rational, personal! All, that is, but one: goodness. The one thing a god of value-free science cannot be is benevolent. It would seem God is not so easily dismissed by man. We push Him out the front door of our mind, snap on a dozen padlocks, and He strolls in the back door.

We have found the new deity, but not the error that invested science with false divinity. Here, the other half of our formula for certainty, *fact*, can shed light. In citing "scientific fact," we unwittingly credit scientific methodology with omniscience. That we refer to a "fact" as readily as less secular generations of the West would have referred to "the truth," is revealing. What is this new unit of reality, the fact? Here is a dictionary definition: "something that has actual existence: *EVENT*; an occurrence, quality or relation the reality of which is manifest in experience or may be inferred with certainty." In usage, "*Fact* in its primary meaning as an object of direct experience is distinguished from *truth*." One might observe that here some of the weightiest questions in philosophy are summarily disposed of, by definition. We need only note the repeated and insistent allusions to certitude: "*actual* existence ... *reality* ... *certainty*." Where does this certitude come from? It is embedded in "direct experience," that is, the perceptions we receive through our senses, as opposed to anything we may learn from revelation or thought. Facts, then, advert to the material world, to events and occurrences in space and time. They are ascertained through the observation and measurement of experience that we call science. With scant liberty, one can say that an event gains facthood and certitude, almost circularly, by the imprimatur of science. Further, the scientific distillations of experience are to be "distinguished from truth." These meanings all boil down to one thing: reality is confined to the observable physical world, and is revealed by science.

This proposition we recognize, of course, as a primary assertion of the modernist philosophies. It errs in exaggerating the scientific method to an absolute. This was understandable three centuries ago. Science was new and its successes were remarkable. It must have seemed that man had finally found the long-sought formula for controlling nature. C. S. Lewis reminds us that science was then in competition with magic. Because the one thrived and the other was stillborn, we forget too easily how similar their guiding impulses were. The scientific method was the magic that worked! It was invested with a mystical flavor from the beginning. Philosophers were quick to assert that this fruitful formula was the *only* formula: mistake number one. We inherit the mistake, but forget there was a good reason for it at the time: the competing "formulas" were alchemy and magic. Those who first asserted it were not as guilty as those who later elevated it to an absolute (and used it as a weapon against religion). It is but a short step from awarding the scientific method an exclusive dealership in knowledge (scientism) to the idea that what cannot be physically investigated with this formula is an illusion or a convenience of the mind, with no real existence (positivism). Mistake number two, and a monster. Here the immaterial is simply *defined* out of existence. Then it is *concluded* rather than proven or observed that the material universe is "all there is." This dubious conclusion becomes the tacit and unexamined assumption of later generations, focusing their science and thought. Man is perforce reduced to an earthbound beast, locked in a material existence, and fully shaped by natural forces (determinism). Our spirit, our will, our moral agency, our thought, and ultimately all human purpose are increasingly called into question, or outrightly dismissed as illusory, by B. F. Skinner and E. O. Wilson, for instance. Note well that these notions are the working premises of the so-called behavioral sciences, which we discuss below.

We have elsewhere examined the contradictions inherent in these modernist formulations—thought denying the validity of thought—and need not expand on that here. But we must remind ourselves that these views are sheer dogmatic assertion. They are neither logical nor scientific, much less revealed truth. What seems to immunize them from philosophic demolition is circularity. Belief in the method (supposedly) validates materialism, and belief in materialism (supposedly) invalidates anything but the method. Smugly imprisoned in this tight little island of thought are the anti-heroic true believers and all their doctrines. Tell them they have a lousy philosophy, and they will reply that there is no such thing as philosophy.

Let them be, and let us be eternally grateful *we* are not marooned in that wasteland. Our task is stripping away all this superstitious nonsense surrounding the word "science," which for centuries has debauched language and thought. Barzun remarks that the scientistic tongue is a pedantic "pseudo-jargon" that does not even rise to the dignity of honest jargon employed by sailors or tradesmen. "The general form of pedantry," he notes, "derives from natural science....the stance and speech of science are everywhere imitated," and "enormous harm has been done by heedless scientism to language."

I will rely on one example to tack down the point. Dear reader, it describes *you*: your loves, your hopes, your dreams, the very mystery of your being.... The British scholar Duncan Williams found it in a scientific pamphlet entitled "Atmospheric Homeostasis by and for the Biosphere," probably composed out on Anti-Hero Island by large anthropoid apes:

> The first cautious approach to a classification of life, reaching general agreement as follows: Life is one member of the class of phenomena which are open or continuous reaction systems able to decrease their entropy at the expense of free energy taken from the environment and subsequently rejected in a degraded form.

Such talk: "subsequently rejected in a degraded form"! Isn't that exactly what happens to human dignity and aspiration after passing through the anti-heroic system?

Sociobabbling

An ugly coinage, isn't it? But that is the point. We need a word for the wanton, indiscriminate and ugly coinage that saturates sociology and related fields. If any other field is half as addicted to grotesque pseudo-jargon, or has done a tenth as much damage to plain English, I know nothing of it.

Here are two recent sociobabbles—one easy, one hard. A new disease has been identified called "performance anxiety," treatable with pills called beta blockers (or more traditionally with a stiff drink). Got it? It is stage fright. Now, everybody knows what stage fright is, and most of us probably suffer this "illness" in some degree, and we understand it perfectly. What does "performance anxiety" say that "stage fright" doesn't say far better? Just one thing: that stage fright has now come to the attention of *science.* "Performance anxiety" sounds scientific and "stage fright" does not. But why would a scientist have to go through such rhetorical convolutions to persuade you his work is scientific? Because it isn't.

Next, the hard one: what is "unconditional positive regard"? Give up? This one is going to give our poets and songwriters fits. Can you hear Curly singing to Laurie, "Let the most complex members of the class of phenomena which are open or continuous reaction systems say our interpersonal modalities are in a state of unconditional positive regard"? Yes, it means "love," and you might not guess that "unconditional positive regard" is a many-splendored thing!

Again we wonder what human soul could do so much damage to a basic and beloved (oops, positively regarded?) word. Clearly it is someone terribly insecure about his status as a scientist. With good reason: sociology is anything but an exact science. The sociologist, desperate to join the club and share the prestige of the physical or exact sciences, resorts to rhetorical legerdemain to insist that his work is equally scientific. If he talked about stage fright and love, we wouldn't even know he is a scientist. So, to get recognition and respect he is obliged to rename in scientific-sounding terms whatever he studies, however ordinary and well-understood it may be. This urge to be "scientific"—demonstrating again the divine power of that word—is creating a whole new language paralleling English: sociobabble. It has long since poured into public usage, muddying speech and thought. Tune in the *Phil Donahue Show,* for example: the language spoken is sociobabble, and at an appropriate level of intelligence. This is what Barzun calls "the clear determination of Western men to translate simple thought into supposedly science-born language."

The elevation of the study of man to a science goes back to the positivist doctrines of Auguste Comte, more than a century and a half ago. (And doubts that it is a science, from within the profession as well as without, have prompted the use of sociobabble the whole while.) The French "positivist" does not translate well; it is really a negative or reductionist idea, making man a natural animal like any other, hence a suitable object for scientific study. Comte thus attached "logy" (science of) to "socio" (society) and announced that it would become the "master science." Having reduced man to a beast, he also founded the Positivist Church with himself as its high priest, devised a liturgical calendar of thirteen months, and decreed the daily worship of man. If this does not make sense, it is no more peculiar than his advancement of phrenology, or his notion that astronomy should extend no further than the orbit of Saturn, the range of the naked eye. After a while Comte went mad and I sometimes wonder how anybody noticed.

Even at its origin, the "science" of man was undertaken "in slavish imitation of the natural sciences," as Frank S. Meyer put it. But can we ourselves be studied with the same experimental methods used to study lifeless matter? If not, sociology is built on a fundamental error; one the social scientist is perpetually obliged to deny with a positivist view: man's essential kinship, as it were, with all things in nature, including rocks. The anti-heroic view is inherent in behavioral science, and practitioners have a clear interest in defending it—at the expense of scientific objectivity. Sociobabble is discharging the waste waters of anti-heroism into the mainstream of language.

But denying the error does not make it go away. We can investigate non-living things, electrons for example, without reference to their consciousness, so empirical and experimental methods are wholly in order. We can, with less certainty, study lower organisms the same way. But we do not know what consciousness they have, or how it might falsify our results. Meyer observes, "A methodology that is richly rewarding when it deals with the 'how' of inorganic processes, and which has moderate results insofar as it considers the lower forms of life, can be applied to human beings only by a perversion of the principle of analogy." Just here, he says, "the prevailing doctrines go astray. The sphere of natural studies contains no element of consciousness with its innate corollary of freedom and moral responsibility. But any study that aspires to throw light upon man must take account of these autonomous aspects of his being." He concludes, "Any 'science' of man which pretends to a fruitful utilization of the methods and techniques of the natural sciences does so and can do so only by ignoring an enormous and decisive aspect of the actuality of men. For men's knowledge of themselves is first of all direct: that which they know of their own consciousness. To attempt to arrive at an understanding of men indirectly, by an examination of their actions, their 'behavior,' is to arrive only at knowledge of a truncated model which resembles man only in externals."

This is what behavioral sciences *do* attempt (recall Wilson's insistence that the "minimum claims" of social or biological sciences were to be "consistent" with the laws of the physical sciences). It will not do. A view of ourselves from the "outside" would be hopelessly distorted. It might see what we do, but not what we refuse to do. It could not penetrate our thoughts, our autonomous selves, or our conscience. Study from the "outside" is circular: it reduces us to animals, which is the same assumption the sociologist started with. This is not science. Our own self-knowledge tells us this view is false, and this cannot be denied as unscientific. Father Stanley Jaki recalls, physicist "Arthur Holly Compton got much closer to the heart of the matter when he vindicated the freedom of the will on the basis that his inner conviction about moving his little finger at will carried far greater and far more immediate evidence than all the deterministic laws of physics put together." In other words, using the wrong methods simply gives us the wrong answers, to the cost of real science and philosophy alike.

There are other problems. Empirical methods can only apply to groups, hence are blind to the uniqueness of the individual person and to any unique occurrence. Weaver,

Barzun and Meyer all remark that interaction between the observer and the observed is not scientific; results would be skewed by the actions of the scientific observer and are therefore unreliable. Analytic or statistical studies are not without value, but are valid only if used without the knowledge of the observed. "... but when a sociologist or a 'political scientist' asks a set of questions whose sole function is to serve his research," Meyer adds, "the scientific character is largely vitiated." This is a basic weakness of all polling techniques, as is also the inherently unstudied and unreflective quality of the answers. "In view of the non-independent character of the questions, the answers can reflect little more than the value system of those who constructed them."

We conclude that empirical investigation has very limited application to the study of man, being confined to independent observation, and can produce an even more limited or auxiliary picture of man due to its externality—"not knowledge *of* man, but simply knowledge of some aspects of their behavior," as Meyer put it. Any effort to go beyond this point is pedantry, or worse, positivist dogmatism in the mask of "science." (Barzun invites us to "think of the huge yearly mass of scholarly research and apply the tests of fitness and significance: clearly pedantry predominates; it is the sea around us.")

The would-be "science" of man never was and cannot be a science: not if, to be so, as it supposes, it must use the methods of the exact sciences. In saying so, I am not questioning the value of behavioral "science," but rather its pretensions. It should be a most fruitful field of study. Russell Kirk observes, "One cannot be a tolerable sociologist until he knows a good deal about humane letters, history, philosophy,

politics and theology—and has had some experience of life."
In this light, sociology should be "the crown, not the
foundation" of studies in the civil order; the end, not the
beginning, of undergraduate study.

Yet the field refuses a role as an honest if only partly
scientific discipline; refuses it with deafening clamor. In the
last analysis, its frantic insistence on belonging to the
fraternity of science is not an argument over methods but a
question of pathology. The kinder explanation is that the
behaviorists very greatly desire to share the prestige of the
physical scientists, whose "success was such that they came to
exert an extraordinary fascination on those working in other
fields, who rapidly began to imitate their teaching and
methods," writes the Austrian economist F. A. Hayek. "These
[subjects] became increasingly concerned to vindicate their
equal status by showing that their methods were the same as
those of their more brilliantly successful sisters rather than by
adapting their methods more and more to their own particular problems." A less pleasant explanation is that the
behaviorists really believe, religiously, the old formula of
scientism that only purely scientific methods produce valid
knowledge. This is anti-religious dogmatism dictating what
methods can be used in academic studies. What it produces is
voodoo sociology, yielding false results from false methodology and trying to cover them up with incantations and
mumbo jumbo in sociobabble (a language only a cultist could
look on with unconditional positive regard).

One has only to ponder the damage done to the word by
sociobabble to concede there is some truth to the latter view.
Which, in turn, is fair warning not to trust anything said or
concluded in that horrible tongue. The pity is, the whole

problem could be so easily solved by a change of definition. If behaviorism were content to be an honest academic discipline instead of a dishonest "science," it could correct its methodology at once and vastly improve its contributions to human knowledge.

Chapter VI
No Two Equals Are Alike

...orders and degrees jar not with liberty, but well consist.
—Milton

True democracy requires...a non-conforming citizenry. Its worst and most dangerous propensity is the impulse to conform. The greatest and most enduring achievements have been due to individual skills and insight.
—Malcolm Muggeridge

My chapter title is a piece of sass I saw painted on a barn in the midwest. It struck me as a priceless rebuke to the egalitarian mania of our times. And it is profoundly true: in the human family, no two equals are alike. We are, or should be, equals only before the law. In every other way we are happily and incurably individual. It is, precisely, the marvelous diversity of our kind that is the central and compelling fact about us. In this indisputable fact lie all our true human potentials and purposes. You are the only you there will ever be. Your life unfolds as no other ever will, and seeks its fulfillment along paths no other can travel. Any philosophy that denies this bedrock truth about the human condition must, in the end, deny all things human and sow everlasting sorrow.

Yet our uniqueness is the truth trampled first and hardest by anti-heroic dogma. In its place, the anti-hero ideologue would impose a rabid and Procrustean egalitarianism that is as false as an idea as it is in the fact (and no fact is more scientifically certain than our biological individuality). Would anyone, upon reflection, be willing to sacrifice excellence, or beauty, or love to an egalitarian idol under which they cannot exist? Indeed, in private, the anti-heroes are themselves elitists who coin the slogans of equality as weapons to bring down the West, and who turn up their noses at their prey. As Richard Weaver observed almost forty years ago, "the most insidious idea employed to break down society is an undefined equalitarianism." Its fruits are today seen everywhere, in wretched manners, in small "d" democratic affectations that shame the Jacobins, and in legal atrocities that would be the envy of Genghis Khan. Of this we shall have much more to say shortly.

Here, yet again, we see the unfailing anti-heroic predilection for reducing life to formulas and, in the process, savaging the richness and purpose of life. Exactly here, says Brian Griffin, "is the tragedy of the democracy that sacrifices the possibility of excellence to the commonly-agreed-upon lie of equality; that in Florence would have paid equal tribute to Leonardo and his apprentice; that in Jerusalem would have given Jesus and Judas the same vote; that in Canterbury would have given equal time to Becket and his killers. It is the pity of the suicidal society that would murder the glory in some hearts because the heat from such glory cannot be felt in all hearts." Long before accepting Christianity, Malcolm Muggeridge gazed hard at the egalitarian nostrums of its enemies. "It would be necessary," he said, "to go back at least to the Dark Ages to find a generation of men so given over to destruction, superstition, and every variety of obscurantism." Non-conforming, he concluded, is a duty: "Against such a trend, the impulse not to conform constitutes a kind of resistance movement"—one in which he personally found delight. Life can in no wise be reduced to formulas, egalitarian or any other: "To a civilized and free mind any enforced orthodoxy must be abhorrent. It is inconceivable that the last word should ever be said about anything, or that history should ever reach any sort of finality." No serious thinker disagrees with this; we hear it only from those besotted with a lust for power.

The war historian William Manchester does not shrink from a symbolism that means much more to our age than all its slogans: the Nazi imprimatur of the egalitarian idol or *Gleichschaltung*—"an untranslatable word and one rarely used until the National Socialists came to power and made it a Nazi imperative," he recalls. "Essentially it means total conformity, everyone shifting gears together at the same time." Or to put it more bluntly, marching in lockstep. "Its antonym is individualism. Today, the *Gleichschaltung* dogma threatens the integrity of our institutions, including the right to be different from one another; our language, our freedom, and the quality of our leadership. German," he adds "is a precise language, but also a harsh one, so I shall henceforth call this driving force egalitarian passion." By empowering this force in the law, the anti-hero subverts our civil order and threatens no less than the meaning of our lives.

It is the same story we have heard before. The anti-hero, so enrapt with his own formulas and so intent, from his supposed Olympian vantage, on dictating how all human beings shall live, cannot see that he is recreating a barbarism older than history. Yet what else did he think—always assuming self-designated intellectuals can think—would result from his willful destruction of civilization? Paradise? But there is no arguing with ideologues. Their ideological handbooks take pains to blind them to all reality and deafen them to all rational argument; they are so at war with life that they march unheeding into fascism, still muttering the anti-fascist litanies of their youth. And there we find them, this very day, if not building their own concentration camps, at least bowing and scraping before every Big Brother who does. It reminds me of Lewis Carroll's delicious proof that if you say a thing three times, it's true:

> Taking Three as the subject to reason about—
> A convenient number to state—
> We add Seven, and Ten, and then multiply out
> By One Thousand diminished by Eight.
>
> The result we proceed to divide, as you see
> By Nine Hundred and Ninety and Two:
> Then subtract Seventeen, and the answer must be
> Exactly and perfectly true.

Let the anti-hero who will, say "I am, I am, I really am an anti-fascist." As the saying goes, "Make my day."

Historical Roots

Egalitarianism is historically recent, the natural offspring of the modernist philosophies and a radical departure from the status societies of the ancient world. Says Weaver, "... rebellion against distinction is an aspect of that worldwide and centuries-long movement against knowledge whose beginning goes back to nominalism." From this movement, in time, emerged the complex of philosophies that have undermined the Western order, and today shape a World Without Heroes. Having examined these elsewhere, we need only note here their affinity for egalitarian ideas.

The naturalism that sees men as accidental beasts spun out by a deterministic cosmos must, perforce, deem them equal: they are all products of the same evolutionary force, and what beast could have qualitative differences from any other? The radical empiricism of Hume simply denies the qualitative, and anchors all knowledge in what amounts to measuring and counting. Small wonder that the latter-day anti-hero can look at men as interchangeable social units, and attempt to "engineer society" with averages and statistics. Scientism, invalidating any knowledge that does not result from the scientific method, is blind to the discrete and unique reality of the individual person: it can only investigate groups and categories. It cannot but reduce human distinctions to statistical trivialities. Logical positivism, warring with metaphysics, takes away our place in the transcendent and even our souls. Man is no longer to be a moral agent with knowledge of right and wrong, but a passive and helpless pawn of events beyond the individual's control. Our equality is that of corks tossed alike on the ocean's wave, without will, without responsibility, and without hope. The egalitarian spirit is thus essentially a denial of personhood, and ultimately a denial of Evil. This is what has taught our times to scorn moral responsibility and to blame all ills or misfortunes on "society" or on deterministic "forces."

The egalitarianism that gathered strength in the mid-eighteenth century did not exceed its rightful meaning: equality before the law, that is, treating everyone justly. The complementary idea of liberty for all arose simultaneously. Indeed, the words "liberty" and "equality" were used almost synonymously at the time. Both, in a sense, were healthy reactions to the abuses of the old feudal order in Europe. The older society had been hierarchical in structure, with a privileged, hereditary ruling class. All men had their status in it assigned by birth, and could aspire to no other. Its vestigial authority was swept away by the claims of liberty and equality. This was a sea change in the affairs of men, and it proved immensely beneficial—nowhere more so than in our own American Revolution.

Not too surprisingly, the anti-heroes of that era, many of them intellectuals and artists, loathed the egalitarian stirrings. Were all men made free and equal, they themselves would be cut loose from their privileged status under noble patronage—turned out into the streets to earn a living on equal terms with all that riffraff! They could and did find a hundred reasons to defend the old feudal order and denounce the vulgarity of the new. What was freedom, they murmured, but base servitude to philistinism? What would become of their prerogative, as Irving Kristol amusingly put it, "to celebrate high nobility of purpose, selfless devotion to transcendental ends, and awe-inspiring heroism"? The original anti-heroic thrust was thus elitist, and so it remains, implacably opposed then as now to a free and open society.

But the world was changing rapidly, and the anti-heroes could not long go on defending the noble birth and beneficence of his decaying Lordship. The early socialists and communists, themselves in the anti-heroic mold, provided ready new arguments framed in "democratic" terms. They pictured a "bourgeoisie," or propertied class, victimizing the "masses." Freedom had not, they argued, produced a classless society—behold the vast disparity between the poor and the rich. The class struggle must continue. In this view, the "common man" was no longer to be feared as an equal, but portrayed as the downtrodden victim of a new oppressor, the "bourgeoisie." Egalitarian democracy was no longer contemptible but a shining new sword to hew down the propertied class and raise up the proletariat. Thus, effortlessly and permanently, the anti-heroes flipflopped their position, and proselytized egalitarianism as insistently as their grandfathers had opposed it. More, the nineteenth-century anti-hero extended its meaning beyond the legitimate to an equality of *condition*—a status never attained on this earth, and a nightmare if it were. This meaning persists in our times, with pernicious effect.

A triumphant science in the past century lent great credence to a naturalist world view. The intellectuals, always suckers for the current razzamatazz, soon had the universe turned into a giant dead Machine just waiting for successful Engineering by Man. (Similarly, in the early part of this century, they would incorporate the Ford assembly line and mass production into their plans.) By some happy fluke, the Machine was inhabited by an intelligent beast that could become master of all by the conquest of nature. Darwinism, and a few decades later, Freudianism, seemed to cement the case for Natural Man, cut loose from any metaphysical moorings and from the traditional Christian basis of Western civilization. The last barrier to a pure and final equality of man had apparently fallen. Unshackled from all past superstitions, man was at last to be free even from God. The conquest of the very stars lay before him. It remained only for Enlightened Man to Engineer the Perfect Society, where equality would free humankind from all envy and contention. Of such was woven the anti-heroic vision at its crest, around the turn of this century. What followed was not the secular New Jerusalem so confidently foreseen, but one of the greatest bloodbaths in history. It is not yet over.

Of course the formulas were wrong. The underlying science had been made obsolete by Planck and Einstein by the time the first shock struck, in World War I. Our certain biological uniqueness awaited later demonstration, but was never really in doubt. An older and wiser philosophy had always insisted on human distinction and the moral value of each person. To ignore human distinctions is to erect totalitarianism—the primary mission of anti-heroism this past century—followed inevitably by the collision of state interests in mass war. To this old story, the anti-heroes have added new chapters in modern times: concentration camps, neo-barbarism and genocide.

Anti-heroism, though much diminished toward the end of the twentieth century, still does not waver from its purpose. Somehow, after acting out their dream for a hundred years, the surviving faithful remain convinced that if only their ideas were in place, all would still be well. But it is precisely their ideas that control a third of the globe under the great slave states. And it is a mark of their parentage that anti-heroes both indulge and pooh-pooh the most heinous crimes behind the barbed-wire borders of these "utopias." Such is the mark of the fanatic, the ideologue insulated against reality. The fiercest faith, if false, must in time succumb to experience; and never have the lessons cost more dearly than in this century. Yet the anti-heroes seem to believe their own propaganda: something else, anything else, is to blame, "society," "reactionary forces," anything but their own false ideals.

I am inclined to think the frenetic egalitarianism in recent years is draining the waning strength of anti-heroism, but that remains to be seen. We must not underestimate crusaders who still affect to an "idealist" or "spiritual" mission, however discredited, and who seem bent on playing on our sense of fair play to institutionalize equality of condition down to the last comma and subparagraph of the law.

The Ideologues

If America is made subject to a new *Gleichschaltung,* the symbolic marching orders might well have been President Lyndon Johnson's crude statement in 1964: "We are going to try to take all the money that we think is unnecessarily being spent and take it from the 'haves' and give it to the 'have nots' that need it so much." Any civilized community would have run him out of town on the spot, wearing tar and feathers. This was nothing more or less than a promise of grand larceny and massive injustice—both of which, as it happens, followed on a grand scale.

The anti-heroes, needless to say, went ga-ga, and descended upon Washington, D.C. like lemmings, rabid to dispense Equality upon the nation through income redistribution. Since that time they have passed out sums unknown but probably approaching two trillions of dollars, no small part of it to themselves and succeeded in creating what is now thought to be a permanent welfare class, who live in dependency off the sweat of taxpayers' brows. Over the period, income disparities actually widened. And there fails another great formula, except it won't go away. The federal government increased its size and confiscation by a factor of more than ten, and you can bet it won't surrender its gains for the health and well-being of the republic.

If this insane centralization, this reckless overthrow of the American constitutional heritage, is causing the ideologues of anti-heroism any misgivings, I do not hear it. What I hear is their unqualified approval and ceaseless clamor for more. We must reckon with an ideology that sets its compass to "march" and is forever after deaf to plain sense. But as Manchester reminds us, "They do not want reason. They want to feed their ravaged emotions. The defeated, not the victor, excites their admiration." Says Kristol, "They may speak about 'equality'; they may be obsessed with statistics and pseudo-statistics about equality; but it is a religious vacuum— a lack of meaning in their own lives and the absence of a sense of larger purpose in their society—that terrifies them and provokes them to 'alienation' and unappeasable indignation. It is not too much to say that it is the death of God, not the emergence of any new social or economic trends, that haunts bourgeois society. And *this* problem is far beyond the competence of politicians to cope with." The anti-heroes, having had their own way, cannot cope either, and plainly make matters very much worse. Let them conquer their terrors and alienation, if they can, by calling off their rebellion against God. In the meantime, it is our own indignation that should be unappeasable.

We must withdraw all sanction for that "visionary," that "secularist worshipper of Progress and Uniformity," to whom, in Russell Kirk's words, "respect for norms and conventions is the mark of the beast. He hopes to sweep away every obstacle to the attainment of his standardized, regulated, mechanized, unified world, purged of faith, variety and ancient longings." What else but this has been the curse of our age? It is not enough, Kirk observes, for the anti-hero to preach that all men ought to be equal. When the fact that they are not proves indisputable, the ideologues tamper even with scientific data to cling to their point: "This is scientism in the worse sense: science enslaved by ideological prejudice." "The ideologue, in brief," he concludes, "is one of Orwell's new-style men 'who think in slogans and talk in bullets.'" The object of his hate—and let us never forget that all utopian schemes, not least the anti-hero's, are built on a fascist-style hatred—is the mythical capitalist, the "bourgeois," precisely the unegalitarian superiority of the most productive in the free marketplace. In other words, their hatred is directed against those who do most to provide for our material needs. "The ideologues are Jacob Burkhardt's 'terrible simplifiers.' They reduce politics to catch-phrases; and because they will tolerate no stopping-place short of heaven on earth, they deliver us up to men possessed by devils."

"And God, how the egalitarians proselytize," Manchester adds. "The objective—the mission—of the egalitarian is to convert you. He is the pious worshipper of the Divine Average, the man who adopts what Robert Frost described as a 'tenderer-than-thou' attitude toward social problems," and

"in supporting his twaddle, the passionate egalitarian tirelessly generalizes from the specific." Exactly. When you hear a
latter-day reformer boasting his own caring, compassion and
concern—always financed with other people's money, of
course—you can bet the rent you have an anti-hero at bay.
Listen on. If he has seen a wino sleeping it off in the gutter
that morning, he will tell you that forty million Americans are
homeless. If the bellboy happened to stutter, he will launch
into a disquisition on mass illiteracy, and he will overlook the
anti-heroic clamps on public education that breed it. The fact
is, as we have seen elsewhere, the anti-heroes claimed public
education for their own before the turn of the century, and the
results are their own handiwork. What they did with it is turn
public education into a course for anti-heroism.

This, surely, is one of the saddest consequences of
ideology gone mad. The schools have been subjected to
egalitarian doctrines in pure form. The order of the day is
leveling, and in practice that means reducing instruction to
the capabilities of the dullest in the class: to the lowest
common denominator. The handicaps of the slow are pam-
pered, while the talents of the gifted are distrusted and
suppressed. Those frustrated kids with something going for
them are bored to tears and often rebel. The dullards plod on
through, and in time, and with every inducement government
aid can offer, go on to be university graduate students and the
new "intellectuals." As Kristol notes, we mass-produce them
nowadays, in absurd numbers, and all weaned on anti-heroic
dogmas. The explosive radicalism and anarchism on public
campuses in recent decades give all-too-ample evidence that
the anti-heroes use public schooling to train their successors.
No one need be surprised if these plods home in unerringly on

a protected career in public service, often, heaven help us, in teaching. And so the mischief continues.

The egalitarian passion produces a mind-set of "alien-ism" among these fresh-scrubbed world-savers, savers in Joseph Sobran's view. Alienism is hatred for the sane, the normal and the traditional in our culture, and a corresponding compassion for all that is failed, divisive or bizarre. In part this is simply due to a loathing for the Western order, but there is an egalitarian reasoning behind it, of sorts. According to their ideology, we all have essentially identical talents at birth, yet clearly we do not perform equally well or reach equal status. Such divergence from the Divine Average must be explained. What these assembly-line intellectuals conclude is that any gain or success above the average must have been *stolen,* and any lag below the average must have been the result of wicked discrimination and injustice. Therefore, they conclude, the successful must *exploit* the failures; the rich can become so only at the expense of the poor. Marx used equally tortuous reasoning to reach the same conclusion, greatly strengthening the anti-heroic prejudice that all personal success or wealth is tainted. Hence the targeting of the productive by the "alien-ist"; hence, too, his feelings of guilt, so often observed, at his own success or wealth. With such logic, the anti-heroes recreate a very old, crude, mercantilist fallacy that Adam Smith demolished two centuries ago: the notion that wealth is static, rather than constantly produced, so that to get it, you have to take it away from somebody else. This is utter nonsense. One need only see that new goods and services are continually created by human skill to realize that the produc-tive earn their success honestly. Far from stealing from the poor, it is the productive who raise the poor out of the poverty with jobs and affordable goods. None of this registers on the "alienist," whose ceaseless attack on the successful on behalf of the failures will in the end destroy both. Yet today our statute books are being filled with his fallacious "compassion."

Sobran gives us another, equally revealing, word: "victimology." This is the ideological art of finding every conceivable "victim" of our brutal and oppressive culture and showering them with government goodies to redress their underprivileged status. This is an anti-heroic Happy Hunting Ground. The victimologists can endlessly indulge their alienist taste for uplifting every sluggard, weirdo or sodomist they can find. Further, they can charge the whole bill—and the amounts are staggering—to that brutal oppressor, the taxpayer. Finally, they themselves draw handsome government salaries for performing this destruction. Any supposed victim will do. All racial or ethnic minorities, of course, qualify, as does the female majority. These are just the normal cases. On the mere assumption—no showing of actual damage is required that they have been wronged by "society" (always blame "society") in the past—they become eligible for legal privileges, such as Affirmative Action. (Note that this overthrows the older, and correct, ideal of a color- and gender-blind society; preferential law is now *based* on one's race, gender or like categories.) Thus, on behalf of "equality," the victimologist takes away freedom and equality alike, with the force of law.

Matters get worse. Groups whose only claim to victim status is how freakish, self-destructive or socially poisonous they are, come in for the same sort of coddling. As noted, one case that came up while I was writing this was the unalienable rights of pederasts. They even boasted a "national organization" claiming it was just wonderful for them to commit sodomy on other people's children, and that it was *good* for the children. In an age without evil, in a time of perfected and delicate equality, we certainly can make no public objection to anyone's "sexual preferences," as we put it now, can we? "Whatever turns you on" is, peachy nowadays, even if it is what used to be called perversion and exploits innocent children. (Lest you think this an isolated case, a few years ago the IRS gave tax-exempt status to a ring of homosexual boys' camps selling kiddie porn.)

Honest people are forced by tax law to pay for these outrages. How long will we tolerate rank injustice posing as "compassion" and "legal redress"? Weaver warned us, "... equalitarianism is harmful because it always presents itself as a redress of injustice, whereas in truth it is the very opposite." Indeed it is. The unalterable meaning of justice is to each his due. Equality before the law means, at a minimum, that we are each entitled to what we earn. The egalitarian ideologue, seeking rather equality of condition, unjustly robs those who earn more, giving the money to people who are not entitled to it (including himself). The entire U.S. tax and welfare system is built on this injustice, and the harm it does pervades every corner of American life. The indigent are rewarded, and waste not a moment claiming it is their fundamental right living off other people's toil. The productive are penalized with so great a disincentive effect as occasionally to bring the whole economy to a standstill. The egalitarians brokering this social civil war with police power wax plump in their bureaucratic posts, and find fulfillment in the damage they are doing to the hated 'bourgeois" beast.

The New Jacobinism

The socialite in jeans or the modern employer who tells his staff to address him by his first name are, however unwittingly, acting out the anti-heroes' egalitarian fantasies. In countless such details, sometimes obvious but often unsuspected, is revealed the spread of anti-heroism in our thought and manners. Social affectations particularly reveal underlying prejudices and assumptions that might otherwise pass without examination. To see how great the anti-heroic grip has become, then, we must review at least briefly the egalitarian premises that are manifest in our cultural and public life. From my vantage, it seems almost as if we were bent on surpassing the Jacobins in "democratic" affectations. It seems only a matter of time until we settle on equally drab, baggy clothing for all and address each other as "citizen" (or "comrade").

From the beginning, even in its science and philosophy, anti-heroism has rejected the qualitative for the quantitative and excellence for equality. Thus, for centuries, any evidence of personal superiority or excellence has become increasingly suspect, and finally a source of outright resentment. Everyman, after all, has long been taught that he's as good as anyone else (which, in a spiritual sense, may well be so, but which does not by any means make his condition or performance equal to anyone else's). When he sees that others are more successful, he begins to think he is being cheated out of the good life the demagogues promise modern man. As Weaver noted, he wants the nice things he sees for sale, but regards having to pay for them as an affront. He becomes a "spoiled child," resentful of the merchants and producers who won't give him what he wants. Similarly, he elects the politicians who promise to confiscate others' money or goods for him. The connection between effort and reward is deliberately played down or concealed by political demagogy.

In these ideological currents, there form almost unconsciously prejudices against achievement. Sympathy is poured on the flop or the fool, while the movers and shakers are subjected to scorn. By a sort of Gresham's Law, the great is driven out of currency by the mediocre, until our culture becomes incapable of artistry and revels in trash. Those who nevertheless succeed must, according to democratic manners, continually apologize for it, "Aw Shucks-ing" their every achievement. As Manchester remarks, "In egalitaria, if you acquire a light, you cast about quickly for a bushel." Where egalitaria is in favor, he notes, the insignia of success disappear: athletes don't wear their letter sweaters, Phi Beta Kappas don't wear their keys, soldiers hide their medals in drawers. Personal responsibility is passe: the business executive is replaced by committees, the sports team captain by revolving captaincies for everyone. And on and on.

The spread of egalitarian elusions into public life is a much more serious matter. Here all decisions are final and enforced by state coercion. The injustices become permanent, and the plain fact is they have metastasize through the body politic like a malignant tumor. "Progressive" taxation, inheritance taxes, welfarism and income "redistribution," Affirmative Action, "fair" this-and-that laws, "equal" this-and-that laws, leveling in the public schools, no-fault insurance, tort law that blames the blameless—these and a thousand other policies institutionalize the anti-heroes' egalitarian fantasies, and incorporate their ideological war against society into law.

The harm done is incalculable. Every positive law creates privilege for some at the expense of others. Those so cheated of course demand redress, and in the process someone else is forcibly disadvantaged. Measure follows measure, each adding new injustice, and creating claims that cannot be reconciled. The country is torn into warring factions, and the politics of envy and resentment replaces civil discourse, even as the state swells in power far beyond its rightful functions. The present obsession with politics and with litigation is but one appalling result of this process. Another is the growth of crime, taking its cue from welfarism, from the egalitarian "right" to help yourself to other people's property. Yet another is racism, not in the sense that a particular group is resented for being too pushy at the public trough, but rather in the much deeper sense that racism is a *form* of egalitarianism. It is not possible to make a derogatory generalization about a given race except as its members are, falsely, seen as equal. So too with other fashionable "isms," such as sexism. Susan Brownmiller's famous formula that all men are rapists is as egalitarian as it is fatuous. When we see ourselves truly as unique individuals, all such grand generalities and abstractions and insults are laughable.

But there is nothing funny in the egalitarian invasion of the public polity. It has already taken us far down the "well-trodden path to absolutism." Historically, this has been a road of no return. We can only pray it is not too late to reverse our course. Once the politics of greed and envy have been unleashed, it is nearly impossible to restore control. Indeed, the foundations of an American *Gleichschaltung* have already been laid. The egalitarian ideologues have long schooled demos in the hatred for "reaction" and "capitalism" that could fuel a future fascist state. Wrote Weaver, "Resentment, as Richard Hertz has made plain, may well prove the dynamite which will finally wreck Western society." Unless we free ourselves of the old egalitarian superstitions and reclaim the joy of human diversity, it is difficult to find any hope for the West.

The American Counterattack

One hope we can still turn to is the restoration of our American heritage. Our country, at its birth, had exactly the right concept of equality, and comes only lately—in the last half century or so—to its egalitarian perversion.

Consider the words of the Declaration of Independence, claiming as self-evident "... that all men are created equal." The Founders did not say that all men are equal, which was obviously nonsense, nor even that they were *born* equal, which would have well expressed part of their meaning: a complete denial of the feudal status society. There was no such thing as "noble" blood, and there would be no privilege by birth in the American republic. All would be equal before the law. But the word chosen, that we are *created* equal, adds a spiritual dimension, a truth, as it were, beyond men's tampering. Our true equality arises from being created alike in the image of God, in being given a rational soul and transcendant purpose. Americans were to be equal under the law of God.

Left behind were the castes and worldly bickering of the Old World. Gone was the society of privilege, holding that kings and nobles were a different *kind* of human, but dragged by that false belief into base affairs. Free Americans knew that privilege was the result of state coercion, not birth. For a thousand years nobility had been little more than a license to steal. The new republic would have none of it. The seeds of despotism were not to be planted in the New World. In America, equality before the law and liberty for all men would bring forth a radically different nation, where men would be free to escape their animal instincts and rise to spiritual fulfillment.

Even so hostile an observer as the Fabian R. H. Tawney fairly gushed over the New World spirit of equality and its liberating effects: "Few principles," he wrote, "have so splendid a record of humanitarian achievement.... Slavery and serfdom had survived the exhortations of the Christian Church, the reforms of enlightened despots, and the protests of humanitarian philosophers from Seneca to Voltaire. Before the new spirit, and the practical exigencies of which it was the expression, they disappeared, except from dark backwaters, in three generations.... It turned (the peasant) from a beast of burden into a human being. It determined that, when science should be invoked to increase the output of the soil, its cultivator, not an absentee owner, should reap the fruits." This principle, this spirit, was the American equality limited to its rightful role, creating a society without privilege. It taught the world, for a time, to live without slavery. But today even that great lesson is being lost to anti-heroism.

To try to extend equality beyond the precise meaning it had in 1776 is inevitably to pervert it and create injustice. Their never was and never will be equality of condition, no matter what kind of society or form of government. Imposing equal conditions on all succeeds only in widening inequalities even as a society of caste and privilege is rebuilt. The further this process is carried, the greater the disparities. This is easily seen in the totalitarian states. The Soviet Union, which claims to be in the vanguard of democracy and egalitarianism, is rigidly ruled by a small privileged party class called the *Nomenklatura,* whose members shop in special stores, dine in reserved restaurants, and revel in such wealth and luxury as a slave state can produce. The great majority of the populace are equal only in their suffering. Such is the reversion to barbarism implicit in anti-heroic dogma. And this very fact is what Soviet apologists regard as the "success" of socialism.

One must repeat, equality of condition, even were it attainable, would be no utopia but a nightmare. What an inconceivably dreary world it would be if we all had exactly the same status and lived exactly the same way! If you and I were really alike, it's been said, one of us would be superfluous. What we all need and hunger for is not physical equality, as an end, but equality before the law, as a means to our unique and individual development in life. We need the liberty to make of ourselves all we can, on our own steam.

Our great American heritage is, or once was, a spirit of liberty and equality that hand in glove liberated our productive energies and built the modern world. Our great mistake was trading them away for a dreary, egalitarian security and a system of state privileges back in the Great Depression days. To reverse our error, we must abandon our legal privileges— *all* of us, and reestablish, as Jefferson put it, "Equal and exact justice for all men." We would do well also to recall his creed, in which Jefferson waxed rhapsodic about the new American republic, its liberty, its geographical advantages, its disentanglement with the snarled affairs of the Old World, and such, promising a virtual paradise. "...with all these blessings," he asked, "what more is necessary to make us a happy and prosperous people?" His answer then is exactly the prescription we need now: "'Still one thing more, fellow-citizens: a wise and frugal Government, which shall restrain men from injuring one another, shall leave them otherwise free to regulate their own pursuits of industry and improvement, and shall not take from the mouth of labor the bread it has earned. This is the sum of good government, and this is necessary to close the circle of our felicities.''

A Few Final Thoughts

An unruly species is man—forever confounding the schemers and dreamers with his irrepressible individuality! The findings are fairly recent, but science not only confirms our uniqueness as individuals but shows a human diversity far greater than had been suspected. Dr. Roger Williams, a biochemist, assembled a wealth of these findings in his 1967 book *You Are Extraordinary*. Our differences, Dr. Williams showed, are by no means limited to such commonplaces as fingerprints, or a unique body chemistry that produces an aroma easily identified by the family pooch. We are, it seems, different in everything, much more so on the inside than in outward appearances. For example, normal hearts may have anywhere from one to six arteries branching out, and variances in normal nervous systems and brains are virtually too complicated to classify. It could hardly be surprising that our physical differences contribute to our mental and emotional distinctions. Not only are no two people built alike, but no two receive the same sensory experience from the outside world. We can hardly expect each other to reach exactly the same understandings about the world, much less find ready agreement about all things. The surprise—and joy—is that we mesh as well as we do: a matter that can be much improved as soon as we really understand how different we are from one another.

Biochemical individuality is a complete and scientific refutation of egalitarian delusions, insofar as equality of condition is idealized. It is one thing, and not a bad one, "to dream the impossible dream." It is quite another to try to put the impossible into practice, by force—that is both insane and brutal. We make no useful philosophy by pretending people can be what they cannot.

The radical egalitarians then are badly mistaken, as in time they may learn from scientific fact, if not from rational argument. But what is right? Here, of course, science can provide no answers. We have to search with just those tools rejected so long ago by anti-heroism, our minds and our moral sense.

We would do well to look first and hardest exactly where anti-heroism focuses its fury: at the Christian underpinnings of our civilization. We would be ill-advised indeed to overlook a conception of man of such accuracy as to maintain civilization for two millennia. If, in fact, we are God's creatures, then our demonstrable individuality cannot be without purpose. Our uniqueness must fit into a greater pattern, whether we see it or no. It may rather be, as Lewis put it, that "we are marble waiting to be shaped or colour to be painted; not a mere seed to be planted." Certainly we may agree with Stassinopoulos that "We are not committed by our genes, as ants and wasps are, to drone away, all together, at the same fixed activity, at some immense, collective work, its outlines hidden forever from our sight. But we are committed by the seed of that divinity which we *all* embody—and which we call our soul—to unfold gradually our own individual, spiritual truth, and through this truth to fulfill our part in the truth and law of the collective existence."

Individuality must count for something. St. Athanasius spoke wisely, many centuries ago, and almost as if he were addressing the latter-day anti-hero: "For if all things had come into being in this automatic fashion, instead of being the outcome of mind, they would all be uniform and without distinction." Our distinction, then, is the gift of God, not nature. Perhaps here we will find purpose. At the very least, we ought to recall the older Christian view that our merits— or elevation above the egalitarian's Divine Average, if you want to put it so—are a worldly illusion. Says Lewis, "The work of a Beethoven, and that of a charwoman, become spiritual on precisely the same condition, that of being offered to God, of being done humbly, 'as to the Lord.'" "...no Christianity, not even the most ignorant or perverse, ever suggested that a baronet was better than a butcher in that sacred sense," Chesterton echoes.

This must be the true spirit of equality: the full contribution of otherwise unique individuals to divine purpose.

Chapter VII
The Unholy Arts of the Anti-Hero

> Genuine art never was created for its own sake, it was always a means of worship, an affirmation of belief, an aspiration pointing beyond itself. The beauty of art is reflected beauty.
>
> —Thomas Molnar

> Modern culture seems to have lost its myths, debased its heroes, and preserved only its demons.
>
> —Harold O. J. Brown

Culture is a cruel mirror in our time, and cruellest to the anti-hero. For nowhere is his handiwork more plainly seen, or more mocking to his pretensions, than in the corruption of Western arts and letters. And indeed this was his intention: tearing down the old Christian culture to make way for the new creator—Man. On the ruins, or so anti-heroes once believed, would be built a higher, more enlightened order, of new greatness. One had but to rid natural man of his primitive superstitions and values to set free his limitless artistic genius.

Of the intended destruction of Western art, we got full measure. Of great new art, we have none. By any index, the best of anti-heroic arts are degenerate, and our popular culture revels in violence and debauchery. Excellence, much less greatness, is to us a withered memory. The best repertoire of our concert halls and theaters is all old, antedating the rise of modernism. But even this is often ignored, while the most incoherent, banal and soon-to-be-forgotten works of anti-heroes are praised as true art. A more precipitous cultural decline than ours is hard to imagine: from the old masters to splatters and splotches and worse; from literature to pornography; from Bach to rock. Were, say, Goethe to come among us today, he would deem us unholy barbarians, the very opposite of the advanced culture the anti-hero boasts. And he might well be bewildered that the magnificence of Western art could be reduced to ruin in a century. He did not know the mind and pride of the anti-hero.

To Goethe, though he was not a Christian, great art was "divinely endowed." "Let anybody only try," he said, "with human will and human power, to produce something that may be compared to the creations that bear the names of *Mozart, Raphael* or *Shakespeare*." It cannot be done. Such works or their like "rose above ordinary human nature, and in the same proportion" as they were touched by God. Without an inner vision of the divine, men have no such power. Thus it is that contemporary art, pursued by the willfully Autonomous Man of anti-heroism, is sterile or worse a death wish. It reveals his rebellion against life as clearly as Christian arts revealed reverence.

How an artist looks at the world and his place in it means everything to his work. His real religion, whether theistic or not, can be neither hidden nor dissimulated in the long run. The wellsprings of art run deep and reflect us truly, not in surface appearances, not as we wish to be seen, but as we are in our own innermost belief. For example, traditional Western culture flowed from Christian piety, and its artists shared a sublime vision of God's creation and man made in God's image. Their works reached out to worship and to glorify their Creator, transcending mere self or art for its own sake. Their art, that is, was not meant as such but as a gift, and it glows with the beauty of one's most precious gift to the Most Holy.

Anti-heroism, in contrast, centers in the opposite view, a denial of God and hostility to Christianity. Anti-heroic art is thus essentially negative, and it can take many forms, from a sour proletarian utopianism to rage to meaningless abstraction to a celebration of chaos to the outrightly demonic. Suffice it to observe that nowhere in the anti-heroic faiths can there be objective standards for art or evocations of transcendant beauty. The anti-hero has nothing to worship but himself and his art, and is inescapably tugged down to the temporal, the mundane and the dark. His work is by nature ugly, and achieves a pale beauty only when he forgets his anti-heroic premises. As Richard Weaver reminds us, "Barbarism and Philistinism cannot see that knowledge of material reality is knowledge of death. The desire to get ever closer to the source of physical sensation—this is the downward pull which puts an end to ideational life." Anti-heroic art, forever imprisoned in materialism, must by its own logic succumb in the end to its own meaninglessness or sink into evil. Having lost all capacity to shock and thereby condemn "bourgeois" culture, it has already reached its dead end. Mindless anti-heroic "art" abounds, and dabblings in the black arts have made an appearance. Surely this is cause for alarm.

What is true of individual writers and artists is true of our whole culture. We answer affirmatively (as he did) T. S. Eliot's query "... whether what we call the culture, and what we call the religion, of a people are not different aspects of the same thing: the culture being essentially the incarnation, so to speak, of the religion of a people."

The question this raises is the cultural mirror and the matter that concerns us: What does this say about America? What religion or religions incarnate themselves in our culture? What inner beliefs reveal themselves in our fascination—to take but a few of the countless examples available—with junkyard "sculpture," atonal and cacophonic "modern" music, kitchen appliances exhibited as art in museums, rock groups named Black Sabbath and Judas Priest, blood movies, porno parlors, *Dallas, Dynasty* and the like, and an obsession with sex that permeates every cultural medium?

One looks in vain through this motley mayhem for any standard of manners or morals not violated or any commandment unbroken. What it conspicuously offers is an unrestrained quest for sensation, especially the physical. What it conspicuously lacks is a higher view of life, seeking beauty, cultivation, character, knowledge and moral redemption. We seem positively intolerant of anything more uplifting than the *Smurfs*. Whatever else we may believe, it is clear that Judeo-Christian belief is today far from predominant. Dr. Harold O. J. Brown writes, "... the climate of unbelief has created the culture of corruption. *Dallas* and *Dynasty* make sense only in a world in which there is no thought of God, of justice, or of judgment." In truth, most American culture makes sense only in the final throes of an anti-heroism that hates God as much for not existing as for existing; for either way, its cause is hopeless, and His gift of moral agency becomes odious.

Yet surely, the serious anti-heroes among us are few. The difficulty of working out this (or any) world view guarantees it. We rightly conclude that most who wallow in decadent culture are the anti-hero's unwitting victims. How, after all, could they discern anything seriously amiss in a steamy soap or in the schoolboyish humor of *Animal House?* It could in no way occur to them that a titillating moment in *Dynasty* was four centuries in the making, through relentless assault on moral authority and our spiritual nature. Nor could they grasp that this long struggle thrust them into a Devil's bargain, trading away the promised fulfillment of whole life for the illusory pleasures of the moment. The many are not to blame; these matters are far beyond *demos.* It is anti-heroism and its long, prideful rebellion against life and reality that must be brought to reckoning.

For this, a few thoughts on the advance of anti-heroism over the past century are in order. A couple of rather funny artistic disputes can help put things in chronological perspective.

Two Fights

On a May Day in 1933, in the depths of the Great Depression, Nelson Rockefeller strode into the main lobby of the gleaming new Rockefeller Center in New York City. There he confronted Diego Rivera, who had been commissioned to paint a mural. Young Rockefeller ordered Rivera to get down off his scaffold, handed him a check for $14,000 to discharge the contract (a small fortune in those days), and kicked him out. Then he had his workmen cover Rivera's half-finished mural with tarpaper. The next day the struggle between "art" and "bourgeois values" hit the headlines.

The question runs deep and is not easily resolved. By traditional standards, art is validated by its aesthetics, by an inner sense that "awakens knowledge of a kind no other means can reach," as Jacques Barzun puts it. Arianna Stassinopoulos adds, "The primary requisite of art is indeed that it shall move us, not that it shall instruct us." Rivera, the firebrand communist, was having none of this. For him (and for anti-heroism at the time), the message made the art and he missed no chance to get his message across. The mural was on stridently Marxist themes. Its focal point was an oversized portrait of Lenin, flanked by Marx and Engels, with many lesser revolutionary lights set below, in suitably smaller stature. These (lest anyone miss the point, one supposes) held a scroll reading "Workers of the World, Unite." Lenin gazes sternly down on a scene of American workers on strike, bearing a sign to "Smash Rockefeller serfdom," being mowed down by the gunfire of obviously American police. In the foreground, as if richly pleased with the slaughter, is a wizened and evil-looking caricature of John D. Rockefeller.

This is, to say the least, tacky. Rivera had tried to paint his utmost curse on an employer who made him rich, and on the very walls of the Rockefellers' own building. Was the mural art, or was it, rather, a bitter, ill-mannered, libelous political cartoon, painted at the expense of its victim? The anti-heroic Aesthetes of the day professed no trouble with this at all. The mural was great art, and the defrauded Rockefellers were Philistines. Then they went on to laud the mural's glowing aesthetic qualities, of which it was conspicuously empty: Rivera was at pains to keep his work ugly and insulting, as part of his message. Not even the artist's plain intent could keep the Aesthetes from their anti-hero duties.

By "Aesthetes" I mean those anti-heroes in the vanguard of redefining art, whose business it has been to attack anything smacking of "bourgeois," and to gush over anything announced to be art by those of like mind. Solzhenitsyn sees them as withdrawn into "self-created worlds" and "realms of subjective whim." Stassinopoulos hears them "complaining in unison about 'how hopelessly warped mankind is, how shallow people have become, and how burdensome it is for a lone, refined and beautiful soul to dwell among them.'" Chesterton dislikes their snobbery: "They circulate a piece of paper on which Mr. Picasso had the misfortune to upset the ink and tried to dry it with his boots, and they seek to terrify democracy by the good old anti-democratic muddlements: that 'the public' does not understand these things...." Barzun describes them penetratingly in the fifties: "Today, after eighty years or more of this open war, most educated men and women have been persuaded that all the works of man's mind except art are vulgar frauds: law, the state, machinery, the edifice of trade, are worthless. More, men and women feel that they themselves are worthless, they despise their own existence, because it fails in loveliness when compared with the meanest objet d'art. The abandonment of Intellect in favor of communion through quartet playing and amateur ceramics has bred a race of masochist–idolaters, broken up into many sects, but at one in their worship of the torturing indefinite." For just such as these I will use capital "A" Aesthete in this discussion. But beware: whom *they* call "Philistines" may be and often are articulate defenders of the older Western culture and higher artistic standards. And even the know-nothings among them rightly sense the fatuities of anti-heroic art.

The assault on Western culture has been dated to about 1870, and was more reformist than radical at first. The anti-heroes were largely bent on replacing "bourgeois" values (a Marxist term they employ relentlessly to this day) with a new and liberated art. Certainly in those times of onrushing industrialism, there were many cultural defects.* But the would-be reformers' shallow analysis wrongly attributed to the mythical "bourgeois" the materialism they deplored, and of which they themselves were the carriers. In truth, the cultural norms and standards had been derived from Christian belief, over centuries. And these covered all the ground, making God the source of beauty, hence linking all human art to an absolute ideal. If perfection was unattainable, at least there was an objective aesthetic standard to direct and measure artistic effort. There were no new standards to be had, for the reformers and no way out except a retreat to sheer subjectivism. The anti-heroes grabbed it, declaring art should exist for its own sake and would be whatever they wanted it to be. Artistic norms were anathematized as inhibitive artifacts

---

*It may shed light on the thinking of Aesthetes that they could feel deprived or offended by a culture that boasted, among many others, Tchaikowsky, Liszt, Wagner, Rossini, Verdi and Strauss; Gilbert and Sullivan; Remington, Van Gogh, Whistler, Saint-Gaudens and Cassatt; Dickens, Tolstoy, Turgenev, Dostoevsky and Hawthorne. (Today they feel at home with Cage and de Kooning.) Also notable in the period was an astonishingly high level of popular literacy, despite limited education, and a culture that enjoyed fine essays and poetry in popular periodicals. Barzun has remarked that the Lincoln–Douglas debates, addressed to the common people of Illinois farms and towns, could hardly be followed by today's college graduate. As striking an example is *Value, Price and Profit* by Karl Marx, described as a "simpler" presentation of the economic views in *Das Kapital*. A doctoral candidate in economics today would have trouble following, much less rebutting, it. In fact, Marx had delivered it, verbally, as an address to a gathering of working men.

of the old regime, to be cast aside with scorn. In this redefinition began the fatal descent of a culture based on transcendant values into the materialist muck it wallows in today. The anti-heroes had paid no heed to Goethe's warning that subjectivism marks an era in decline and bent on its own doom. Neither did they heed the contemporary warning by Nietsche that the non-Christian in the modern world did not realize the travails he faced in a world unredeemed by Christ. The shocks were not long in coming.

Even as the arts and letters cut themselves adrift into experimentalism, the poisons of the larger anti-heroic vision—that of Autonomous Man taking control of the godless cosmos—was permeating the whole of Western society. An aggressive Darwinism provided the new anti-heroic creed.* So strong was its influence that one of its adherents, William Kingdon Clifford, could invert the words of the Bible to gloat: "The dim and shadowy outlines of the superhuman deity fade slowly away from before us; and as the mist of his presence floats aside, we perceive with great and greater clearness the shape of a yet grander and nobler figure—of Him who made all Gods and shall unmake them. From the dim dawn of history, and from the innermost depth of every soul, the face of our father Man looks out upon us with the fire of eternal youth in his eyes, and says, before Jehovah was, I am!"

The fine arts, having deserted their duty to inform man of his moral nature, could only reinforce the rebellious and

---

*Darwinism, implying the subjection of the weak to the strong, is—and was from the first understood to be—an invitation to militarism. This impulse loomed large before the first World War; moral authority had been too weakened by anti-heroism to resist it successfully. And, in 1937, only two years before the bloodbath began again in the second war, we find Sir Arthur Keith, an eminent Darwinist, still publicly lamenting the prospect of centuries of peace!

increasingly warlike mood in the West. Cubism, for instance, reducing the human form to an ugly, anti-heroic geometry, only detracted from the higher view of life needed to avert disaster. One year before the "guns of August," Marcel Duchamp thumbed his nose at the older West by inverting a bicycle wheel on a stool and proclaiming it art. The poisons, accumulating over decades, did their work; Europe marched as one into the unspeakable carnage of the Great War.

The second World War was fiercer and bloodier, but the first was a shock like no other to the Western mind. In the prologue to his *Heartbreak House*, written just a year after the war had ended in exhaustion, George Bernard Shaw acutely laid the blame for the catastrophe on the rise of the anti-heroes' Darwinist "religion." But the anti-heroes were in no mood to listen.* The shockwaves had split their ranks, and both camps sunk deeper into the anti-heroic swamps. One, misreading the new Einsteinian universe, turned to a rabid moral relativism which haunts us still. In their eyes, all creation had gone mad, and life had no meaning. From this despair emerged surreal art and the bitter rebuke of dadaism, acting out the insanity seen. A new and equally surreal literature was led by Joyce and Kafka, who made their protagonists actual anti-heroes for the first time. The other camp turned militant, seeking secular salvation in the collectivist state, and putting its hopes especially in the fledgling Soviet experiment. Many made the pilgrimage to Russia, even at the height of the Stalin purges, and saw exactly the wonders

---

*They had also ignored this wise and accurate observation by Dr. Albert Schweitzer: "Our civilization is going through a severe crisis. . . . Most people think that the crisis is due to the war, but they are wrong. The war, with everything connected to it, is only a phenomenon of the condition of uncivilization in which we find ourselves."

they desperately wanted to see. (Their ecstatic reports are one of the great testaments to self-delusion on record.) A young Thomas Merton, for example, would later write, "I had in my mind the myth that Soviet Russia was the friend of all the arts, and the only place where true art could find a refuge in a world of bourgeois ugliness. Wherever I got that idea is hard to find out, and how I managed to cling to it for so long is harder still, when you consider all the photographs there were, for everyone to see, showing Red Square with gigantic pictures of Stalin hanging on the walls of the world's ugliest buildings. . . . " This camp, naturally, adopted the tenets of "socialist realism," and its art took a hard, proletarian flavor. The Great Depression of the 1930s signalled to the anti-heroes that "capitalism was done for," and they reunited in militancy. Clifford Odets, John Dos Passos and James T. Farrell, along with Rivera, were perhaps the best known of the many who lent their talents to the cause and left an indelible socialist imprint on the arts of the day. Malcolm Cowley, literary editor of the *New Republic*, would later recall, "Even the left-wing writers of the time were not much interested in Marx as a philosopher or in Marx as an economist (whatever did he mean by surplus value?) or Marx in his favorite role as a scientist of revolution. Instead, they revered him as a prophet calling for a day of judgment and a new heaven on earth. . . . They bisected and bifurcated, either–ored: either light or darkness, Socialism or Fascism . . . either the glorious (Communist) future or a return to the Dark Ages." That is, either the final attainment of anti-heroism or a galling return to the hated house of the Father.

Thumbing through the thick catalogue of "isms" spun out by Modernism, one is impressed most by the considerable ingenuity shown by artists, over a century, to sustain a hopeless cause. (One is also impressed with the similarity to visiting a freak show.) Experiment after experiment, school after school followed the new freedom from rules. Seemingly everything was tried, and tried again, save only reaching beyond self and art for beauty: that was the old aesthetic standard, its banning the one rule the modernists observed. But nothing lasted long—discouraging to artists fiercely determined, through imagination or materials, to create a work that could "in its power, transcend its time," as Daniel Bell put it. This desire, a paltry envy of the greatness of traditional Western culture, went unfulfilled. Arts intended to subvert the older order triumphed in their moment, but soon lost all power to shock. The experimental, through repetition, soon evoked yawns—or worse, the Philistine query, "Oh, another experiment?" However art was redefined, whatever new concept was read into it, boredom with it was not far behind. The power of Modernism was spent long before its most anti-heroic spasm in the counter-culture of the 1960s, which celebrated its own incoherence and urged the faithful to seek "pre-rational spontaneity" in "the shaman's rhapsodic babbling," as Bell noted. It is hard to get any freer than that.

The simplest explanation is that none of these frenetic efforts were, in truth, great and enduring. When we ask why not, perhaps it will be realized that, for all the damage done, the game was lost at its first stirring. A game of baseball or bridge without rules would quickly become chaotic, and quite possibly violent. Why should anyone suppose that arts and letters can be sustained—much less advanced—without aesthetic standards rooted in objective reality? When the anti-heroes first sought to free the arts from their traditional mooring, they put the very definition of art at the mercy of the moment, to be claimed by any fad, fancy or whim. Or to put it more bluntly, they stripped the arts of all definability: which, in the end, is a decisive statement that art is nothing at all. As the faddishly supposed aesthetics of protest, experiment, concept and the like fade away, the issue becomes stark. At the end of the road is the self-denying art of meaninglessness. It rightly represents a time in which the larger anti-heroic vision, though very late in the realization, questions all meaning, including its own. We see both among us today. The aesthetic questions have finally been defined out of existence. All we can ask now is ludicrously, "Is it art?"

Such was the nature of the recent furor, between the Aesthetes and Philistines, over a Richard Serra sculpture titled *Tilted Arc* in the plaza of a federal office building in New York City. The controversy was actually aired at a meeting called by the General Services Administration, owner of the work in question—which reminds us of the servility as well as undefinability of the arts in our time. Before proceeding, let me say that *Tilted Arc* is a wall-like sheet of rusty Cor-ten steel, appropriately curved and tilted, 120 feet long, 12 feet high, weighing nearly eighty tons, that stretches across said plaza. It was commissioned by the GSA on the advice of several Aesthete experts, and cost the taxpayers $175,000.

The federal workers, affected Philistines all, were not altogether pleased with the sculpture, and it was on their collective objection that the GSA bureaucrats held the meeting. Among the Philistine objections were that *Tilted Arc* blocked all passage across the plaza, imposing significant detours on workers; and that it invited nasty grafitti, could shelter terrorists, and made the plaza useless for lunching. They called it "overbearing," "depressing" and even an "iron curtain," and made references to a rusty piece of junk and even more references to an "eyesore."

Naturally, the Aesthetes turned out in force to defend their own and put down this churlish Philistine reaction. "I have to tell you it is beautiful," said one. Another likened it to walking through Stonehenge, or a cathedral, or an Egyptian temple. None missed an opportunity to deplore the attack on artistic freedom, and sculptor Claes Oldenburg repeated the old litany, denouncing the vigilantes who were trying to "override the opinions of better-qualified persons."

Mr. Serra himself came to the meeting, and of course was the star witness. One was reminded of Chesterton's stricture that if the art was intelligible, it could be intelligibly described in English.

He had, Serra reported, spent two and a half years on *Tilted Arc* (doing heaven knows what), and hadn't made a dime on it, and furthermore, the work was "site-specific," meaning its art could exist nowhere else. (One of the Aesthetes, taking this perhaps too seriously, later suggested razing the federal building to create more suitable sur-roundings for the immortal rusty steel wall.) Further still, Serra could offer a crystalline statement of the artistic conception of the work:

> As you cross the plaza on the concave side, the sweep of the arc creates an amphitheater-like condition. This newly created concave volume has a silent amplitude which magnifies your awareness of yourself and the sculptural field of space. The concavity of the topological curve allows one to understand the

sweep of the entire plaza. However, upon walking around the convexity at the ends, the curve appears to be infinite. Understanding the simple distinction between a plane leaning toward you that is curved and concave, and a plane leaning away from you that is curved and convex, is crucial. This establishes new meaning among things.

Perhaps; or is this perhaps too much blather to bear about a piece of curved, rusty steel? As I write, the issue is undecided. I can only report that the Philistines sat stunned in their new amphitheater-like condition, reverberating with silent amplitude. The GSA board, turning pale, immediately decided that *Tilted Arc* would not be judged on "aesthetic" grounds, but only on whether it hinders the workaday function of the plaza (which, if you try walking through the plaza perpendicularly to either the convexity or concavity of the sculpture, you will learn at once). What remains is Mr. Serra's promise of "new meaning," which sounds rather too much like the old trick of spinning doubletalk to gull the rubes and pass off one's latest inanity as art. Barzun offered some choice specimens, and I could add more.

Apparently it worked again. The Aesthetes got in the last shot. Remove one work of art anywhere, they said, and it is the beginning of the end. Never again would an artist trust the government (they are the last to learn) or accept a large tax-financed grant to create a work of art on government property. Serra himself promised to go into exile if anyone messed with his steel wall. No one heeded a St. Louis observer's recollection that Serra had razed a nice little park in that city to install, in the name of art, a rusty steel pyramid. The park, once popular and planted with flowers, was now deserted except by derelicts who used the pyramid as a public convenience. Adding to the rust.

It might be asked whether this is not an exaggerated or isolated incident, unrepresentative of our culture overall. The instinctive answer is that if the art world is in such disarray that "is it art?" can be asked of a work, we won't have far to look for more disputes. Nevertheless, I reviewed the mutterings of the cultural milieu for a few weeks, and with a minimum of malice, to be sure *Tilted Arc* was not one of a kind. Here are a few of the more interesting stories:

—A controversy erupted over a sculpture in Paris called "Long-Term Parking." The work was a stack of junked autos sandwiched with concrete into a towering obelisk. Irritated Parisian Philistines succeeded in having it re-zoned from artwork to a building so it could be torn down.

—An exhibition of art by the mentally ill was held in Chicago, complete with references to such avant-garde European painters as Jean DuBuffet who draw on insanity as inspiration for their work. No ironies were observed.

—The Whitney Museum of American Art held its biennial exhibition, including such items as household objects, ultraviolet lighting in the bathrooms, and one work done on an erector set.

—Prime-time television showed its own version of Tolstoy's *Anna Karenina,* omitting nothing but the moral stuff. According to TV, Anna is fulfilled by her adultery, not remorseful and consumed with "disgust and horror." After all, what sort of sin is sex nowadays? Of course, if Anna did not stray, her sin and true repentance cannot be compared to her husband's greater sin in refusing to forgive her, and one is left wondering what was the point of the book. One welcome touch was that Anna's sex scenes were restrained by TV standards; but then, there weren't any sex scenes in the book.

For anyone of healthy instincts, such flaps and rumbles are just plain funny. But it would surely not seem so to those Aesthetes of furrowed brow who worship Art. Their idolatry is rich in irony. It was their own anti-hero ancestors who painted the abstract universe that drained all meaning from their lives; so now they kneel before what they see as the last tangible verity—Art. Yet they cannot even say what their god is, for the same anti-heroes stole the meaning of Art, too. Thus they are made to worship the void. Lastly, as Stassino-poulos points out, elevating art to an end in itself is a trap. We must not, she argues, mistake our raptures at great art for our fulfillment as whole persons. The arts are only reflections of the true beauty we seek; they are but the signposts that point to our destination: "It is this living effect of art on man that makes art at its highest what Goethe believed it to be: a sister of religion, by whose aid the great world scheme is wrought into reality; no mere amusement to charm the idle or relax the careworn, but a mighty influence, serious in its aims and joyful in its means."

Just as surely, by the corruption of art is the great world scheme undone. The anti-heroes, meaning to subvert the traditional Christian culture, subverted all culture. Seeking the glory of art for themselves, they unmade art. Denying that beauty lay beyond themselves, they killed it with their hands and brushes and words, and call ugly things beautiful. Thinking to set the arts free in a brave new world, they tore down all the signposts. In place of joyous music and paintings to lift our souls, they give us steel hulks that tell us life is a wearisome joke. *Demos* does not know he has been swindled, and would not much care if he found out; he's having too much fun with the vulgar delights of his barnyard. The Aesthetes, likewise, are undismayed by their handiwork; they are too entranced with the torturing indefinite.

Yet we cannot say, "If that's what they want, let them have it." The loss of an ennobling culture is real, and it is without measure, and it is a loss to us all. Similarly, a corrupt culture corrupts everyone. We have lost more even than the greatness of Western arts and letters, for we have surrendered our own participation in our culture. We are chair-bound spectators, letting anti-heroism foist its counterfeits on us instead of creating a culture ourselves. Bernard Iddings Bell observed thirty years ago that we Americans "do not make nearly as much music today as our grandparents did." Neither do we decorate our homes with our own crafts and art as they did: "We buy what mass producers tell us is in the best taste. It may or may not be good; but it is not ours, no matter how much we pay for it." The art of conversation is practically lost; we no longer make our drama, leaving it to professionals; few of us take part in sports any more—the list goes on and on. Earlier generations pursued all these cultural strands for sheer enjoyment, and theirs was a healthier, happier art than ours. In a word, undoing the damage of anti-heroism starts at home. It is a lot more fun to sing together, even if we do it poorly, than to have an expert do it for us. When we leave these pursuits to others, we let them dictate not only our tastes but our morals. Letting the Aesthetes dictate cultural directions leads not only to art at its lowest, but to infection by its materialism. If we are to escape the present cultural morass, it is important that we take the responsibility on ourselves, but more important still to remember that true art is worship.

Toward Cultural Norms

Said Chesterton, in one of those astonishing insights that he seemed to have at his fingertips, "The only two things that can satisfy the soul are a person and a story; and even the story must be about a person." Other pleasures are many and deep, to be sure. But they satisfy only mind or body, not the whole person. With maturity we learn that the delights of the moment can never fulfill our lives or bring us happiness, no matter how greatly we multiply them.

Every human life is a story, and of our stories are woven the cultural fabric. To get inside a story, then, can tell us much about life, and much about our arts: at the very least how to distinguish *The Last Supper* from *Tilted Arc,* or the choral movement of Beethoven's Ninth Symphony from Ozzy Osbourne's *Speak to the Devil.*

Life, like a tale, begins in creation and ends in judgment, but its outcome is not predetermined. "A story has proportions, variations, surprises. . . ." It must be told and cannot just occur to anybody or be worked out like a sum. If we add two numbers there is only one right answer. But if we tell a story, we can have it end any way we wish. That numinous gift of choice is the crucial ingredient of every story, and every life. Perhaps alone among all creatures, we humans are truly born free; else we would have no art or tales to tell. But we do. Our kind are born poets and artists and story-tellers. That, if nothing else, tells us the anti-hero philosophies are dealing in snake oil. Our free will points to purpose beyond the world, and fills our choices with meaning. Will we choose well or ill? Will we fall or be saved? Such is the essence of our true drama, whether in life or on stage. Real life is thus ever at the crossroads, and we cannot with certainty see beyond. But we can choose the right road.

Anti-heroism does violence to life and art alike by denying human will. It tells us there is no such thing as choice, that all is determined by nature, or history, or economics, or social forces. It tells us that creation had no Creator, that the material universe is all there is, that our lives are a brief and meaningless event between two eternities. Such are the planted axioms of our times; such form the spirit of the age. Yet if ever a human being has told a story or drawn a picture, all of it is nonsense. A dead cosmos tells no tales.

The ultimate act of courage, it has been said, is to see ourselves as we really are. Yet nothing less is demanded of us in the flood tide of anti-heroism. We must look deeply and well into the mirror of culture. If the reflection be cruel—and surely it is—it is only because we at last see ourselves as very much less than we should be. This is not cause for despair. It is the first, hardest step toward recovery. But, as in a story, we ourselves choose the outcome. So let us be about it.

We peer at the mirror and see anti-heroism everywhere triumphant. We see ourselves as mere beasts, enchanted with our rutting and fodder and fresh straw. We are portrayed, rightly by anti-heroic lights, as meaningless, as chips of wood tossed about randomly by a maelstrom of forces beyond our control. Nowhere in the cultural mirror can we escape our image as materialistic, undisciplined, amoral and irreligious people, with *demos* sunk even further into what has aptly been called pornotopia. (When, if ever, have the soaps dramatized anyone going to church to worship?)

What we see is too often true of us, yet not what we want to be. Nor are the anti-heroic depictions true to life. We are, underneath all the garbage tossed our way, an heroic people, in heart and soul. And we are not the helpless victims of fate that the anti-heroic dogmas make us out to be. Many years ago Malcolm Cowley observed that our young writers had never heard of the cardinal sins and virtues, and that consequently they treated crimes and sins as mere mischances. In their fated and anti-heroic drama, no real love or hate could appear. Characterization died, as art dies in the dadaist's fur-covered toilet seat. But we still know love and hate, don't we? Life is real, and our culture will be what we want it to be.

If we would have a higher culture, we must seek it first in excellence, or as Matthew Arnold put it, "the acquainting ourselves with the best that has been known and said in the world." But excellence alone will not guide us. We cannot, armed by our desire alone, achieve excellence. This has been demonstrated beyond doubt in short-lived rusted steel. Art can never be an idol. To capture it is to catch a soap bubble and see it pop in our hands. We shall have no art until we remember that it is a reward, given us only when we reach beyond ourselves to the Author of beauty.

Chapter VIII
American Schooling:
The Training of Anti-Heroes

If the object of education is the improvement of man, then any system of education that is without values is a contradiction in terms. A system that seeks bad values is bad. A system that denies the existence of values denies the possibility of education. Relativism, scientism, skepticism and anti-intellectualism, the four horsemen of the philosophical apocalypse, have produced that chaos in education which will end in the disintegration of the West.

—Robert Maynard Hutchins

In these few words, Dr. Hutchins offers a profound insight and a bitter choice. True education and the anti-heroic view cannot co-exist. They are literally sprung from different worlds and embrace different modes of thought, different views of man, and contradictory conceptions of all human dealings. They are natural and indeed implacable enemies, between which no compromise is possible. In plain words, we cannot have it both ways. We can indulge our anti-heroic pipe dreams, or we can, through education, give our children richer lives: but not both. Never both.

The anti-hero's formulas, we see over and over, reject all values and deny even our humanity. This posture has gathered force for two centuries and more, not from science, but from would-be philosophers of science and a few scientists dabbling in philosophy. Buoyed by the early successes of the physical or "exact" sciences, it has sought illicitly to extend the methods of the laboratory into the moral realm—as if courage or a prayer could be described by complex differential equations. Despite this glaring contradiction, the anti-heroes have had immense success asserting that empiricism alone gives valid knowledge; that all we can really know is sensory experience reducible to numbers and measurements. They assume that, in Richard Weaver's biting phrase, "experience will tell us what we are experiencing." Reality itself is thus shaped by definition, by an anti-hero formula that ruthlessly excludes our self-knowledge of our rational and moral nature. The assault on our values and our higher nature is seamless and complete. The philosopher David Hume, patron saint of anti-heroism, set the tone for it long ago by urging readers of his *Enquiry Concerning Human Understanding* to raid the libraries and assess every book by its adherence to pure empiricism. Should a book betray any hint of humane or religious values, said Hume, "Then commit the book to the flames; for it can contain nothing but sophistry and illusion." By such thought and utopian crusading, we are made to think of ourselves in our own times as mere animals without meaning or purpose, lost in a dead and uncaring cosmos.

The damage caused by this monstrous doctrine is incalculable, and nowhere more hurtful than in the field of education. A system that denies values, as Dr. Hutchins observes, makes education impossible. Education is precisely the preservation, refinement and transmission of values from one generation to the next. Its tools include reason, tradition, moral concern and introspection: the examination from within of what can never be seen from without by scientific methods: ourselves. Where anti-heroism pretends to be *wertfrei* (value-free), education is value-laden, and, in the end, concerns nothing but our higher nature and moral purpose. Education seeks truth; anti-heroism denies its existence. Education seeks meaning in human life, justice in human affairs, dignity in human aspirations; anti-heroes deny all human purpose save evolutionary survival. There is no common ground between them. To accept anti-heroic dogmas is to define education out of existence. Beasts cannot be educated, can they? Beasts can only be trained for relatively simple, vocational tasks.

And training is virtually all the American school system has been concerned with for nearly a century. It should not surprise us that our schools, largely under anti-heroes' control, use our children for social experiments and train them to be anti-heroes. We suppose them to be getting an education, however inferior. But arguably they are never exposed to real education at all. The vestiges of American education, in its traditional meaning, were swept away before the turn of the century by anti-hero "reformers." So thorough and savage was their victory that the meanings of the word education have been forgotten and lost. As early as 1931, Albert Jay Nock could say with assurance that not a single undergraduate college or university in the country could still be counted an educational institution. The revolutionary overthrow of what he called "formative education" in favor of "instrumental training" was total. We will return to these crucial concepts in a moment.

Neither should it surprise us that as disciplined education fades from memory, even the training substituted for it grows ever feebler and more dilute. We do not educate our teachers. We train them with a smattering of "subjects" and instructional techniques. How—and what—are they to teach? It is to their own great credit that no few of our teachers manage to do well through extra diligence and devotion. But many cannot overcome the handicap their poor training imposes. And their students in turn are even more handicapped when their generation enters the teaching profession. So it is that the results of public schooling have worsened steadily for as long as anyone can remember. The unbroken twenty-year decline in Scholastic Aptitude Test scores (the most widely used placement test for high school students planning to enter college) is just one measure of many.

Horror Stories

Not a week goes by but what we can read in the newspapers some item like the following. They provide a melancholy index of the long reach of anti-heroism in America, particularly among the academics. It is no consolation that the war against education was over long before we were born. The casualties are here and now and disspiriting:

—A Ford Foundation study found that 23 million adult Americans could neither read nor write, and that as many as

60 million were "functionally illiterate." (Reading and writing are first-grade material and can easily be taught to any normal child.)

—The Department of Education—a clear contradiction in terms—reveals its own handiwork with the statement that 72 million Americans are illiterate. It also predicted that 90% of the high school graduates in coming years would not have entry level job skills. (A reflection that the schools deal in vocational training, not education, and do even that very badly.) Citing the above statistics, the B. Dalton Company, a private bookseller, determined a few years ago that it would use 5% of its pre-tax profits to fight illiteracy—that is, to try to remedy the damage done by the schools.

—The United States was found to rank 47th among Western nations in literacy.

—Over half (53%) of the teachers employed in Texas failed a basic competency test. In Florida, a group of high school students did better on a similar test than the teachers, all college graduates.

—The then new Secretary of Education, William Bennett, met with a group of 70 of our best high school students. He asked how many of them had heard of *The Federalist Papers*—only 7 (10%) raised their hands.

—Writer Benjamin Stein, who deals with many teenagers in his work, spent a couple of years informally surveying their attitudes and what they knew—or as it turned out, their "astounding ignorance."

Stein wrote in *Public Opinion* magazine, "No amount of preparation could possibly cushion the blows of unawareness of even the most elementary current events, history, politics, economics or just what goes on each day outside of Los Angeles which lurks in the cheerful minds of these children.... I can offer a few examples that might just make you wonder where all that money for public education is going." Here are a few of his examples. Stein found not one student in either high school or college who could identify the years World War II was fought; and some could not identify who fought whom, or who won. No one could identify the dates of World War I or the Civil War, either. None could name all the presidents of the last forty years, and only one could name the right decade for the Eisenhower administration. "Of the (at least) 12 whom I have asked, none has known within 40 million what the population of the United States is. Only two could tell me where Chicago is, even in the vaguest terms." None had ever heard of Lenin, none could name any of the first Ten Amendments, none had any idea when Lyndon Johnson was president, none could identify the Warsaw Pact or NATO, and one endearingly thought Toronto must be in Italy.

Unnerving as Mr. Stein's article is, complaints about the ignorance of public school products has been around a long time—as long, in fact, as the schools have been engaged in anti-hero training. (There were, to be sure, plenty of complaints about the traditional education before that, but at least the schools were not charged with turning out ignoramuses.) More than half a century ago, Nock, for instance, found these specimens of writing by university upper-classmen majoring in *English:*

—"Being a tough hunk of meat, I passed up the steak."
—"Lincoln's mind growed as his country kneaded it."

—"As soon as music starts silence rains, but as soon as it stops it gets worse than ever."

Needless to say, many of those students went on to teach English to a new generation of students, who in turn taught our present-day teachers. Small wonder that the National Education Association has—so help me—been debating in all earnestness, "Is it time to give up on grammar?"

Before we take leave of these depressing matters, let me offer one more reflection, stirred by a couple of items in the news. The first concerned a youngster who was booted off a sports team at a major Eastern university after a brush with the law. That does not concern me, and I have no wish to speak ill of the boy. What does interest me, as revealed in the ensuing fuss, is that he had been admitted to the university with an SAT score of 470—the equivalent of 70 on a scale of 1200—far below the minimum entrance requirements at any college in the country. A case of rule bending for a prize athlete, of course; and the fans wanted him back despite his legal and academic problems. That does not concern me, either. My question is, what on earth did he do in class? How could the university arrange classes for a youngster of such limited academic capacity?

The other item, in a column by George Will complaining about the loss of core curricula in higher education, recalled that the *freshmen* courses at Fisk University, an all-Negro school, had, at the turn of the century, included Tacitus and Horace in Latin and Sophocles and the Bible in Greek. How many of us today can boast an education of the excellence of this relatively poor minority school back then?

How far we have fallen! What makes it particularly sad is that anti-heroism destroys the achievement of such as Clinton

Bowen Fisk, who founded the school in 1866 in an army barracks in Nashville. It was a daring and principled act, creating for freed slaves one of the first (if not the very first) schools in the south. Within a few years its students were getting a far better education than the "prestige" universities offer today. I have a special reason to care about it. Fisk was a member of the first class to attend Hillsdale College, back in 1844—a class of five. Another of those first five was Livonia Benedict, the second woman in the country ever to win a college degree and first to earn the more coveted Bachelor of Arts degree. Her glowing achievement was, like Fisk's, sullied by the anti-hero "reforms" to follow. I cannot help feeling that had the young athlete not been so grossly disadvantaged by today's inferior public schooling, he could have had a real education anywhere in a less meretricious age. Certainly he would have been welcome at Hillsdale, whose charter from the first forbade discrimination by race or sex, and which was graduating women and blacks a century before anyone thought to codify such ordinary human concerns into the law. Any *educational* institution ought to do the same without a second thought, for the educator is concerned with justice and the values that derive from seeing all humans alike as children of God. It is only when we see ourselves as the meaningless "end products" of an equally meaningless evolution that we forget our standing in the human community and reject values. And that is simply barbarism.

Education vs. Training

There is no nobler impulse in the American character than our shared desire that every child be offered a good education.

This impulse runs very deep in our history, and we guard it today as zealously as ever. We gladly and generously bear the burden of the staggering cost of our schools (about a quarter of a trillion dollars a year), with no more than a hope, often dashed, that better facilities will produce better education. Yet it has become apparent to everyone that something is fundamentally and badly wrong with our schools, and that their product, by the kindest estimate, is mediocre. Moreover, the more we innovate, adjust, overhaul and spend, the worse the results become.

In all this tinkering, it seems the one thing we never question is what education really is. And the one reform we never try or even consider is restoring "the grand old fortifying curriculum" of education as it was always understood for centuries before our time. Yet our own deep faith in the value of education is wholly derived, not from the modernist experiments, but from precisely that traditional curriculum we abandoned long ago. For all that we may now think it quaint or impractical to read Homer in Greek, on such foundations was the modern scientific world built; and in this long-ago success was forged our certitude that education is the answer to almost any problem. It is, on the contrary, our present system, *designed* to be practical and teach useful skills, that turns out to be maddeningly impractical—a seeming paradox we will have to unravel.

Education is customarily defined as a preparation for life; but what sort of preparation, and for what final purpose, makes all the difference. Aristotle thought the purpose of education is to make the pupil dislike and like what he ought—to "be just in rendering to things their due esteem," in Traherne's words. Plato had said as much, and, as Nock pointed out, "made it the mark of an educated man that he should be able, and above all that he should be willing, to 'see things as they are.'" According to Weaver, "all education is learning to name (things) rightly." To British novelist and essayist Dorothy Sayers, "the sole and true end of education is simply this: to teach men how to learn for themselves; and whatever instruction fails to do this is effort spent in vain." These seemingly diverse views are really aspects of a shared view that the aim of education is to prepare one for the life of a whole person, in all things mental, physical and spiritual. Such education is not "practical" in the sense of preparing one to earn a living. Rather, it seeks to make one ready to take advantage of the total potential of human life.

Nock's own example may make this clearer. Born in 1870, he was, and knew himself to be, one of the last beneficiaries of a full classical education in America. "Considered as a vestigial survival, the college I attended is worth a good many words," he wryly noted later, "but I doubt that the tongues of men or angels could convince the modern American mind that such an institution actually existed, short of the Jurassic period, if then; still less that a person now living actually attended it and remembers it and knows that it was real" (and this in 1943!). Before college, his only brush with formal education had been a private preparatory school he entered "just turning fourteen." He had learned to read by himself, and with but a little assistance from his father, also learned Latin and Greek. (He was at pains later to deny that he was any sort of intellectual prig, being, rather, a healthy, outdoorsy boy with enough athletic skill to play semipro baseball for many years.) None of this is as unusual as it sounds. All that was needed to begin classical education was the "Three R's," which could be, and often were, learned at home. Many students didn't enter school until 12 or 13 years old, and occasionally they finished college at ages that seem startlingly young to us. Bacon was graduated from Trinity College at 15, "unusual" but not unheard of.

Nock's college was "small, never running quite to a hundred students," and out in the middle of nowhere. Students were "strictly on their own," neither encouraged nor discouraged in the extracurricular activities. Food was plain, and they took care of their unpretentious quarters, or not, as they pleased.

> The authorities had nothing to do with us in a social way; our only contact with them was in business hours and for business purposes. They were men of vast learning, great dignity, always punctiliously polite, but with no affectation of cordiality. For our part, we put up no pretense of fondness for them, but our respect, pride, admiration of them, knew no bounds.

The most important extra-curricular lesson was justice, and

> We learned this, not by precept, but by example.... In all circumstances we were treated justly, never coddled or pampered, but never overborne or sat upon. Each day's work was a full day's work, union hours, but we could never say we were overtasked. In my four years there I never heard of any one getting a word of commendation for a piece of good work, though I saw a great deal of good work, even distinguished work, being done.

Perhaps most important, "We were made to understand that the burden of education was on us and no one else, least of all on our instructors; they were not there to help us carry it or to praise our efforts, but to see that we shouldered it in proper style, and got on with it."

It is readily seen that education is socially beneficial, a means of expanding knowledge and transmitting culture, values and norms between generations. Here Nock reminds us that education is, first of all, strictly the student's own responsibility, and for his own private benefit. It only later, and secondarily, repays its benefits to culture and society with well-honed minds skilled in right reason and able, disinterestedly, to "see things as they are." We may not be able to point, with statistical indexes, to the specific contributions of the educated; but their value is great beyond measure. Indeed, we may yet learn to our sorrow that no civilized order is possible without them. What is it that they learned that we no longer teach?

Nock continues, "Our academic course was as fixed and unchangeable as the everlasting hills. You took it or you left it.... Elective courses, majors and minors, 'courses in English,' vocational courses, and all that sort of thing, were unknown to us; we had never heard of them.... Readings and expositions of Greek and Roman literature; mathematics up to the differential calculus; logic; metaphysics; a little work on the sources and history of the English language; these made up the lot." Why should such a curriculum be anything special? Nock left no doubt about the reason, in a memorable passage I will quote in full:

> The literatures of Greece and Rome comprise the longest, most complete and most nearly continuous record we have of what the strange creature known as *Homo sapiens* has been busy about in virtually every department of spiritual, intellectual and social activity. That record covers nearly twenty-five hundred years in an unbroken stretch of this animated oddity's operations in poetry, drama, law, agriculture, philosophy, architecture, natural history, philology, rhetoric, astronomy,

logic, politics, botany, zoology, medicine, geography, theology—everything, I believe, that lies in the range of human knowledge or speculation. Hence the mind which has attentively canvassed this record is much more than a disciplined mind, it is an *experienced* mind. It has come, as Emerson says, into a feeling of immense longevity, and it instinctively views contemporary man and his doings in the perspective set by this profound and weighty experience. Our studies were properly called formative, because beyond all others their effect was powerfully maturing. Cicero told the unvarnished truth in saying that those who have no knowledge of what has gone before them must forever remain children; and if one wished to characterize the collective mind of this present period, or indeed of any period—the use it makes of its powers of observation, reflection, logical inference—one would best do it by the one word *immaturity*.

Latin and Greek are thus not an end, but a key to a vast storehouse of knowledge about the human creature and his every important activity. They are a key, the only key, to an immense literature more to be enjoyed than "studied." Immersion in this long record of the past is formative and maturing; and the educated, in whatever fields they enter, are a civilizing force, a brake on the tendency of human society to self-destruct when left solely in the hands of the immature "collective mind."

The student of this regime may seem to fare poorly alongside the product of a training institution. He may, for a time, be exposed to fewer "subjects," learn fewer "facts," master fewer "skills." The objection will be made, "All this classical stuff is very well, but can he change a spark plug?" No, he cannot. And with just such cheap points, the traditional curriculum was very easily routed. But what the student did have was self-discipline, the training to turn to any trade or profession and learn it twice as fast, and the maturity to make the most of his whole life, not just his job. His education conceived him to be not a future auto mechanic but a future adult, with adult perceptions and responsibilities. His knowledge was formative and fulfilling, where today's student receives only instrumental training: useful skills at best, a depersonalizing "adjustment" to society at worst.

Do not mistake me. There is nothing whatever wrong with general or vocational training—except calling it education, and then, in our confusion, expecting it to produce what only education can. Not everyone has a taste or aptitude for education, and for many, training is an obvious and correct alternative. Moreover, the classical curriculum, in poor hands, can become rigid or stultifying, and is never a panacea (with which problems we will deal in a moment). For the moment let us only observe the distinction. If we wish to continue training courses in our schools, then we will have to deal with their manifest problems in terms of training. But let us neither mistake it for education nor expect it to offer that enrichment of the whole person that is the aim of education. The nature of this enrichment was elegantly summarized by W. J. Cory, a master at Eton in the last century:

> You go to school at the age of 12 or 13; and for the next four or five years you are not engaged so much in acquiring knowledge as in making mental efforts under criticism. A certain amount of knowledge you can with average faculties acquire so as to retain; nor need you regret the hours that you spend on much that is forgotten, for the shadow of lost knowledge at least protects you from any illusions. But you go to a great school, not for knowledge so much as for arts and habits; for the habit of attention, for the art of expression, for the art of assuming at a moment's notice a new intellectual posture, for the art of

entering quickly into another person's thoughts, for the habit of submitting to censure and refutation, for the art of indicating assent or dissent in graduated terms, for the habit of regarding minute points of accuracy, for the working out what is possible in a given time, for taste, for discrimination, for mental courage and mental soberness. Above all, you go to a great school for self knowledge.

Clearly, these are arts and habits that will serve one well in every area of life, and certainly not least in almost any occupation one can imagine. And these are to be acquired *in four or five years,* and with *average faculties,* where we frustrate our own children with twelve years of pabulum.

Two Revolutions

Toward the end of the last century the power of anti-heroic thought was gathering, unchecked. Ironically, only a few decades before Planck and Einstein overthrew the foundations of the mechanistic sciences, it was believed that science had nearly all the proofs of the naturalist cosmos in hand. All but a pair of minor problems, ether flow and black-body radiation, had been solved, and young men—including the youthful Max Planck—were advised not to go into physics, there being nothing left to do! In Europe, facile philosophies invoking this powerful science had put moral authority, and Christianity in particular, into headlong retreat. Darwinism, in full flower, promising automatic progress in a limitless future, was the new holy of holies. It was a time to turn ideas into power, and one did not have to be terribly radical to dream of rooting out the mistaken thinking and institutions of the past to build a brave new world.

America was little perturbed by these Old World ferments, yet its pragmatic and democratic views would prove congenial to anti-hero "reforms." Americans in the post-Civil War period were on the move, impatient with Victorian gentility, eager in their own way to build a new world. Old standards gave way until even the poet of America's common life, Walt Whitman, would complain that whatever its other successes, "our New World Democracy is, so far, an almost complete failure in its social aspects, and in really grand religious, moral, literary and aesthetic results." Classical education, never any too strong, was failing. Something had to be done about it, and in the good old American reformist tradition, something was. Education was discarded.

The educational system, said the reformers, was out of touch with the times. It gave far too much attention to the dead languages and literature of the ancient world. Of what use was that to the young people who would be the men and women of the twentieth century? How could it prepare them for life in a practical and progressive America? Furthermore, the old curriculum smacked of elitism, affronting our deep-rooted egalitarianism. Not all students, indeed, perhaps but a few, had the aptitude to seek higher education and attain to "the republic of letters." It was unfair for the system to provide a privilege for the few that could not be had by all. Besides, the rigors of education were too severe. It wasn't any fun. Obviously, the thing to do was dispose of the old curriculum, and introduce in its place the sciences and living languages and more useful vocational arts in a more relaxed atmosphere. Who could argue? Few did. The spread of the then-still subtle infection of anti-heroism had left education without capable defenders. Accordingly, near the turn of the century, the schools simply, and in very short order, abandoned the old ways of teaching and turned to new ones. It could hardly have occurred to many at the time that the change was far more drastic and portentous than merely changing curricula. Thus ended the first revolution against American education, in a near-total victory, seemingly a bloodless coup.

In, very promptly, came the Instrumentalism of John Dewey—relaxed discipline, and dabblings in "progressive education." And problems. The newly installed machinery coughed and sputtered and produced no better results than the old methods. And in truth, the product got worse.

Nock, a keenly interested witness, observed that what followed was "incessant tinkering, the like of which probably has never been seen anywhere in the world," with the new teaching. Plan after plan, devised by the great universities, was introduced, adjustment after adjustment made. "Yes, yes, we kept saying, let us but install this one new method in the secondary schools, or this one new set of curricular changes in the undergraduate college, or this one grand new scheme for broadening the scope of university instruction...." But nothing worked. The results were "admitted to be anything but satisfactory," said Dr. Nicholas Murray Butler, president of Columbia, echoed by the presidents of Brown, Haverford, Princeton, and many others. It is no doubt providential that these gentlemen, themselves educated men of the old school, did not live to see the sort of mindless, frantic "innovation" that has marked American schooling in the last few decades.

The first revolution, which destroyed the classical curriculum, was at least under some tutelage by educated men who could compare the new system with the old, and see the failings of their handiwork. The second, overlapping the first

in some respects and harder to define—but far bloodier—
slowly took root in the post-World War II period, as even the
traces of the old ways were forgotten. The marks of the second
are statism, rank monopoly, and an articulated anti-heroic
doctrine. Where the first revolution ventured a gentle sin,
trying to keep in touch with the freshening vision of a
dynamic new world, the second had drunk deeply of the anti-
heroic Old World doctrines and was frankly ideological. It had,
and has, no humane reform in mind, but rather has sought to
turn classrooms into laboratories and to use schoolchildren—
our children—as guinea pigs for social engineering. Under it,
the older moral concept of education as a tool for human
betterment gives way to a steely, unscrupulous advancement
of the anti-hero society. Schoolchildren are not to be educated
but "adjusted" or even conditioned to conformity in a
centralized new order. Evidently no stratagems to impose
adult designs on children's minds are to be abjured for just or
moral reasons. To the anti-hero, the name of the game is
winning, Darwinism writ large, the strong to control the weak
for exploitation. Thus our children become helpless pawns in
the game, victims of covert striving toward an authoritarian
order already far too familiar around the world today. Should
this be thought exaggerated, one would do well to pay more
heed to the endless prattle about service to "the cause" in
Academe, and to the political outlook in that rarefied
atmosphere. The radical explosion in the 1960s and early
1970s is ample witness to the nature of what is being
thought—and taught.

In structure, the second revolution is a pure bureaucracy.
From its protective womb, anti-hero "educationists" seek ever
to impose monolithic standards on schooling: an exact

inversion of the first purpose of education, to develop unique individuals. This assault is not limited to public schools, but aims also to bring private schools to heel with teacher certification and other regulatory intervention. Schoolchildren are molded to be identical "social units," their individuality and creative freedom stifled. They are, moreover, *deliberately* held back in what they can learn, to the level of the dullest members of the class, the least common denominator. Thus the class advances in lockstep at the pace of the slowest, with promotion virtually automatic and given by age, not achievement. This leveling process is centrally controlled by the mandating of curricula and textbooks that have been properly censored and approved by the anti-hero authorities in the state capitals and in Washington, D.C. The amount of anti-hero dogma that seeps into approved texts, in the form of behaviorism, statist indoctrination, hostility to religion, moral relativism and the like, is, well, heroic. Small wonder that so many parents, at great sacrifice, are sending their children to private or religious schools, to escape the indoctrination and mediocrity of public schools. But no broader answer is available until the public school system is completely decentralized and returned to local control, or more drastically, dismantled in favor of free market education.

As an extra, supreme attraction to the anti-hero activists, you and I as parents are to be taxed ever more lavishly to support the anti-heroes and their cause. The worse the results of the so-called education they offer, the more we pay. The truth is, there is nothing so unique or demanding in the teaching business as to demand high salaries. It is the other way around. Where teaching was once, not long ago, a dedicated calling, paid in part by honor and personal satisfaction, high salaries have turned it into a mere job that attracts the dull, uninspired, bureaucratic types who couldn't hope to do as well anywhere else. It is a commonplace that students in education schools are the poorest in higher education, averaging an incredible eighty SAT points lower than those in other studies. Future teachers are thus "just at the borderline of educability," says Dr. John Silber, president of Boston University. Yet standards are so low in the public schools— what Dr. Silber calls "no-fault pedagogy"—that even such as these can be employed at generous salaries. And despite all the poor-mouthing one hears, teaching salaries are high, as is obvious from the fact that demand for jobs far exceeds the supply. With the rewards of teaching measured in dollars rather than dedication, no one need be surprised at the low-grade, lackadaisical, bureaucratic sort of instruction so common in public schooling. What astonishes me is that we still have a courageous minority of teachers whose dedication is undiminished, and who achieve what little success there remains in the school system.

Compounding the problem is the descent of teaching into the patterns on monopoly trade unionism. The National Education Association, the teachers' union, is the largest in the country, with some 1.7 million members. It is vociferous in its demands for higher pay, and implacable in its opposition to any kind of merit testing or placing for teachers. It is also blatant in its political activism for anti-heroic causes. Can we really feel safe entrusting our children's schooling to bureaucrats more interested in money than in teaching—much less to political activists? So long as we hold to our present course, we get both.

Two centuries ago, the great economist, Adam Smith, himself a teacher, pointed out that a teacher's natural income should come from fees students pay to be taught. True education, therefore, should have little or no cost in taxes (imagine!): "the endowment of schools and colleges makes either no charge upon (public) revenues, or but a very small one." He then questioned whether public funding was beneficial in education, and answered, decisively, no. A teacher's performance, he said, would deteriorate precisely to the extent he was paid indirectly (as by public salary), instead of earning it directly by serving "the consumer," the student. Where "the teacher is prohibited from receiving any honorary or fee from his pupils, and his salary constitutes the whole of revenue which he derives from his office," Smith wrote, "(h)is interest is, in this case, *set as directly in opposition to his duty* as it is possible to set it" (emphasis added). Our present system does precisely this, set teachers" interests against their duty to teach well. In other words, the rules of the marketplace apply as much to education as to any other occupation. Free and open competition brings out the best; monopoly brings out the worst. Surely it is time we broke the educationist monopoly.

Chapter IX
Darwin and the Descent of Man

Social progress means a checking of the cosmic process at every step and the substitution for it of another, which may be called the ethical process; the end of which is not the survival of those who may happen to be fittest.... but of those who are ethically the best.... I do not see how selection could be practiced without a serious weakening, it may be the destruction, of the bonds which hold society together.
                                        —Thomas Henry Huxley (1893)

The distinguished philosopher Mortimer Adler once termed evolution a "popular myth," which is just what it is. "...[T]he evolutionary epic is the best myth we will ever have," affirms sociobiologist E. O. Wilson, the Frank B. Baird Professor of Science at Harvard. Writer Martin Gardner thought otherwise and was sufficiently miffed to include Professor Adler in his *Fads and Fallacies in the Name of Science,* "The Curious Theories of Modern Pseudo-Scientists and the Strange, Amusing Cults that Surround Them. A Study in Human Gullibility."

It remains to be seen whose gullibility will be a study when the last chapter on evolution is written. Certainly, the subject has excited more pseudo-scientific jabber over the past century than any other—much of it from scientists. This would be inexplicable if evolution were a matter of innocent and disinterested science. What controversy could that provoke? Yet the furor over evolutionist doctrines has hardly diminished since the time of Darwin. To the detached observer, the ongoing feud between so-called creationists and evolutionists has all the marks of holy war between two—repeat, two—fundamentalist sects. Even the scientific aura surrounding the question is invoked for clearly religious reasons. To the anti-heroic faithful, science itself is quasi-divine, and its revelatory gospel is not to be questioned.

Let us be blunt, outrageous as it will sound to modern ears. Evolution is and always has been a religious vision. It is a vision that denies God, but is no less mystical or mythic on that account. It is a vision that may claim more reproductive success is our reason for being, yet move men to such faith that we see once again the truth that man is bred to worship. Evolutionism must be taken on faith, and that is the whole of its strength. The only relevant question about it, in the end, is whether it is the true faith.

Let's be blunter still. Evolution has never been more than a working hypothesis for science, and a dubious one. It cannot meet the simplest tests for being called "science." There is almost no empirical evidence to support it. Practically all the evidence disappeared without a trace in ages past. Only an infinitesimal fraction has been or ever will be found. To the contrary, there is what the renowned geneticist Richard Lewontin calls "a vast weight of empirical evidence" against evolutionary theory; and the eminent biologist du Noüy raised a number of theoretical problems that almost certainly cannot be solved. Moreover, evolution is virtually immune to scientific testing, so nothing much ever will be known about it. So far as science goes, the question is whether *anything* can be rigorously known about evolution. According to Colin Patterson and the cladists, the scientists who classify fossils, the answer is no. A minority of respected scientists think evolution is flatly impossible on other scientific grounds.

It is revealing that the scientific content of Darwinism is commonly and grossly exaggerated. The modernist and anti-heroic insistence on empirical science is so great that Hume called for burning all books in the libraries not based on empirical evidence. Yet when their own evolutionist holy writ is in question, believers not only ignore their own rules but become unbelievably forgiving of adverse evidence. This leap in faith is apparent in such statements as Ernst Junger's: "Evolution is far more important than living." Or this, from a reviewer: "Dr. [Gertrude] Himmelfarb knocks holes in his [Darwin's] data and logic, but even if she took the bottom out of him altogether, . . . I should still find him satisfying, even if not right." Such professions say nothing about the facts, but a great deal about the human creature, including no few scientists who put their hearts before their heads. It reflects a most endearing quality in us, and a source of enduring hope for us, if we will think it through. We did not acquire this character evolving from the muck.

In the heat of controversy, even scientists can forget that evolution was in no way a scientific discovery. Darwin himself admitted, though only in private, that he had no empirical evidence that natural selection had ever produced a new species. The word evolution does not even appear per se in *Origin of Species,* though in the form of "evolved" it was added to the sixth edition a dozen years after publication. At the Darwin centenary (marking also the fiftieth anniversary of *Origin*) August Weismann stated, "It is not upon demonstrative evidence that we rely when we champion the doctrine of selection as a scientific truth; we base our argument on quite other grounds." This remains true today, as witness the heated debate over evolution even within the scientific community. Facts are not debatable: if "demonstrative evidence" were available, a demonstration would resolve the question. The dispute, rather, is over scientific methodology and the validity (or invalidity) of knowledge inferred from the fossil record. Though seldom aired publicly, the debate goes to the heart of evolutionary theory. (Journalist Tom Bethell observes, "When they see themselves beleaguered by opponents outside the citadel of science, they [scientists] tend to put their differences aside and unite to defeat the heathen.") That the most serious objections to evolution are still being raised by scientists a century and a quarter after Darwin is also revealing: as Jaki points out, resistance to a true scientific breakthrough almost always dies out within a generation.

If evolution was not a scientific discovery, where did the idea come from? It was simply a deduction from what T. H. Huxley accurately termed the "doctrine" of natural selection. And to believe it, he said, requires "an act of philosophical faith." Surely nothing less can sustain the belief that life arose spontaneously from dead matter, a central necessity of the Darwinian view. But if this be so, how could the glorified apes that we are in the Darwinian perspective possibly profess a faith? Natural animals show no disposition towards faith, nor towards the analogical reasoning needed to conceive matter and claim it is the source of life and intelligence.

Even were materialism demonstrably true, natural selection is not a necessary, hence scientific, explanation. Huxley states, "That the doctrine of natural selection presupposes evolution is quite true. But it is not true that evolution necessarily implies natural selection. In fact, "evolution might conceivably have taken place without the development of groups possessing the character of species." Note the circularity. Evolution, once deduced from the "doctrine of natural selection," is elevated to a mystical entity and *its* course need not be dictated by natural selection. Its deductive origin is glossed over for what amounts to a profession of faith. Darwin also conceded that other explanations of past life were possible, but chose to exclude them entirely from his theories. This was the fateful departure from open scientific inquiry to an exclusionary formula, one which still directs and focuses research. This was the visionary act that turned evolution into a rebellion against exact science in favor of theory and philosophy, as Robert E. D. Clark observed. Darwin's own words have an unmistakably mystical flavor." ... it is *certain*," he said, and I emphasize the unscientific language, "that if we can see any advantage in a small variation (and sometimes if we cannot), *selection sees more*." Poobah. The theory insists selection is blind, statistical chance. It is not some divine, seeing entity. All we have here is sloppy rhetoric which has somehow been mistaken for revelation.

Seeing "advantages" is to this day the principal form of evolutionary "science." I do not exaggerate at all. Scientists make up stories, called "Darwinian scenarios," purporting to explain what *might* have occurred in a largely unknowable past, as if anything they can contrive to imagine actually *did* occur. In the absence of solid empirical evidence, there isn't much more one can do. Knowingly or not, they are engaged in philosophical speculations, and indeed speculations in which they have an obvious self-interest. We "laymen" need not be cowed from exploring the subject for any technical reasons, and it is we who can see it with detachment. Colin Patterson puts it plainly: "It is easy enough to make up stories of how one form gave rise to another, and to find reasons why the stages should be favoured by natural selection. But such stories are not part of science, for there is no way of putting them to the test."

On the Descent of the West and its Origins

Were we to try pinpointing the words most responsible for the collapse of Western civilization, we would find no stronger candidate than this preachment by Charles Darwin at the conclusion of the *Origin:*

> As all the living forms of life are the lineal descendants of those which lived long before the Cambrian epoch, we may feel certain that the ordinary succession by generation has never once been broken, and that no cataclysm has desolated the whole world. Hence we may look with some confidence to a secure future of great length. And as natural selection works solely by and for the good of each being, all corporeal and mental endowments will tend to progress towards perfection.

Ye shall know heaven on earth, effortlessly, automatically, and all guaranteed! What backwater Bible-thumper ever promised so much? Christians are at a minimum required to repent their sins and believe. The new Darwinian fundamentalist need not lift a finger. Albert Jay Nock loved to remind us of Epstean's law, "Man tends to satisfy his needs with the least possible exertion." Surely here is a classic example. As between the rigors of religion and an evolutionary salvation that didn't even require us to see the evils we do, it was no contest.

All 1,250 copies of *Origin* sold out on the day of publication, Thursday, November 24, 1859. The world was waiting for Darwin. The idea of evolution had been in the air for a century. Darwin, awaiting the advance of a materialist philosophy he had come to believe (as he stated in his private notebooks), was shocked by an outline of A. R. Wallace's rival theories greatly resembling his own, and rushed *Origin* into print. "If you can realize," said George Bernard Shaw later, "how insufferably the world was oppressed by the notion that everything that happened was an arbitrary personal act by an arbitrary personal God of dangerous, jealous and cruel personal character, you will understand how the world jumped at Darwin." Strained as this caricature of Christian love is, Shaw was not mistaken about the period's hostility to the heroic view of life, nor about its immediate infatuation with Darwinism.

Sales of *Origin* stayed brisk, thanks not least to a glowing review, a month after publication, by the eminent biologist, T. H. Huxley. But this can by no means account for the work's popularity. Three centuries of growing scientific success had imbedded the idea of man's mastery over nature into popular lore, and elevated "progress" to an effortless certainty. That the progress observed resulted from the breaking of feudal chains, increasing liberty, the repeal of mercantilist laws, capital investment, risk-taking, reduced taxes and state interventions, entrepreneurship, ingenuity and human will, all within a necessarily moral context, was pushed aside in favor of sweeping, fatuous philosophies that conceived the efforts of men as automatic. History moves in upward stages, said Hegel. Nature moves towards perfection, said Darwin. Humanity draws inexorably nigh to a socialist heaven on earth, said Marx, drawing heavily on both and not coincidentally setting back economics to pre-Adam Smith statism (Marx asked to dedicate *Das Kapital* to Darwin, but the latter refused). Such were the ascendant ideas in the mid-nineteenth century that put the waning Christian order to rout, and put the civilized world on a course to auto-destruct.

Says Muggeridge,

> It is interesting to reflect that now, in the light of all that has happened, the early obscurantist opponents of Darwinian evolution seem vastly more sagacious and farseeing than its early excited champions. There must be quite a number today who, like myself, would rather go down in history even as a puffing, portentous Bishop Wilberforce than, say, a Herbert Spencer, or a poor, squeaky H. G. Wells, ardent evolutionist and disciple of Huxley, with his vision of an earthly paradise achieved through science and technology; those twin monsters which have laid waste a whole world, polluting its seas and rivers and lakes with poisons, infecting its very earth and all its creatures, reaching into Man's mind and inner consciousness to control and condition him, at the same time entrusting to irresponsible, irresolute human hands the instruments of universal destruction. It must be added that, confronted with this prospect when, at the very end of his life, the first nuclear explosion was announced, Wells turned his face to the wall, letting off in *Mind at the End of its Tether* one last, despairing, whimpering cry which unsaid everything he had ever thought or hoped. Belatedly, he understood that what he had followed as a life-force was, in point of fact, a death wish, into which he was glad to sink the little that remained of his own life in the confident expectation of total and final obliteration.

Darwin himself had no inkling of the anti-heroic genies he was letting out of the bottle; nor had he much hope for the success of *Origin*. "...[I]t will be grievously too hypothetical," he wrote George Bentham some months before it appeared. "It will very likely be of no other service than collocating some facts; though I myself think I see my way approximately on the origin of species. But, alas, how frequent, how almost universal it is in an author to persuade himself of the truth of his own dogmas. My hope is that I certainly see very many difficulties of gigantic stature."

Difficulties there were and are. Darwin practiced dis-simulation to brush them aside, perhaps deceiving himself as well. For instance, as Jaki notes, "In (his) notebooks he set for himself the rule to avoid stating how far he believed in materialism. He would merely say that 'emotions, instincts, degrees of talent, which are hereditary, are so because the brain of a child resembles parent stock.'" He also warned himself, "Never use the words higher and lower." Much the greater difficulty, however, lay in his professed ineptitude with metaphysical reasoning. He was, he said, uncomfortable with "metaphysical trains of thought," and later complained, "my theology is a muddle." Darwin was thus ill-equipped to see the contradiction at the heart of his doctrine. Purposeful man cannot be the product of an evolution that Darwin—purposefully—defined to be purposeless.

Assigning an exclusive role to the purely mechanical process of natural selection was a metaphysical declaration; or more accurately, counter-metaphysical. There was no scientific basis for doing so. It was a deduction from Darwin's materialist philosophy, not an induction from the evidence. He did not even care so much about natural selection as in destroying the idea of special creation, hence creation itself. Jaki observes, "He realized that creation and evolution are not mutually exclusive, but materialism and creation certainly exclude one another." To this day it is a particular article of faith with Darwinian fundamentalists that the separate creation of species by God did not occur. Such evidence as there is—species always appearing "suddenly" and without known transition forms—gives the opposite impression, but it is not a point one need argue. We note only the dogmatic view.

Darwin was fully aware that the human mind was "the citadel" that had to be conquered to make his case for materialism, and that it could not be done "by attacking the citadel itself." But here the theory derails. "Why is thought, being a secretion of the brain, more wonderful than gravity, a property of matter?" he asked, thinking it mere prejudice. But thinking is something we do, not something that happens to us. It apparently never occurred to Darwin that only minds capable of thought could see "properties" of "matter." "He was no longer alive," Jaki remarks, "when better physicists replaced gravity with something more recondite and reliable, and began to marvel at the power of the mind." But Darwin did live long enough to entertain the alarming thought that, if his own mind was descended from a monkey's (not to say an amoeba's), how could he be any more confident of his own conclusions than of a monkey's?

By Darwinian logic, Jaki says, "the notion of matter which thinks is respectable, the distinction between matter and mind is not." Man's implicit liberation from God meshed perfectly with the anti-heroic temper of those bygone times: "That Creator and absolutes had no place in the vision presented in the *Origin* was a key to its tremendous popularity. The *Origin* supplied the already strong craving for the elimination of all metaphysics with a support which through its massive factuality appeared scientifically unassailable. The objective of that craving, as articulated mainly by Spencer for the second half of the century, was repose in the endless flux and reflux, a happy acceptance of the prospect that man and mankind were but bubbles on unfathomable deep and dark waves, bubbles free of eternal purpose and unburdened with eternal responsibilities." The anti-hero's rebellion had received its most perfect expression.

Further Descent

We should not take leave of Charles Darwin without brief note of his second work, *The Decent of Man, and Selection in Relation to Sex.* Here, Darwin boldly launched into the subject of human origins, in a deductive and "vast commentary" on ideas he had formed thirty years earlier. Among the thoughts he had jotted in his notebooks were these: " ... if all men were dead, then monkeys may make men." And, "Origin of man now proved—Metaphysics must flourish.—He who understands baboon would do more toward metaphysics than Locke.... Our descent then is the origin of our evil passions!—The Devil under form of Baboon is our grandfather."

There are those who find the idea of hereditary sin self-excusing, and therefore comforting, but I am not among them. This view, expounded by a Professor Dart and popularized in our time by Robert Ardrey, invites us to sit back and welcome the next war, which is, after all, biologically inevitable. More nonsense. A mechanistic biology that denies us the free will to choose our fate does not see humans as we are. More importantly, it denies the moral responsibility that all mankind knows, and that is the one brake on our temptations to sink into the dark.

Let us recall Weaver's warning that knowledge of material reality is knowledge of death. It is the sense of potential goodness in us that guides us toward civilized life. Unless we are better than nature, life is no comfort. No less a Darwinian than Huxley argued repeatedly, and powerfully, that civilized human life contravened natural selection. Once we get to the point that all members of society can survive, he said, "the struggle for existence" is "ipso facto at an end." "Social progress means a checking of the cosmic process at every step and the substitution for it of another, which may be called the ethical process; the end of which is not survival of those who may happen to be fittest...but of those who are ethically the best."

We do not deduce Mother Teresa from nature. Human goodness is a rebuke to Darwin. E. O. Wilson rightly sees altruism, which by definition reduces natural survival ability, as "the central theoretical problem for sociobiology," which is the cutting edge of neo-Darwinism. It is an interesting question. How could the principle of reproductive success of the fittest conceivably lead to the development of humans who sometimes risk and sometimes lose their lives trying to rescue pets? Professor Robert Trivers, a gung-ho evolutionist, thought he had a nifty answer a few years ago with the idea of "reciprocal altruism," which translates to you scratch my back now, I'll scratch yours later. This is an invaluable idea, to be sure, but it isn't altruism. It is economics, complete with a law of contract and a futures market. The problem is a lot tougher than this to the evolutionist view. Altruism is not a scientific concept. It is a metaphysical reality that is simply unaccountable to a materialist philosophy. Or to put it another way, had men evolved naturally from dead and amoral matter, there wouldn't be any altruism for scientists to worry about, and for that matter, there wouldn't be any science to do the worrying. Science itself is built on metaphysical foundations, and is not self-explanatory. It cannot answer philosophical questions, and should not try.

Richard Leakey and Roger Lewin, in *People of the Lake,* applied the "reciprocal altruism" concept to their reconstruction of ancient human or pre-human life in Africa. From a few bits of fossil bone and stone tools at apparent campsites, they could infer a division of labor. Women did the (vegetable) gathering, men did the hunting, in the main, both later sharing the food. Survival advantage can easily be seen in this economic advance, and it does have a uniquely human sense to it. But Leakey was clearly troubled with calling it altruism, and stressed that at some point humans became capable of real altruism: of goodness without a price tag. It is a pity we can never know what was on those ancient "hominid" minds. Jaki sees in this an evolutionary advance by man's becoming better in an unmistakably moral sense; and Huxley, with his arguments that mankind has risen to civilization precisely by overruling natural selection in favor of ethics, would have agreed. There is, moreover, a clear moral sense to economics, involving sympathy and trust, which has been brought out in the work of George Gilder and others. "Capitalism begins with giving," Gilder states. This is apparent from growing studies of "economic anthropology," which, like other anthropological investigation, draws on the practices and legends of primitive peoples to shed light on the prehistoric past. "The capitalists of primitive society," writes Gilder, "were tribal leaders who vied with one another in giving great feasts.... The gifts, often made in the course of a religious rite, were presented in hopes of an eventual gift in return. The compensation was not defined beforehand." This is not explainable as mere value-for-value trading. "These competitions in giving are contests of altruism. A gift will only elicit a greater response if it is based on an understanding of the needs of others. In the most successful and catalytic gifts, the giver fulfills an unknown need or desire in a surprising way.... In order to repay him...the receiver must come to understand the giver. Thus the contest of gifts leads to an expansion of human sympathies."

Might we not equally hypothesize that the altruism of ancient humans was real, that they loved one another in a human sense, and that the sharing of food and work and life marked joy and sympathy toward a beloved, rather than a contract? Alas, there is little or no evidence either way that is not speculative. But at least we can say that if these ancients were fully human, then we may suppose they were much like us and already capable of genuine goodness. Stassinopoulos, Lewis and many others have argued that the real evolution of mankind is toward spiritual growth, not mere physical development, and that this advance is by choice, not mechanical chance. We become more human precisely by rejecting the "cosmic process," as Huxley termed it, and reaching for the moral life that is our birthright.

Civilization, the opposite of natural processes, is sustained only by shared moral understanding and effort. The scientist, in the protected atmosphere of Academe that I too know well, may forget that it is not he who holds nature and barbarism at bay. Worse, he may forget that his philosophic dabblings in the name of science may have dreadful consequences. Jose Ortega y Gasset understood well: "But if the specialist is ignorant of the inner philosophy of the science he cultivates, he is much more radically ignorant of the historical conditions requisite for its continuation; that is to say: How society and the heart of man are to be organized in order that there may continue to be investigations.... He also believes that civilization is there in just the same way as the earth's crust and the forest primeval."

We help ourselves not at all by positing purely material processes to life, when our own behavior and culture belie it. And surely it is irresponsible to pass off metaphysical pleading as "scientific," enhancing the popular myth that "science" has the whole question squared away. Do we really find the Devil in a Baboon? Should we, as a forgetful Darwin said elsewhere, prefer as our ancestor that baboon which rescued its relative from "a pack of astonished dogs" over a human ancestry drenched in bloody sacrifices? A man who can see altruism in monkeys, not to mention free will in "oysters, polyps and all animals," and who assumes human reverence took the form of bloody sacrifices in the ancient past, is best ignored on philosophical questions.

Descent did not work out its own radical implications, but other writers soon did. "A happier coming race will cast out miracles," said one. The inverted biblical language of another, William Kingdon Clifford, is quoted elsewhere, as is Sir Arthur Keith's lament at the prospect of centuries of peace. Yet another is Ernst Haeckel, whom Darwin admired, and whose work was later invoked for the theories of Nazism.

Marx and Engels likewise invoked Darwin. That Darwinism would attract such motley company is hardly coincidence. When we trade traditional morality for nature "red in tooth and claw," as Tennyson put it, barbarism must soon follow, and in our age it takes a totalitarian form.

Chesterton, with his healthy intuitions, saw the danger at once. It is not that we are dismayed at seeing our supposed ancestors in a zoo, he said, but at seeing ourselves as something changeable and less than human; for thereafter we will be subject to the manipulations and controls of slave-masters. Lewis called it, candidly, *The Abolition of Man,* and so it is. Darwin clearly understood what it meant to replace moral law with "survival of the fittest": "Looking at the world at no very distant date, what an endless number of the lower [!] races will have been eliminated [!] by the higher civilized races throughout the world," he said, and applauded Caucasians for having "beaten the Turkish hollow in the struggle for existence." Somehow, when Hitler's very civilized master race set out to follow this blueprint in a civilized and efficient way, the world was shocked and deemed it one of the great crimes of history.

It is an error to put all the blame for this on Hitler, as if he were some evil mutant who arose unaccountably from the muck to brutalize the world. He was, on the contrary, no original, but one who took all too seriously the evolutionist spirit of those times. By 1908, as a young man, he had already formed a view hauntingly reminiscent of Darwin's own: "There is absolutely no other revolution but a racial revolu-' tion. There is no economic, no social, no political revolution. *There is only the struggle of lower races against the higher races"* (emphasis added). W. Heitler, one of the architects of quantum mechanics, noted that a false concept of science in the Darwinian mold had helped create the tragedy of World War II: "In the decline of ethical standards which the history of the past fifteen years [the period of Nazism] exhibited, it is not difficult to trace the influence of mechanistic and deterministic concepts which have unconsciously but deeply crept into human minds." Jaki adds, "... reference should be made to the crucial role played in the formation of Nazi ideology by the physicalist interpretation of biology as championed by Ernst Haeckel and the German Monist League. This role is amply documented by D. Casman, *The Scientific Origins of National Socialism....*"

No more than anyone else could Charles Darwin deduce our humanity from lifeless matter and natural selection. In the end he had to turn to scientifically discredited Lamarckism for the wistful hope that concluded *Descent:* that "after long practice, virtuous tendencies may be inherited." What in truth we inherited from this thinking was war without mercy.

Chapter X
Evolution as Religion

Evolution is a good example of that modern intelligence which, if it destroys anything, destroys itself. Evolution is either an innocent scientific description of how certain earthly things came about; or, if it is anything more than this, it is an attack upon thought itself.

—Chesterton

It seems at times as if many of our modern writers on evolution have had their views by some sort of revelation.

—G. A. Kerkut

A funny thing happened to me recently. I realized that I had lost my belief in evolution.

—Joseph Sobran

Darwinists admit the history of life has many unsolved mysteries, but insist "evolution is a fact." The "fact of evolution" was even cited by the defense back in the Scopes "monkey trial" in 1925. One is hard put to compress more confusion into few words; but let's try to set it straight.

Evolution, we have seen, was a deduction from "the doctrine of natural selection," not a discovery from "demonstrative evidence." But a "fact" gets its facthood precisely from confirmable experience, or at the very least, from empirical evidence so overwhelming that inferences therefore can scarcely be mistaken. Now, we know there were no scientists around observing, measuring and testing evolution for the past billion years, so we can rule out first-hand evidence. We know, too, that evolution is a process so insensibly slow that it is all but impervious to present observation or testing through replication. Some minor successes with microevolution have been claimed with these methods, but one would be hesitant to say what they mean, much less apply them to the staggeringly complex processes of nature. One safely concludes there is practically no direct, replicable evidence—the kind that is supposed to give science, not to mention a fact, its credentials—supporting and evolutionary explanation that must account for the entire history of life on earth. So far the qualities of a fact are absent.

But then, we have second-hand, inferential evidence in the fossil record. Or do we? There is precious little. The processes of nature do not favor fossil formation, virtually all soft tissue do not favor formation, and virtually all soft tissue is lost to decay. What survives is bits and pieces, mainly shells and a few bones. Gaps in the "record" are the rule, not the exception; key pieces are everywhere missing. Taking the presumed ancestry of humans or human relatives, Richard Leakey notes that all the fossil evidence from one to three million years ago could be displayed on a couple of average tables; and all the fossil remains from before that would fit in a shoebox. Paleontologists surely draw remarkable stories out of these scraps of bone, but as their work is ultimately untestable, it is open to contention and error. For one example, scientific encyclopedias for two generations accepted the Piltdown Man as an authentic human ancestor. We know now (don't we?) that it was a hoax using a relatively recent human skull and an ape's jaw. That the hoax was not discovered until recent times (1953) is ample evidence that paleontology is more an art than an exact science. The scientific method is not supposed to be susceptible to hoaxes.

In any case, and contrary to popular belief, the fossil record is meager, and yields scant knowledge of evolution. If the cladists (discussed earlier) are right, the concept of ancestry cannot be inferred at all from the fossil record with the present tools of science. They make an impressive case that not nearly enough is or can be known to fit together the myriad links of the evolutionary chain. What this means is that the "evolutionary epic" is a story without characters.

More than a century of searching has at best barely improved the hard evidence. The case for evolution remains deductive, not factual. There is no "fact" of evolution. Insisting on the "fact" is simply the anti-hero's way of saying he believes in evolution, regardless of the evidence. Earlier Darwinists were more forthright in admitting that the "demonstrative evidence" didn't really matter. What has been important from the first is the evolutionary story, "the best myth we will ever have." The word evolution means a series of related changes in a certain direction. In the Darwinian sense, it means an unbroken progression of life forms from the start: popularly from "lower" to "higher," more accurately from simple to more complex organisms, ending with man. Mere change in the past would be meaningless. Evolution *must* be progressive. The change has to be going somewhere, and it has to be taking us with it, to invest the story with meaning. And it must be easily understood. The inexorable upward progress of nature renders this story flawlessly.

Natural selection, so goes the myth, molded us from the dust, raised us to the highest form of life, and promises our future salvation. Working "by and for the good of each being," it slowly but certainly perfects our "corporeal and mental endowments."

Like all anti-heroic myths, evolution is, transparently, a retelling of the stories that have animated Western civilization for two millennia. Otherwise, it could scarcely be understood, much less welcomed with hosannahs. We may even take some comfort that modernist heresies remain faithful to the traditional ideas of creation and salvation, and still inspire faith, however misguided. But, like all anti-heroic myths, the evolutionary epic changes the story to push God off His throne and make Man the new ruler of the universe. This too is true to Western belief. It is the recapitulation of our first temptation: "Ye shall be as gods." The rebellious men of the West, tempted as of old to deny God, and thinking themselves in possession of some powerful new magic called science, leapt at the chance to trade life eternal for Darwinism and the dust. They forgot that the end of the story was man's banishment from Eden. Like Wells, they fancy they have discovered a life force, but court a death wish.

Darwin's fateful choice of natural selection as the exclusive mechanism of development thrust the biological sciences into a blind alley. This choice, we repeat, was no scientific necessity, but a materialist declaration. Had Darwin's interest been an open search for truth, Jaki observes, "natural selection would not have been given an exclusive role in the first edition of the *Origin,* and the history of modern biology might now be told with no reference to an inordinate craving to 'deify natural selection,'" as P. G. Fothergill justly put it. Men may deny God with their voices, but cannot escape His presence or judgment with fanciful theories and exculpatory formulas. Barzun writes, the doctrine of natural selection immediately put Christian opposition into a minority and "superseded all other beliefs." "Nor is it hard to understand why it did," he adds, "for it fulfilled the basic requirement of any religion by subsuming all phenomena under one cause."

This "one cause" is a Procrustean strait jacket for evolutionary science, forcing it to account for every phenomenon of life, from spontaneous generation to Shakespeare, with one chance mechanism. This poses almost unbelievable problems for the theorists. Legitimate scientific findings that bear examination have posed severe obstacles for evolutionary theory.

The evolutionary epic necessarily begins with the natural genesis of life from non-life in the distant past. Nothing is or can be known about how, or whether, this occurred. No evidence remains, and no test-tube recreation, should scientists ever succeed in this, can be more than a possible explanation of the actual event. We will never know. One must take it on faith. Why prefer this faith to one that sees our beginning as an act of creation by God? Science has no test to rule out the latter, which has other evidence in its favor.

The subsequent development of life progresses unbroken from the simplest organisms to the mind of man. We can easily imagine such a progress—a requirement of the faith. But the "tree of life" is not like this at all. The evolutionary story is full of twists, regressions, dead-ends and mysteries. Clearly, only one strand of past change represents the progressive evolutionary story. Many simple organisms have not evolved at all, and if they were not still around, men never would have had a guess at evolution. Where does the progress in "our line" come from? Modern theory, if I do not misunderstand its meaning, denies any direction to genetic changes. No "progress" inheres in the genetic coding passed from one generation to the next. Steven Jay Gould, among the most outspoken of evolutionary scientists, dismisses the whole idea of "progressive advancement" of past life as incorrect. It was all simply the chance struggles of organisms in their environments. But surely this strips the very meaning out of the "evolutionary epic." What myth is to be spun from meaningless change? How do we celebrate our emergence from a chaos of chance without undermining the validity of human thought?

The distinguished evolutionary biologist Lecomte du Noüy refused to accept the contradiction of purposeless evolutionary forces. Some thirty years ago, in *Human Destiny*, he assembled a wealth of evidence against the thesis of evolutionary progress by chance. In case after case, he argued, the necessary transitions involved numbing improbabilities. Blithely to accept that evolution succeeded against all odds is to believe in a long series of miracles.

The first and greatest mystery is the spontaneous arising of life from dead matter. The odds against this happening cannot be directly calculated. But Charles-Eugene Guye was able to calculate the probability of the random emergence of a single molecule of a protein necessary for life. The odds against this, he found, are almost infinitely too large for humans to grasp; too large for any measures we could imagine in space and time. This calculation deliberately used assumptions favorable to spontaneous generation. But even had Guye erred by a factor of a trillion trillions in the other direction, the odds against random life would swallow the history of the universe as the oceans swallow a raindrop. Du Noüy emphasizes, it is *"totally impossible."*

Useful as the calculation of probabilities is to science, it "cannot take into account or explain...the fact that *the properties of a cell are born out of the coordination of complexity* and not out of the chaotic complexity of a mixture of gases. This transmissible heredity, continuous coordination entirely escapes our laws of chance." Thus any hope that future science can explain present mysteries "is an act of faith and not a scientific statement."

Time and again evolutionary leaps occur so anti-chance that the resort to chance to explain them "amounts to admitting a miracle," du Noüy continues. Spontaneous generation of not one but hundreds of identical protein molecules needed for life is such a problem. The transition from non-cellular organisms (and some still survive, weighing up to a pound) to the complex cellular basis for life is another. The apparent change from blue algae based on phycocyanin chemistry to green algae based on chlorophyll, in the plant kingdom, might as well have been a "miracle." The change from plant to animal forms, involving a leap from the chemistry of chlorophyll (built on a magnesium atom) to hemoglobin (built on an iron atom), is impossible to conceive. Yet it must have begun almost immediately; another chance, du Noüy says, best not subjected to a calculus of probabilities. The transition from asexual to sexual reproduction is similarly unimaginable, yet a necessary "chance" in the evolutionary epic. Changes in the number of chromosomes must have occurred often in transitions, but imply simultaneous "Adam and Eve" mutations difficult to account by chance (otherwise the offspring would be sterile). The development of homoiothermism (constant body temperature) "stands out today as one of the greatest puzzles of evolution."

Other problems with the familiar evolutionary story involve timing. Darwin mistakenly believed evolutionary change must occur very slowly and always gradually. However, du Noüy among others point out, " . . . each group, order, or family seems to be born suddenly and we hardly ever find the forms which link them to the preceding strain." ("Hardly ever" is understating things. Only one fossil specimen exists, the archaeopteryx, so it is said, and the case that this represents a transition is hardly indisputable.) Du Noüy continues, "When we do discover them they are already completely differentiated. Not only do we find practically no transitional forms, but in general it is impossible to authentically connect a new group with an ancient one." (This is precisely the problem that the cladists stress.) About these abrupt emergences he remarks, "We have put the word 'suddenly' between quotation marks so as to make the problem stand out." Gould now offers the theory of "punctuated equilibria" to describe such departures from the Darwinian timetable, meaning that species vegetate for long periods, then, boom, turn into something else. Whether this is description, sound theory or guesswork, I do not know.

Similarly, many transformations occur which do not confer an immediate advantage and are thus not accountable by survival pressure. Rather, says du Noüy, this represents "a necessary step to attain a still distant but superior stage." The development of air-breathing apparatuses by amphibians is an example. More dramatic cases are the evolving of bipedalism (walking upright) in pre-hominids (apparently), and the "sudden" appearance of the human brain. Darwin erred in tying brain size to body weight under survival pressure, as Wallace pointed out to him even before *Descent* was published. Gould had reason to ruminate on this: "Our brain has increased much more rapidly than any prediction based on body size would allow.... We are indeed smarter than we are." This is, of course, metaphor. What he is saying, and it is a remarkable admission, is that Darwinian theory isn't working. Moreover, linguist Noam Chomsky, also an outspoken evolutionist, rules out language as an instrument of human evolution. The brain has to have a uniquely human neuronal structure *before* it can use symbolic language. If we can believe all this, man emerged "suddenly" with fully human intelligence and linguistic capacities—but far too soon for the evolutionary schedule. That is, on a Darwinian basis, there was not nearly enough time for the development of human characteristics. No, of course we are not "smarter than we are." But we are much smarter than evolutionary theory predicts.

Still further problems remain. There are cases of "mimicry, parasitism and adaptation of organs," Jaki notes, "which to account for in terms of natural selection amounts to explaining miracles by magic." Evolution of plant life poses even greater problems than those of biology, and "[defies] even the proverbial powers of Darwinian imagination." The dispute, as Jaki puts it, is about "living machines" that do not consciously choose an evolutionary goal. Reproduction—

never mind its necessary success in the scheme of natural selection—has been examined with the methods of exact science, and is "well-nigh impossible." Can a mechanism of chance preempt purpose "in spite of the fact that the more complex an animal machine is, the more overwhelming is its evidence of working for a purpose?" This is a "perennial thorn in the side of the Darwinists" and "hardly any of them [have] failed to voice...perplexity" about it. Well might they be perplexed. If one event at bad odds succeeds another at bad odds, the result is the two improbabilities multiplied—or much worse odds. When we have a whole long series of these events so improbable as to invoke the word "miracle" from scientists, the product is an improbability too vast for words or thought.

Science is supposed to show "what is" in the natural realm, not multiply miracles by miracles. It is only the human spirit, however misled by bad evidence, that seeks the miraculous. Du Noüy, the scientist, would have none of it. "The laws of evolution," he insisted, "are *teleological,* whereas those of the transformation of each species *simply tend toward a state of equilibrium with the surrounding medium."* (Gould may have been thinking of this, and I hope he has a good theoretical answer for what "punctuates" the equilibrium.)

"Evolution, we repeat, is comprehensible only if we admit that it is dominated by a finality, a precise and distant goal. If we do not accept the reality of this orienting pole, not only are we forced to recognize that evolution is rigorously incompatible with our laws of matter, as we demonstrated above, but—and this is serious—that the appearance of moral and spiritual ideas remains an absolute mystery." Indeed; and inventing "reciprocal altruism" does not solve du Noüy's mystery.

Jaki observes that "opposition to the main trend" of scientific advance "usually dies out with the generation of the original dissenters." But scientific opposition to evolutionary theory remains strong more than a century later. Some while back, the fifth volume of the *Encyclopedie française,* "written with the collaboration of all leading French biologists, came to a conclusion almost impossible to believe and just as impossible to find quoted: 'It follows from this presentation that the theory of evolution is impossible. . . . Evolution is a kind of dogma in which its priests no longer believe but which they keep presenting to their people. So much about a matter which it takes courage to spell out so that men of the coming generation may orient their research in a different way."

Great faith have they who will not accept miracles in the religious sense, but who will believe what their peers term the impossible.

Creationists vs. Crusaders

One interesting thing about the feud between "creationists" and "Darwinists" is that it is still going on. How can this be? The issues were supposed to be resolved in Darwin's favor long ago. The most sensational clash in the feud, the Scopes trial, took place sixty years ago (1925). And at least a generation before that, the Darwinists could without exaggeration foresee complete victory. It remained for them only to mop up the remnants of opposition. The last resistance to Darwinism, they hooted, came from a handful of Christian fundamentalists who could easily be ridiculed as backward

yokels and know-nothings. This statement by Woodrow
Wilson summed up well the attitude prevailing even before
Scopes: "Of course, like every man of intelligence and
education, I do believe in organic evolution. It surprises me
that *at this late date* such questions should be raised"
(emphasis added).

Wilson would be shocked that "such questions" are still
being raised today, not least by scientists. Equally curious, all
the old Darwinist platitudes, in their fading sepia turn-of-the-
century tones, are still trundled out to do battle with that same
misguided handful of creationists. One often finds them in the
papers, as if they were "news." Only now, they have the ring of
a pastoral exhortation to the Darwinist flock to remain
steadfast. In our time there clearly are fundamentalists on
both sides of the barricades, Darwinist as well as Christian.
This is worth exploring. In one of the Sherlock Holmes
mysteries, the key clue was a dog that *didn't* bark. Ours is like
that: what became of the Darwinist triumph, once—a lifetime
ago—almost within grasp, yet now more elusive than ever?

Sobran advises: "Events always fool those who are too
sure of destiny's course." At the dawn of our century, the
whole Western world had just such certainty that progress
toward a limitless, golden future lay before it. Had not the
tenets of Darwinism guaranteed it? One voice alone, Chesterton's, was raised in a most remarkable warning that went
unheeded: "Earnest free-thinkers need not worry themselves
about the persecutions of the past. Before the liberal idea is
dead or triumphant we shall see wars and persecutions the like
of which the world has never seen." The First World War was
then less than ten years hence.

Experience, if nothing less, reopens questions once deemed closed. This century of Darwinist ascendancy has indeed seen "wars and persecutions" without precedent. The reflective mind, aware that men act on their inner beliefs, can in no way absolve the prevailing Darwinist faith in these tragedies. "A good tree cannot bring forth evil fruit...." In view of its evil consequences, we cannot but question the truth of evolutionary doctrines, however "scientific" they are represented to be. Events have thus shaken the old certitudes in Darwinism, raising grave doubts for many, if not for the Darwinist true believers.

The progress of science has further eroded the faith. For a homely case, the Scopes defense assembled a blue-ribbon panel of scientists to prove that "evolution is a fact" with a wealth of "scientific" evidence that would make any evolutionist today wince. They were, for instance, quite sure that no plants could evolve until there was soil for them to grow in. They also put the oldest (pre-fossil) rocks at 100 million years old, defending their dating techniques as accurate. Later methods indicate they were wrong by a factor of more than forty, and also suggest the evolutionary epic was not possible in the much-too-limited time span they gave it. Yet they believed the epic just as their successors believe it with a wholly different picture of the facts. It is all very well that mistakes have been corrected (we think), but one may profitably ponder a belief that can thrive regardless of the facts it is supposed to be based on. Of course it was other, epochal advances in science that undermined the older mechanistic view, and with it the materialist basis of Darwinism. In particular, Einstein's relativity and the "Big Bang" theory give us a new picture of the universe emerging, as the old creation story had it, at a specific moment, and in a most specific, finite, almost palpably purposeful form. This is not evidence against evolution per se, but it evokes a powerful argument against the materialist and purposeless "evolution by chance" that Darwinism insists on. Other advances discussed below, within the sciences concerned with evolution, cast doubt on the validity of past assumptions about ancestry.

The case for Darwinism, never nearly as strong as its adherents claim, grows weaker. It was the success of its belief, not its evidence, that made the old battles appear more one-sided than they were. The "fundamentalists" are still painted as its hated enemy, but were never alone in opposition to Darwinism. The more orthodox denominations can (but need not) accept God's creation on an evolutionary basis, while rejecting the materialist assumptions of Darwin.

What interests us in all this are the clear earmarks of a growing fundamentalism in the Darwinian faith. The anti-religious underpinnings of its view turn from a mere working premise to an aggressive, unreasoning dogma, harshly enforced within the flock and actively proselytized without. Their numbers dwindling, the remaining faithful increasingly crusade to regain lost dominions. Cross a Darwinist on duty and he becomes a thundering evangelist. Let the heathen "creationists" even mention the word science, and his mask of cool scientific rationality gives way to rage. Such dogmatism has serious implications for the scientific community and for public policy. To question Darwinism in the academy is to risk excommunication from the body of Enlightened scholars, and possibly blacklisting. Steven Jay Gould has observed this: "We have persecuted dissenters, resorted to catechism, and tried to

extend our authority to a moral sphere where it has no force."
A memorable article by John Pfeiffer, himself a Darwinist,
reported that "strong emotions" and perhaps "deep personal
insult" were rife in the academy over interpretations of
evolution. Orthodoxy was demanded:

> Not long ago a professor wrote an article questioning a
> former teacher, in the mildest possible terms, about the
> authenticity of a certain find—and ended a friendship of 30
> years. On another occasion an eminent anthropologist arose to
> speak at a meeting given in his honor, and began reminiscing
> about the early days of his career when his ideas concerning
> human evolution had been ignored. But he managed to
> complete only a few sentences of his talk. Then, overcome by
> the recollections of years of frustration, he lowered his head and
> burst into tears. Investigators have stalked out of meetings,
> indulged in personal vituperation (in technical journals as well
> as privately), argued over priorities, accused colleagues of
> stealing their ideas.
>
> Such behavior . . . is by no means unknown in other areas of
> science, but its incidence is strikingly high among pre-
> historians. The reason for this occupation ailment is obscure,
> but it may have something to do with the shortage of solid
> evidence.

Such behavior is also the opposite of—and obviously hurtful
to—scientific disinterestedness. It is just as obviously faith,
not science, that glosses over the admitted "shortage of solid
evidence" to insist on orthodoxy.

The same intolerant faith spills into public life to wage
war on all religious expression. Though it affects a concern for
constitutional principle, there is no doubt the purpose of this
campaign is to exterminate religious influence and impose a
secular philosophy on our public institutions. To do so, it
twists the Constitution into interpretations the Framers

never imagined. For instance, on a given day, you are likely to read about a skirmish such as this one, reported by the UPI: "Pressure from fundamentalists and religious groups [uh-huh] has led publishers of the nation's major biology textbooks to provide 'a watered down version of biology,' a study charges.... 'The quality of biology textbooks has declined drastically,...' the co-author of the study said. '...in recent years, publishers have given in to pressure from the ultra-fundamentalists and watered down references to evolution and other scientific theories.... The study was commissioned by People for the American Way... [a] citizens group founded... to protect First Amendment rights from threats from the new Religious Right.'"

Crusaders on duty and their media accomplices seem to have no scruple about passing off their philippics as "news." Nor are they too fussy about their arguments. The language here is interesting. Textbooks that do not hew to Darwinist dogmas are said to be watered down and are equated with a drastic decline in quality. The infidels responsible for this outrage were *ultra*-fundamentalists, leaving us to wonder how one can be more fundamental than a fundamentalist. (Or at least we might wonder if we did not know that "ultra," in all anti-heroic tongues, signals that something horrid and reactionary is afoot.) The targets of this PAW assault are blackguarded with opprobrious labels and stigmatized with capital letters; whereas their assailants are canonized as "citizens" highmindedly defending the First Amendment and the American Way. It is nowhere recorded in the "story" that PAW is an ultra-liberal group, or that it sees in the First Amendment only a "wall of separation" between the state and religion (which the Constitution somehow neglected to mention), and denies the clear intent of the Amendment to guarantee tolerance and the "free expression of religion." Themselves intolerant of religion, the crusaders have for years used the Amendment to do precisely what they affect to deplore in others: to dictate public school curricula and, indeed, impose their anti-religious views in all tax-funded areas. One recent result: the denial of tuition aid, otherwise routine, to a blind student because he wanted to attend theological school. Only let some unenlightened legislator try to legalize a moment of voluntary prayer for schoolchildren, and the crusaders sue to block it. Such guidance as *Matthew* 18:5-6 is prohibited by law—just when it is needed most.

Or again, were you in the trenches with these humorless souls, you would be exposed to a flood of letters and leaflets and tracts with all the flavor of the pamphleteering by the old temperance movement. One example brought to my attention is the *Creationist/Evolutionist Newsletter,* a wide-eyed and misnamed tract purposing to warn the faithful about dangerous "creationist" activities. One revealing item in it was an abstract of a study conducted at Ohio State University by Paul F. of the department of genetics: "Students were questioned about their views on the creation/evolution controversy, especially their concept of Darwinian evolution and *the concept of equal time for 'creation science'"* (emphasis added). Note that this does not pose evolution against creation, but evolution against giving "equal time" for "creation science," which is damned in quotes. Students were clearly expected to cleave to revealed Darwinian doctrine and stoutly reject any examination of other views—and this at the university level! The students' faith was found sadly wanting: they voted four to one in favor of open inquiry and academic freedom. Darwinist teachings—that is to say, "biological education," Prof. F. and the newsletter editors reported disspiritedly, was "not very successful" in Ohio.

The nearer one gets to the scientific establishment, the more one hears the evolutionary myth embroidered and invested with quasi-religious hopes and fears. The myth is a staple in popular magazines about science. Here is promised everything from meeting extraterrestial intelligences to immortality through genetic engineering to building our own sun when the present model burns out. A survey by Dr. Jaki finds that scientists are usually far off the mark predicting what will happen in their own fields fifty years hence; yet foreseeing a human future fifty billion years from now does not strain the Darwinist faith!

Or, looking backward, the litany of evolutionist belief was frankly stated in an article titled "Ancestors: A Family Album," which purported to trace human lineage through all known hominid fossils. As usual, the language is revealing:

> Today we are not shocked that our distant ancestors *were not*
> [N.B.: not "might not have been"] people but animals that
> looked like apes....In the 120 years since Darwin's assertion
> those who have followed have shown him to have been largely
> correct. Except for those who believe in miracles of special
> creation (events that, by definition, can neither be proved nor
> disproved), *no one doubts* that our heritage can be traced back
> nearly four million years to little creatures [eh? created
> beings?] that, as adults, stood only about as tall as a five-year-
> old today. (emphasis added)

A ritual declaration of faith is thus observed, and the audience is led to a comfortable certitude that the case is closed, "proved" in a way that "miracles" cannot be. Man is unquestionably descended from *Australopithecus afarensis* (meaning "southern ape from Afar, Ethiopia"), whose fossil remains were first found only three years before this article was written. "No one doubts" this. Well, it's a nice story. The trouble is, nobody has any idea whether it's true. Maybe so, maybe not; the problem lies as always in sanctifying sheer conjecture as scientific knowledge. In short, the claim vastly exceeds the evidence. When one gets into the main text of the article, one finds large doubts and disclaimers expressed at every stage, and "some paleoanthropologists" don't believe it at all. Read more closely and you learn that the first member of genus *Homo* appeared "suddenly," with no known lines of descent from *A. afarensis* after all. Even the pretty color pictures accompanying the article—"family portraits"—are admitted to be "Unfortunately...based more on imagination than evidence." The same could be said of the whole evolutionary myth.

Extraterrestial intelligence (or at least life) is another article of Darwinian faith likely to pop up in these media. For example, one magazine reported some years ago on space probes to Venus and Mars. The surface of the former was found to be extremely hot and *"lingering hopes* that Venus might support life *received a blow"* (emphasis added). What hopes were these? Suppose the life form on Venus had been deadly viruses? The second report, oddly titled "Obituary of a Planet," somberly announced, "Mars is dead." At mission control, "When the analysis committee saw the clear photos that came in later, they were *'shocked really beyond belief'"* (emphasis added). This is certainly strange language for scientists. Science is supposed to deal in facts, not in metaphysical cravings. But it is everyday stuff for the Darwinists. Believing that life sprang naturally from dead rock on earth, though we know not how, they hope that biogenesis is a simple process that has occurred a zillion times in a trillion–zillion star systems out there. So goes the theory, and that is why the government spends boodles of money on radio telescopes, evolutionary biology and other projects born of Darwinian faith. The hairsplitters who argue voluntary prayer in schools is "establishing" a state church, have no such qualms about funding Darwinist enterprises with tax dollars extracted from people of different religious views. Meanwhile, it is worth noting in passing that if there is Intelligence out there, and if it evolved as Darwinists suppose through successful predation in the struggle for existence, we had better think twice about trying to communicate with it. If it is not a fellow creature of God, we might well be in the position of a mouse greeting a cat: food.

One last, amusing example of Darwinist proselytizing will serve to introduce a growing breach in the "church of science." Recently a famous advice columnist was asked—by someone signed "I am serious"—which came first, the chicken or the egg? Now, if this wheeze is to be taken seriously, it is a conundrum about form, posing being against becoming: is a chicken one thing, or is it different things at different points in its reproductive cycle? Is an egg an embryonic chicken, or does it have its own essence? This sort of debate has gone out of style since Occam banned universals. (And a pity it is, for the same question arises in the debate over abortion: is a "fetus" fully human, or only potentially human, hence "terminatable" without moral offense?)

The columnist, steeped in modernism, mistook the question for one about origins, and was so incautious as to cite *Genesis* 1:20 in favor of the chicken. Whereupon a "deluge" of mail reciting evolutionist catechisms poured in to correct her, advise that the scripture was no match for science, and assert hotly the "scientific" "fact" that "birds" evolved from "reptiles." (One wonders if these are the folks who buy rattlesnake eggs at Wyoming tourist traps.) A reader, signed "2 B EGGSACT," vouchsafed that "The egg preceded the chicken by several hundred million years" in the evolutionary scale, apparently confident that a few hundred million years is state of the art eggsactitude. Other readers cited the old chestnut that everyone in the flock seems to know by heart, to ridicule the "creationists who believe the earth was created in 4004 B.C." There may be creationists who believe this; I wouldn't know. If so, they can claim a highly respectable scientific imprimatur. The date is famous. Though widely attributed to Bishop Ussher, it was actually calculated by the great scientist Kepler *(Mysterium cosmographicum)*—in 1596! One looks in vain for any hint that the Darwinists can laugh at themselves for believing a long series of scientific mistakes, not least our descent from Piltdown Man—a view still prevalent only thirty-five years ago.

Rebellion of the Cladists

Such claims as that "birds" "evolved" from "reptiles" are the backbone of the evolutionary myth. They are taken to be true, not only by the columnist's readers, but by countless textbooks on biology and related fields. They are the essence of the "scientific fact" of evolution. No Darwinist disputes them, or can, in the scheme of things.

Nevertheless, it is precisely such claims that are now being put to the severest test, from within science. For the last decade, perhaps more, an increasingly heated debate has rent the complacency of standard evolutionary theory. It is, in the words of the perspicacious writer Tom Bethell, "One of the least publicized and least understood challenges to Darwin and the theory of evolution—and surely one of the most fascinating, in its sweep and vigor...." (I am indebted to Mr. Bethell for these reflections, particularly his lucid February, 1985 article in *Harper's*, "Agnostic Evolutionists.") The dispute, involving such arcane scientific concepts as plesiomorphy and paraphyly, is not easy to follow. But the gist of it is that the traditional methods used to classify fossils (or present life forms) are in question. The challenge is to the ultimate meaning and validity of scientific classifications that have hitherto been routinely accepted in evolutionary scholarship. What is at stake is scientific knowledge of evolution.

The dissenters are called the cladists, spoken of earlier, or sometimes "pattern" or "transformed" cladists. Cladistics (the word is too new for my Webster's Unabridged; it derives from the Greek *klados*, meaning "branch," and the A has a long pronunciation, as in glade) is a school of taxonomists—the scientists whose job it is to classify fossil remains into scientific categories. (Taxonomy, if you will pardon further confusion, is part of the larger science of classification called systematics.) Cladists, says Bethell, "are rigorous, scrupulous labelers." Their task "is to discover and name the various groups found in nature—a task first assigned to Adam by God, according to *Genesis*—and put them in one category or another." But taxonomy was not rigorous in the older scheme of things. As one observer put it, "Whoever wants to hold to firm rules should give up taxonomic work. Nature is much too disorderly for such a man." The cladists, insisting on scientific rigor, dispute this, and there is the rub.

What is all this about? It goes down to what we mean when we invoke such groupings as "fish" or "reptiles" or "primates." What, really, is a dog? We can get to know one dog, one specimen, the family pet. We may know a dozen dogs. But there are hundreds of breeds of dogs, all in one species definable by its ability to interbreed, and nobody can really know them all. But this is just one species. In scientific classification, there may be thousands of species in one genus. The classification, which is man-made and in a sense arbitrary, deals in larger and larger categories of families and orders and phyla, and such. How do we deal with it? There are 35,000 known, and perhaps three times as many unknown, species of spiders in the rachnid genus (which also includes daddy-long-legs and scorpions)—and some fifteen scientists to sort them out. It can't be done. "Laymen," rarely if ever discouraged in this view by the scientists, suppose all this has been squared away and firm—but science has hardly scratched the surface.

So we ask again: what are "fish"? What are "birds" or "reptiles"? They are *ideas:* categories devised by the human mind. The categories are supposed to lump together in some recognizable form vast numbers of, say, simple genera, that in turn include even more immense numbers of bewildering species. Multiply the problem of lumping St. Bernards with Chihuahuas, take away any present knowledge that they can interbreed (this cannot be known about fossil organisms), multiply it all by thousands of species, allow only scattered scraps of evidence, and you begin to get an idea of what is involved in producing rigorous scientific knowledge of evolution. But only a trace of the real thing. Such categories as reptiles or primates, say the cladists, are too nebulous to yield any real scientific information. How, then, can category A (which is a human concept full of staggering uncertainties) be described as the ancestor or descendant of category B (likewise)? What the cladists say, with great force, is that it cannot be done. As Bethell quotes it, a sort of rallying cry among cladists is: "The concept of ancestry is not accessible with the tools we have."

Let's look at this another way. Human ancestry can be traced, at least for a few hundred years, with written records, family genealogies, parish books. But in nature, of course, there is of course no history, and all must be reconstructed from the scanty and disputable traces of past life. What evidence there may be must be sorted out and dated, or else it can hardly be of any use to science. The dating techniques, as noted earlier, have in living memory been revised by a factor of close to fifty—hardly a source of confidence. The classification of past life forms poses far greater problems. First, most of the evidence is gone forever. Second, what we do find must be rigorously classified, which is almost as hopeless. Before you make the statement that species X is descended from species Y, you certainly have to know that species X and Y are related. You have to know more than that. You have to know indisputably that X is the closest relative of Y. That is where the job of cladistics comes in: establishing that X and Y are related, and if so, how closely. Without this, there is no evolutionary theory. Without this, you cannot claim as scientific fact or in any legitimate way that the one species descended from the other. Without rigorous taxonomy, without cladistics, you never get to first base.

The cladists' rebellion thus centers on what can be known in a scientific way. They deny that classifications can be made in the older mode, what Gould calls the "admittedly vague and

qualitative, but not therefore unimportant notion of similarity" of life forms. To the cladists, similarities do not begin
to tack down scientific categories. Again, these are merely
ideas, far removed from the real scientific business of dealing
with what limited evidence there is. Accurate classification
may take thousands of years (a reasonable proposition from
the human resources involved), or it may never be achieved.
The point remains: unless the fossil evidence is properly and
scientifically classified, we can literally know nothing of
evolutionary ancestry. The whole evolutionary myth is left
without a scientific basis. The dissenters are perfectly described as agnostics: their whole claim is that nothing can
realistically be known about orthodox evolution with the
present tools of science. On the testimony of precisely those
scientists who have to do the dirty work to make the case, the
whole myth is going up in smoke.

The story by no means ends here. The cladists have
shaken the tree of orthodoxy, and thus evoke evolutionary
fundamentalist wrath. The dispute takes on the religious
overtones we have already seen. Bethell perceives that
cladistics "was saying that evolutionists—like the creationists
they periodically do battle with—are nothing more than
believers themselves." Says Colin Patterson, a paleontologist
with the London Museum of Natural History and a leading
cladist, "I really put my foot in it. I compared evolution and
creation and made a case that the two were equivalent. I was
all fired up and said what I thought. I went through merry hell
for about a year. Almost everybody except the people at the
museum objected. Lots of academics wrote. Deluges of mail.
'Here we are trying to combat a political argument,' they said,
'and you give the ammunition.'" Is it not at least strange that

these supposed scientists should be concerned with combat-
ting political arguments? This is not the attitude of science,
but of belief; and what they so lightly dismiss as "politics" was
faith.

The question, as Patterson and other cladists soon found
out, and as we have already seen, concerned religion. To the
cladists, evolutionary theory is simply irrelevant, and, for the
foreseeable future, unscientific. To the flock, it remains the
holy of holies: what Patterson terms "the unified field theory
of biology." "Once something has that status, it becomes
something like religion" in scientific chambers, he said.
Queried about evolutionary ancestry, Patterson replied, "I
don't think we shall ever have any access to any form of the
tree [of life] which we can call factual." Questioned further
whether he believed it all to be unreal, he replied, "Well, isn't
it strange that this is what it comes to, that you have to ask me
whether I believe it, as if it mattered whether I believe it or
not. Yes, I do believe it. But in saying that, it is obvious it is
faith."

As we close, I would like to quote a passage from remarks
by Patterson to his peers at a systematics meeting in the
American Museum of Natural History in New York City a few
years ago. By that time Patterson was well advanced in his
doubts about evolution and had, as a thought experiment,
tried to start thinking like a "creationist." His remarks were
titled "Evolutionism and Creationism." To wit:

> I think always before when I've got up to speak on a subject I've
> been confident of one thing—that I know more about it than
> anybody else in the room, because I've worked on it. Well, this
> time it isn't true. I'm speaking on two subjects, evolutionism
> and creationism, and I believe it's true to say that I know
> nothing whatever about either of them.

One of the reasons I started taking this anti-evolutionary view, or let's call it a non-evolutionary view, was that last year I had a sudden realization. For over twenty years I was working on evolution in some way. One morning I woke up and something had happened to me in the night, and it struck me that I had been working on this stuff for more than twenty years, and there was not one thing I knew about it. It's quite a shock to learn that one can be misled for so long. Either there was something wrong with me or there was something wrong with evolutionary theory. Naturally I know there is nothing wrong with me, so for the last few weeks I've been putting a simple question to various people and groups.

Question is: can you tell me anything you know about evolution? Any one thing, any one thing that is true?

A century and a quarter after Darwin, this is a dumbfounding question. A scientist asks his colleagues if they can provide a single true statement about the faith that has moved men for all that time—and there is no answer. However confident its postures, Darwinism is an empty faith.

Reflections

Some perspectives are in order at this point, to avoid any misapprehensions. The evolutionary debate has been marked from the beginning by a confusion of wholly different scientific and philosophical questions. Darwin himself muddied the issue by grafting his amateur philosophizing onto his innocent factual findings. As Jaki observes, "The *Origin* was a vast offering of one final, more philosophical than scientific, truth based on the contemplation of nature, namely, that all development of life was mechanistic in such a sense as to render unnecessary all philosophy, to say nothing of theology, however natural." Adherence to an anti-religious interpretation of evolution remains the distinguishing feature of Darwinism, and marks it as a cult, not science.

We, in turn, must insist on preserving the distinction between mere scientific data and ultimate meanings. Our whole concern is with contemporary belief—Darwinism in particular—and its consequences. Neither the factual questions of evolution nor the present feebleness of scientific evidence for it are directly at issue. We base no case for a heroic view on either, but rather examine them to contrast the extravagance of Darwinist claims to the dearth of supporting evidence. Whether men actually did evolve from some other life form is of no moment, and is an innocent empirical question, safely left to science. We are at no pains to deny the possibility. *Genesis* itself repeatedly affirms that "the Lord God formed man of the dust of the ground...." (2:7). Certainly this poses no difficulty for the theist who knows creation and evolution are not incompatible, and who is aware that if the "why" of creation is understood, the "how" becomes, by comparison, trivial. What we do deny, emphatically, is the Darwinian thesis of a random, mechanistic evolution. Such a thesis cannot derive from fact, however "scientific," and dead-ends philosophically in a fatal contradiction. Darwinists' work, says Jaki, "is a life-long commitment to the purpose of proving there is no purpose. Every Darwinist is a living refutation of a philosophy, Darwinism, for which purpose is non-existent."

For like reasons, we have no immediate quarrel with Darwin's deductive theory of selection. The gradual change of life forms through reproductive success of "the fittest" is a plausible and scientific hypothesis. The world might never have seen Auschwitz or A-bombs had he quit there and heeded his own advice about a mistake in an earlier paper: "My error has been a good lesson to me never to trust in science to the principle of exclusion." It was precisely in asserting natural selection to be the exclusive agent of biological change that Darwin abandoned science. As we have seen, this step cannot be justified by induction from empirical evidence or by deduction from his theory. This was the fatal departure into philosophic speculation. But Darwin went farther. He also stipulated that selection must be a chance mechanism, effectively (and intentionally) denying any metaphysical explanation of life. In this he became blatantly the preacher of the materialist view he had come to believe. Little excuse can be made for this on grounds that Darwin was merely trying to put his biological science on an equal footing with the more prestigious exact sciences, which he ill understood. In essence, he was dictating what science could believe—a dogma that put Darwinism on a collision course with future scientific discovery. With such crude, counter-metaphysical posturing, Darwinism, at its own origin, became the principal agent of the anti-heroic reaction to Western belief.

Here again we see the anti-hero's resort to blinders, to an exclusionary formula, so that we may not see the evil of his apotheosis of Man. The irony, in the instance, is that his formula is an assault on science itself. Suppose, many centuries from now, that a Darwinian explanation is held to account for all biological change. Have we answered any of our questions? Not at all: we have merely buried the mysteries of life under a pile of loose and unscientific conceptions: "natural," "mechanistic," "spontaneous," and the like. If we are natural, what is Nature, and why do we invest her with

supernatural, creative powers? Science cannot establish ultimate meanings. In the meantime free inquiry, the whole spirit
of science, is trampled by the Darwinists' flat declaration that
theirs is the One True Explanation. How can they possibly
know?

A scientific theory, however attractive, must have ob-
servational evidence. Einstein proposed three tests for general relativity, and announced that unless the theory passed all
three, it was horsefeathers. (It passed.) In contrast, neither
Darwin nor any of his followers has ever produced any
empirical evidence that natural selection has been the origin
of any species. Never mind the title of his book; nothing is yet
known about how species can originate "naturally." Hume's
dictum to burn all books not based on empirical evidence
would burn *Origin*—and countless thousands of biology
textbooks based on it. Here, Darwinism is in conflict with
even the minimum demands of science. For our purposes,
what is interesting is how much empirical evidence the
Darwinist is willing to ignore, to go on believing his quasi-
religious myth.

By the original hypothesis, change must occur infinitesimal, imperceptible degrees over endless periods. This
didn't work, so the theory of punctuated equilibria was added,
stating that species vegetate for vast periods, then pop into
something else. If Mr. Gould is right about the latter, Mr.
Darwin's theory flunked. The two theories cannot be reconciled. Nature, that charming but unruly myth, seems to have
reservations about fitting her ways to any mold, Darwinian or
neo-Darwinian. Some creatures change, some do not. New
creatures emerge in the most fantastic leaps. Some simply
bypass present advantage for a progressive change needed in

the future; others take no advantage of selection at all. Such biologists as du Noüy and Lucien Cuénot—and let us remember another distinction, that not all evolutionists are Darwinists—are led by their investigations of these incredible twists to denounce evolution-by-chance as preposterous, and to insist on a finalist or teleological direction to evolution—in scientific terms: anti-chance, and exactly what Darwinism denies. Whatever else we may say about it, these investigations were in the framework of empirical science, and cannot be rejected by a deductive Darwinist theory.

The scientific case against Darwinism by no means ends there. According to the cladists, there is simply no scientific means—at least with our present tools—to establish ancestry in the presumed tree of life. Darwin's happy vision of an unbroken progression of life comes apart at all its seams. All we really have left is the assumption—not contradicted by present evidence, but not proven or provable for the past— that living organisms have a parent or parents. It certainly seems a reasonable assumption, at least until we get back to the first organisms that had no parents. But it is only as assumption, without empirical evidence, without a scientific imprimatur. Bethell quotes the Harvard geneticist (and Darwinist) Richard C. Lewontin: "The only way you can know that some fossil is the direct ancestor is that it's so human that it *is* human. There's a contradiction there. If it is different enough from humans to be interesting, then you don't know whether it's an ancestor or not. And if it's similar enough to be human, then it's not interesting. So, look, we're not ever going to know what the direct ancestor is." Nicely put. How then can we ever know, with scientific certainty, that there *was* an ancestor? We can't. It is strictly an assumption, an article of faith: not a fact. Believe it or not as you wish, but don't call it science.

The Darwinist cult still thrives by portraying itself as scientific, but it never had such credentials to begin with, and now lies in ruins before the real thing.

A bit of doggerel by an anonymous wag realizes the full absurdity:

> Behold the slime primeval!
> That lifeless muck
> From which, by luck,
> Evolved the Church Medieval

Darwin's *Origin*—that is to say, the original *Origin*—never mentioned evolution at all. We have T. H. Huxley's assurance that evolution is not a necessary, hence scientific, deduction from Darwin's theory. What then is this interloper, evolution, that Darwin did not even mention in the *Origin*?

If we want to be fastidious, evolution is far more the expression of Herbert Spencer's philosophy than Darwin's biology. But it is a vague idea, of scant use to either. Evolution serves one purpose only: it is the creation myth of anti-heroism. It is advanced to turn the complexity and mystery of life into a *story*—a story so simple that all the flock can understand and put their faith in it. Nobody understands this better, or states it more brazenly, than sociobiologist E. O. Wilson: "The core of scientific materialism is the evolutionary epic ... is probably the best myth we will ever have. It can be adjusted [!] until it comes as close to the truth as the human mind is constructed to judge the truth. And if that is the case, the mythopoeic requirements [!] of the mind must somehow be met by scientific materialism so as to reinvest our superb energies." Hear, all ye faithful: your masters give you an epic to live by (subject to revision from time to time)! Thereby the mythopoeic requirements of your minds will be fulfilled, and your superb energies harnessed for the great cause of scientific materialism! Scrutinize Wilson's words, for they are stark witness not only to Darwinist contempt for the mind, but also to willful deceit for its cause.

Such dealings in illusion did not fool Chesterton. "There is something slow and soothing and gradual about the word [evolution], and even about the idea," he wrote.

> As a matter of fact, it is not, touching these primary things, a very practical word or a very profitable idea. Nobody can imagine how nothing can turn into something. Nobody can get an inch nearer to it by explaining how something could turn into something else.... But evolution really is mistaken for explanation. It has the fatal quality of leaving on many minds the impression that they do understand it, and everything else.... But this notion of something smooth and slow ... is a great part of the illusion. An event is not any more intrinsically intelligible or unintelligible because of the pace at which it moves. For a man who does not believe in a miracle, a slow miracle would be just as incredible as a swift one.

Darwinian theory requires vast, unthinkable spans of time to hide its miracles (recall Darwin's dismay when geologists of the time set the age of the earth at 100 million years—not nearly enough for natural selection to do what he wished it to). The idea is simple: given enough time, enough throws of the dice, something will "go right"; chance will overcome anti-chance. And thus a thousand miracles accrue by imperceptible degrees. Yet, to believe this does not help at all. The contradictions of a chance universe remain. In the Darwinist view, "an aggregate of inappreciable increments is simultaneously equated—in its cause to *nothing*, in its effect to the *whole of things*," as J. Martineau put it. He noted that "a logical theft is more easily committed piecemeal than whole-sale. Surely it is a mean device for a philosopher to crib causation by hairs-breadths, to put it out at at compound interest though all time, and then disown the debt." Jaki adds, as we noted earlier, "...evolution was a process insensibly slow.... The issue was between a divine creation which is inherently specific and a man-made chaos which is intrinsically hazy." In seeking refuge thus in haze and shadow, Darwinism reveals that its true motives go beyond science: "The chief additional ingredient is a craving for the absence of metaphysics, a craving which should not be left immune to scrutiny." We have examined this craving before: it is the anti-hero's dark desire to dethrone the Creator and be free of moral responsibility.

And so it is, through the Darwinist century, that the "evolutionary epic" has been put forward by purposeful men as a refutation of purpose. Of course the Darwinist who so declares is invalidating his own words by making them the meaningless and empty product of chance. "In this," said Chesterton, "he questions the brain itself, and endeavours to remove all reality from his own assertions, past, present and to come." Defenders of reason need no misgivings in asserting that the human mind sets us apart from the purely natural. Animals do not devise theories of evolution, or make what Huxley termed an "act of faith" in believing that life developed from unlife by chance. Nor can men construct materialist philosophies with the random secretions of an epiphenomenal brain. No rational philosophy can deny reason itself. Are we to heed the man who thinks there is no basis for thinking? Darwinist materialism may claim foolish hearts, but can make no appeal to the mind. Justly is it termed "a celebration of incoherence," its adherents not scientists but "philosophers who revel in the denial of logic and values."

All this might have been laughed off as coffeehouse babbling long ago, were it not for the alleged scientific seal of approval for Darwinism. But it is pseudo-science that assumes a mechanistic, determined universe, and seeks to study stars, atoms, sardines and men with the same tools. This view, which we examine in the next chapter, is in truth a veiled attack on science. It poses real problems for the would-be scientist who feels obliged to follow the Darwinist blueprint. Professor James Gray of Cambridge risked his reputation to say, "No amount of argument, or clever epigram, can disguise the inherent improbability of orthodox [evolutionary] theory; but most biologists feel it is better to think in terms of improbable events than not to think at all." Evolution or nothing: this choice is forced on them, not by evidence, but by doctrinal Darwinist materialism. The dilemma dissolves merely by allowing creatures to have a Creator. The conflicts between seeming purpose found in nature, and the denial of purpose by hypothesis, disappear. Even Wilson seems to concur by referring to the "construction" rather than the "evolution" of the human mind. Jaki observes, "The deepest source of scientific knowledge of the universe is a most purposeful commitment to the tenet that the universe is the embodiment of design. One should therefore be on guard against taking too lightly the varied phenomena of the animal world which are strongly suggestive of a striving designed for purpose. Qualms about recognizing purpose will quickly lose their scientific coating if one considers that even man's conscious striving for purpose is a metaphysical reality which leaves intact the laws of physics and chemistry."

Problematic as it is within science, a dogmatic denial of God wreaks havoc without. With the spurious blessings of science, the Darwinist assaults the heart of Western tradition, morality, order and belief. At a practical level, the Darwinist denial of moral purpose can only glorify the principle: "Might makes Right." Liberty and the sanctity of life depend on our moral nature as creatures of God. Only moral restraint holds back the jungle and its law. This lesson has not been lost on Darwin's admirers, and the Darwinist roots of militarism, Bolshevism and Nazism in this century are explicit. Ernst Haeckel, a German biologist who expanded on Darwin's work (and whom Darwin praised), declared we must surrender to the "cruel and merciless struggle for existence which rages throughout all living nature" and to the fact that "only the picked minority of the qualified 'fittest' is in a position to resist the struggle successfully, while the great majority of the competition must necessarily perish miserably." Long before the Nazis came to power, natural selection had given way to planned selection—despite Huxley's warning that this could lead to the destruction of civilization. Haeckel himself prescribed the "arrest and destruction of the remaining majority," and assigned elite status to the Nordic race. Thus was Hitler given his blueprint. The logic of Darwinism is inherently totalitarian. No one need be surprised that its adherents to this day tend to be politically sympathetic with the totalitarian systems; or that this century has been "cruel and merciless." Power is victory in the amoral struggle for existence. The Darwinist comes easily to worship power and the State, its repository. The cruelty will not subside until human life is resanctified, and we treat each other as moral men.

The price we pay for tolerating "a celebration of incoherence" is barbarism. The final irony may yet be this: that scraping off the materialist excreta may yet restore the theory of evolution to innocence and vigor. If evolution proves, in the end, to be a success for genuine science, its very success will raise our eyes to the law and singularity of the universe that bespeak purposeful creation. If the universe reveals its order to us through rational science, it is because the universe is so ordered by the Author of reason.

Chapter XI
The Origins and Basis of Science

Nature is the art of God.
> —Sir Thomas Browne

In the great seas of being, all things preserve a mutual order and this it is that maketh the Universe like unto God.
> —Dante

We are not sufficiently astonished by the fact that any science may be possible.
> —de Broglie

Every time a scientist works in his laboratory, he assumes the reality of God though he denies God with his lips.
> —Rev. R.J. Rushdoony

Most people say it is the intellect which makes a great scientist. They are wrong: it is the character.
> —Einstein

"RAINBOW: see Atmospheric Optical Phenomena"
    —*Van Nostrand's Scientific Encyclopedia.*

There was an awful rainbow once in heaven:
We know her woof, her texture: she is given
In the dull catalogue of common things.
Philosophy will clip an angel's wings.

                                        —Keats

When Keats penned these lines in 1819, he somehow peered into the inner fears of our age. For us, seemingly, it is science that threatens to engulf the mysteries of our being, and add the souls of men, like so many pinned butterflies, to the conquests of its inexorable advance. Are we ourselves, along with the rainbow, to be reduced to the "dull catalogue of common things" by a science without limits? Or is there permanent sanctuary for the human spirit, golden meadows beyond all scientific reach where men may yet rightly glory in the rainbow?

This question is posed, not by science, but by anti-heroic philosophies of science. (Keats was right about that, too.) From our view it is a false dilemma: there is no conflict between science and the heroic dimension to life; quite the contrary. Nevertheless, the power of science is much to be feared—now, not in some distant future—unless it is the tool of moral men. In undermining morality, the anti-hero unheedingly attacks science, or worse, turns its awesome power to dark purpose. For all that we have benefited by advances in technology, industry and medicine, bills are coming due in the form of toxic waste, pollution, carcinogens and the like, not to mention thermonuclear weapons. The challenge set to us is establishing the rightful basis and role of science. Symbolically, the last battle for the West may be fought over all that a rainbow means to us. If so, let it begin here.

On the one side are the anti-heroic philosophies, from scientism to logical positivism to scientific materialism, all which elevate the methodology of science to an absolute. It is they that tell us the rainbow is a triviality, whose only meaning is complete in its scientific description—a physical phenomenon in a universe that admits only a physical explanation of reality. One way or another, they all declare that the only valid knowledge, nay, the only reality is that which can be determined by science. We have encountered such reductionism before. The anti-hero cannot claim omnipotence for the science of fallible, mortal men. So, instead, he defines all reality to fit his petty formula. This is a form of ideological warfare, and sophomoric. But insofar as he succeeds, he can jeer at larger visions of life as "superstitious" or "ignorant"—a tactic still standard after two centuries of overuse.

In the small, circumscribed world of scientism, there are by definition no limits to science. It is from this view that we inherit our fears of scientific engulfment. Over four centuries, science has become a nearly suprahuman force, too vast for any individual to understand, too uncannily successful to accept at our ease. With "unlimited" potential to penetrate and control the natural world, this force takes on the quasi-divine quality of omnipotence. It is as if we were creating a god with our human powers. Unfortunately, this new "god" is as likely to shower us with acid rain as with blessings; it does not have only our best interests at heart. More ominous, we, as "natural" creatures (according to this same philosophy), must in time fall under the control of this uncaring "being" that is evolving from the servant to the master of men. The anti-heroes today are increasingly alarmed at this prospect, forgetting that they themselves created this Frankenstein monster.

We, on the other side, can take amusement rather than alarm at this chicken coming home to roost. Science never has been and never will be unlimited. No definition will make it a god. Its methods cannot reach beyond the physical, the measurable and the quantifiable. Yet we know there is more to men—and to rainbows—than this.

Why *do* we take pleasure in seeing rainbows? Why do we go outside at the end of the storm to revel in their beauty? It is a fact, unaccounted by Darwinism, that we do, even though there is negative survival value in risking a bolt of lightning for this satisfaction. Wordsworth spoke more to our purpose in life than the whole of science ever will with these familiar words:

> My heart leaps up when I behold a rainbow in the sky;
> So was it when my life began;
> So is it now I am a man;
> So let it be when I shall grow old, or let me die!

This, to a mind unduly seeped in scientism, must seem rubbish. How can some alleged aesthetic experience have greater value than life; or more precisely, how can either have any value at all? Science admits of no values. It deals in mechanism, not purpose. The rest of us can agree that this is the nature of science, yet shake our heads in pity at the acute emotional poverty of this view. Shall we surrender beauty and purpose for the value-free procedures of the laboratory? If so, we must be consistent and, following Hume's advice, throw our poetry and drama and literature, our Homer and Virgil and Goethe and Moliere and Shakespeare into the fire.

Which view will we have? Which rings true to life? "A rainbow, described in the symbolism of physics," said Eddington, "is a band of aetherial vibrations arranged in systematic order of wave-length from about .000040 cm. to .000072 cm." Moreover, he warned (though siding with Wordsworth and the heroic view), to see it as anything else is "paltering with the truth." From this view, we should "attune our minds" to get the same pleasure from a table of wavelengths that we get from seeing a rainbow! Now, the better mathematicians assure us that equations are sometimes elegant, or aesthetically pleasing. This we may well believe; but not that this sense of elegance derives from mathematics, much less that anyone will go into raptures over a table of wave-lengths.

We can hardly expect more than "Atmospheric Optical Phenomena" in a scientific encyclopedia. I also checked a couple of unabridged dictionaries and another (standard) encyclopedia. All provided the routine scientific explanation of the refraction of water droplets, where we might have expected more. There was no hint in any of these sources at any qualities of the rainbow that can make the human heart leap. Nor was there any mention that Keats's "awful rainbow" was God's covenant to man (*Genesis* 9:12–15). Why not? Are we so sunk into scientism that we disdain the formative myth of Western civilization? I think it is, rather, that for all our vaunted science we can answer only the "how" question, never the primal "why." We never get an inch beyond saying that the rainbow is because it is a "property" of things that are. Why there is water, why droplets reflect light, why there is light, why the refraction forms a bow, why we discern the result as color, why "matter" has properties, why humankind both asks these questions and thrills at the sight of a rainbow: these are the imponderables for science. The wisdom of mankind, and the record of our inner feelings, is far older than science, and cannot be gainsaid by examining "hows." Again, we learn more from our historic teachings than from Atmospheric Phenomena:

> Look upon the rainbow, and praise him that made it;
> very beautiful it is in the brightness thereof.
> It compasseth the heaven about with a glorious circle,
> and the hands of the Most High have bended it.
> —(The Apocrypha, *Ecclesiasticus,* XLIII: 11–12)

The anti-heroic philosophies may deny this, but only by contradicting themselves. There will never be a laboratory test for God or what the Most High may do. These are matters that will never be known to science or to scientistic philosophies. But the human mind is not helpless at the failure of this supposedly "complete" form of knowledge. If we open, say, *Bartlett's Familiar Quotations* instead of *Van Nostrand,* we get a wholly different picture of life and purpose. Here are some twenty references to rainbows, most of them poetic, none of them "scientific."

Again, I ask which view is true to life? The poet says what the scientist may not:

> You may grind their souls in the selfsame mill,
> You may bind them heart and brow;
> But the poet will follow the rainbow still,
> And his brother will follow the plow.

How very unscientific! John Boyle O'Reilly clearly has not been advised by Darwinism that brothers with identical hereditary and environmental backgrounds will turn out alike. Whatever could warp the one into becoming a kamikaze poet bent on pursuing the useless aesthetics of atmospheric illusions? This sort of declaration mocks all the fashionable pseudo-science of the past century, and our only problem is that we all know it's true. The preacher's son may be a rotten apple, the hippie's son a capitalist. Never does the same pod produce identical peas. All sober people know this, especially those parents, like my wife and me, who have had the direct experience of raising several children to adulthood. Just let anybody try to tell me that children are wholly shaped by environmental influences and genetics!

Empirical science is supposed to be nothing more than learning from experience. There's nothing new, exclusive, encompassing or sacrosanct about that. We all learn from experience, and we can all, unlike science, learn from unreplicable experience—not least from raising a brood of one-of-a-kind children. The truth to tell, though, science is much more than the quantities and measurements of empiricism. But that part of science doesn't lend itself to the tidy formulas or pat philosophies of anti-heroism. When the great scientists cite the role of character, intuition, mathematical elegance and deductive intelligence in their work, they are crediting qualities that can neither be justified by the scientific method nor allowed by a physicalist interpretation of reality. Science itself, with a capital S if you wish, flunks the first test of scientism: it came into existence without any help from the scientific method that is supposed to validate all knowledge.

But then, science is not at all what it is represented to be in the anti-heroic philosophies. It is too small to be a god and too large for anti-heroes to grasp. Whether they like it or no, science cannot be contained on the sterile island that the anti-heroes define as existence. It was born in a grander vision, survives on nothing less, and pays back all with a dazzling affirmation of the words of the prophets. It has done so already; we have only to disentangle sloppy philosophy from real science. Ideas move slowly, but relentlessly. It may take fifty years or a hundred, but I tell you with certainty, even if I am not here to see it, in due course the world will look back on scientistic philosophies as quaint, ignorant superstitions.

Meanwhile, I'd like to recall Eddington's unsuspecting phrasing that the rainbow is wave-lengths "arranged" in "systematic order." An ordered universe, a certainty in the order of the cosmos, is the fundamental requisite of all science. Science emerged from this certainty, and cannot survive without it. If two plus two could equal five in some remote region, as Mill and Spencer have hypothesized, all scientific calculation loses its credibility. Whatever scientists may say philosophically, they always assume a perfect order to nature in their work. Whether they know it or not, this assumption has the nature of a prayer. If there is such a thing as natural law, there is a Lawgiver. This is a purely Western idea. The Eastern religions do not believe in a natural order or in a universe—and never developed science.

The West won the world because we know better. Yet, among ourselves, we quarrel over this: how can the rainbow be "arranged" in "systematic" order of wave-length by insensate, random "natural" forces? And how can this set of "vibrations," whatever its cause, excite scientifically inexcusable emotions in a peculiar, scientifically unexplainable animal that invented science? The answers, I think, will be reassuring as soon as we take the Lawgiver back into account. I have a modest question of my own in reply to all this.

To be sure, the world does not ride on this, but perhaps our lore and literature are to be believed. I'd like to know: does any animal see the rainbow *exactly* as we do, in its full and gentle and perfect gradation of color? Some animals have, of course, the apparent receptors of color vision, so we infer that they see in color. But have they a range identical to ours? Maybe their sight is heavy on blue or light on red. So, out of curiosity, I ask any scientist who may be reading this and knows, what other animal, if any, can see the rainbow just as we do?

It is more or less an innocent question. We knew, long before there was science, that only one creature takes delight in and writes poetry about rainbows. That is distinction enough. Yet if the rainbow colors are ours alone, our Western tradition may be wiser than we think. If, as Cuénot put it, "it is not daring to believe that the eye was constructed to see," it is no more daring to believe the rainbow was constructed for us to see.

On the Origins of Science

It is almost never observed what an immense advantage the historical approach confers on Western scholarship. To us nothing could be plainer than that we must see our subject in its full historical context to make sense of it. Imagine, for instance, trying to understand America without knowledge of and reference to her roots, the settlers, the Declaration of Independence and Constitution, her struggles, ideas, traditions and the formative events of her past. It cannot be done.

A view formed thus would be hopelessly superficial and could add nothing to useful knowledge.

Yet this approach is unique to the West. It was unknown or rejected in the ancient world, and is still rejected in other cultures. Greece, for example, had excellent and perceptive historians—insofar as they were recorders of events—but they scorned the question why history exists or what meaning it might convey. The pagan world, then and now, has always fixed its eyes on the ebb and flow of things, the cycles of all existence. It saw the cycle of life and growth, death and decay, and rebirth. It saw the stars wheel in the sky. It saw the fortunes of men and empires rise and fall as unfailingly as the unchanging change of the seasons. It is easy from this perspective, much too easy, to relate all existence to the ceaseless and eternal motion of the heavens, to the Great Year endlessly repeated where Socrates is condemned to take the hemlock at every turn through an infinite future. One steeped in this ancient vision would ask, why bother with "history"? What goes will come again. You learn nothing.

Appropriately, the radical departure from the pagan world is found at the beginning of the Bible: In the *beginning,* God created heaven and earth. With these words the eternal cycle was broken. Creation itself and all things have a beginning and an end with the meaning of absolutes. The importance of this idea cannot be overstressed. With it, history ceased to be an idle record and became the one-time story of humankind: "philosophy teaching by example," in Lord Bolingbroke's memorable phrase. And with it, as we shall see, science became possible for the first time. Yet this unintuitive idea had to be sheltered, nourished and brought to maturity by the power of the Gospel before it could be accepted in a world steeped in paganism. Jaki observes, "The writings of Origen and especially of Saint Augustine clearly show that it was belief in the Gospel truth of a once-and-for-all redemption in Christ that gave strength to the Christians to jettison the doctrine of the Great Year[,]" the doctrine which foretold only destruction for the world.

These seemingly roundabout thoughts should help us tackle a most obvious question and a mystery. The question is, how did science originate? Or to put it another way, why was science stillborn in every civilization of the ancient world? The mystery is that it is nearly impossible to get a straightforward, historical answer to this. Few questions of this importance have ever been so thoroughly evaded, overlooked, fudged or falsified. A long progression of historians of science, or more accurately, pseudo-philosophers posing as such, from Condorcet, Comte and Hegel to Mach and the logical positivists in this century, have tendered ludicrous answers. Science, they have said, originated by sheer luck, or was an intellectual "mutation," or was born in the ancient world, or was not because of bureaucracy or sexual repression. All of this is sheerest nonsense.

We are left with a glaring gap in our historical knowledge. We have little or no idea how it came to be that we live in the first scientific age of man. That we do is the foremost fact of our times. In the three centuries since reaching maturity in Newton, our science has utterly transformed the world. It has lifted men, especially in the West, from lives as mere beasts of burden to standards of living undreamt by ancient kings. It has enlarged our knowledge of nature beyond all measure, and improved our production of food and other necessaries enough to support an enormous increase in world population.

Science may today be reckoned the largest employer in the world. Yet, that is less than no answer. But if we cannot say how science originated, we cannot hope to understand it; no more than we could pretend to understand American politics without knowledge of the Constitution. Worse, if we do not understand science in its roots and development, we must certainly be uneasy about its future course.

Of course, nothing like this has ever happened before, and this too wants explanation. There have been many great, complex and mature civilizations before us. Men, then as now, had clear sight and intelligence. All had the beginnings of science, but these led nowhere. The simple fact is that never in the vast ancient empires of China, India or Egypt, not even in Greece and Rome, did science rise to a viable, self-sustaining enterprise. Some writers mistakenly place the birth of science in classical Greece, but cannot explain its failure to develop beyond an embryonic form. Only Greek geometry reached a scientific level, and that too dead-ended (it would be many centuries before geometry was advanced again, and never in the realms of the ancient world). This is surprising: certainly Greece boasted the inquiring spirit and familiarity with experimentation needed to nurture a viable science. Yet some critical factor was missing, and even there these promising scientific beginnings flickered and died out.

More than a thousand years were to pass before the flame of science was first successfully kindled. Those years encompass the history of Europe, from the dark days of the fall of Rome to the emergence of the first fully Christian culture in the Middle Ages. That is to say, a civilization emerged in Europe based, like no other before it, on Judeo-Christian dogmas and belief in the Christian Gospel. This view was sharply at odds with the eternal cycles and infinity of being in the pagan world. The Mediaevals believed the dogma of Creation in time. The Universe was limited, heaven and earth. It had a beginning and it would have an end. It was a thing, an artifact, a product chosen and given order by a perfect God. When Mediaeval universities taught the learning of the ancients, it was from this perspective. And so it was that the Mediaevals took issue with Aristotle, when his theories of eternal motion became known to them in the thirteenth century.

"In intellectual history, actual starting points are difficult to specify," Jaki notes. But "it is fairly easy to identify the first modern physicist. He was Jean Buridan, professor of philosophy at the Sorbonne around 1330." Alarm bells will go off for the anti-hero reading this. According to his formative myth, that honor should go to Galileo (or at least his teachers) almost three hundred years later. The myth insists, moreover, that generally and in Galileo's personal example, science took root only by defying the dogmatic superstitions of the Mediaeval Church. There *was* no science in the Middle Ages, says the myth. There couldn't be. Men's minds were locked in superstition.

It is so easy for non-historians to write off whole ages with scarcely more knowledge than a few catchwords and cliches! Yet if the Mediaeval scholars, as alleged, knew nothing of science, then we have a latter-day miracle of Immaculate Conception: science suddenly springing to life *ex nihilo,* without roots or development. And some scholars argue this: it was sheer good luck or the happy curiosity of the European mind, as opposed to the sluggish or bureaucratic thinking of all men before. And—zip! out of nowhere you have science with a capital S.

But early in this century, a French physicist and scholar named Pierre Duhem tackled this question with the historical approach that is the center of Western studies. Specifically, he sought the origin of the concept of virtual velocity, which underlies the science of dynamics. And he found it was older by far than Galileo or Galileo's teachers. But let Jaki, himself the consummate historian of science, tell the story:

> Duhem's was not an easy and straightforward search. He had no previous scholar to lead him. He had no printed material to rely on. He had to go through countless medieval manuscripts that nobody had touched for centuries. He had to teach himself medieval handwriting, or rather the many forms of medieval Latin stenography, which varied from area to area, from century to century. He had no secretaries, no research assistants, no eager graduate students, no interlibrary service, not even ballpoint pens. At every half-line he had to dip his pen into the inkwell, adjust the measure of ink taken up by the pen, shift the blotter, and resume writing. He had no photocopying machines, no dictaphones. He filled 120 notebooks, of two hundred pages each, with long excerpts from medieval manuscripts. He did all that with an often-trembling right hand which he had to steady with his left so that his handwriting might be decipherable not only by himself but also by the printer.

It was Duhem who traced what is essentially Newton's first law of motion back to Buridan—a formulation in defiance of Aristotle's eternal motion. When God created the world, said Buridan, He set the stars in motion "as He pleased, and in moving them He impressed in them impetuses which moved them without His having to move them any more...these impetuses were not decreased nor corrupted afterward, because there was no resistance [to them]." Newton, long afterwards, might have said this in fewer words, but not better. Buridan's disciple, Nicole Oresme, later the Bishop of Lisieux, defended and disseminated this principle of motion, until it was copied in countless students' notes and passed along to Galileo and Newton centuries later.

Startling to say, these matters were not known to historians until the first years of this century. Even now, the monumental scholarship of Pierre Duhem is systematically ignored, glossed over or denied by would-be philosophers still in the thrall of the anti-heroic myth. But the myth also had its beginnings, which can be traced. The myth came along much later when the French *philosophes* of the eighteenth century, so enraptured with themselves as to declare themselves "geniuses" and "Enlightened," tried to appropriate science for themselves and force all knowledge into scientific patterns. Their efforts produced the guillotine in their times and the totalitarian mind in ours. Their contempt for religion and its supposedly debilitating effect on Mediaeval thought is echoed even now by countless academic ignoramuses, not all of them undergraduates.

These enlightened ones, saints all in the anti-heroic pantheon, were not mistaken in seeing that science could strip away superstition—but they never imagined it would penetrate their own. In their pride, they believed that science had attained its final and perfect form, and that they grasped all its secrets. (Similarly, a century later, Max Planck, father of quantum mechanics, was told not to go into physics because there was nothing left to discover.) Such self-anointed seers of science seemed to follow the maxim of the James Garner character, *Nichols:* "If you want to know the truth, make it up." Make it up they did, wholesale, with hilarious rewards for the latter-day reader. Condorcet, for instance, expanding on empiricism as the ultimate knowledge, proposed an empirical system of justice such that miscarriages of justice should not exceed the risk of taking a mailboat from Calais to Dover in fair weather, or the chances of dying between ages 37 and 47 of a disease that lasts less than one week. Kant solemnly defended the Buddhist idea of an infinite, cyclical existence and declared the universe to be so much wishful thinking (it's safer to do that a century before Einstein). This is the scientific equivalent of flat earth theory, which survived in the loftiest realms of thought long after navigators stopped worrying about sailing off the edge of the world. Such thinking never freed itself from Euclidean geometry, where surfaces are perfectly and conveniently flat and straight lines go on to infinity: concepts useful in the abstract, but not for describing a finite, curved universe. Comte defended phrenology as the scientific equal of Newtonian cosmology, and decreed that astronomy should not be pursued beyond the range of the naked eye because there was no use looking for planets other than those his numerical tables had revealed. There are no end of these foolish predictions on record: fair warning, surely, that neither the science nor the Enlightenment of that era are to be swallowed without a beer chaser.

Our principal legacy from all this is the sheer fabrication that Christianity had to be vanquished before science could arise—"a lie of gigantic proportions," in Jaki's words. The strength of this lie has been such as to prevent us from finding the invention and development of science in the distinctively Christian milieu of the High Middle Ages. "The natural philosophers of Latin Christendom in the thirteenth and

fourteenth centuries created the experimental science characteristic of modern times," states science historian A.C.
Crombie. The Southern novelist Walker Percy adds, "So much
for the relationship between Christianity and science and that
fact that, as Whitehead pointed out, it is no coincidence that
science sprang, not from Ionian metaphysics, not from the
Brahmin–Buddhist–Taoist East, not from the Egyptian–
Mayan astrological South, but from the heart of the Christian
West; that although Galileo fell out with the Church, he would
hardly have taken so much trouble studying Jupiter or
dropping objects from towers if the reality and value and
order of things had not first been conferred by belief in the
Incarnation." Pierre Duhem's massive documentation of
these true origins of science has been deliberately downplayed
and attacked by anti-heroes who know the truth will collapse
their myths and their illicit claims to science. They may
succeed, for a short while, in obscuring history; but they
cannot hide from the advances of science itself.

It is, then, sweetly fitting that twentieth-century science
has vanquished the mechanical cosmology of the anti-hero
and restored a conception of an ordered universe that the
Mediaeval theologian would be comfortable with. To do so,
scientists have had to push aside bad philosophy as well as
obsolete scientific ideas. They had to ignore anti-heroic
formulas and methodological limitations. They had to clear
the last cobwebs of the pagan Great Year, of infinities and
eternal cycles. They had to make a magnificent effort of mind,
shaming the materialist's loopy claim that thought is an
illusion. I certainly do not pretend that science has reached its
height in our time. But after Einstein, it will never go back to
the eternal and supposedly "self-explaining" universe—in

truth a chaos, not a cosmos—so loved by the ancient world and by the modern anti-hero. Nor will it ever again perceive the universe as infinitely cyclical or "oscillating" as we put it now. Physics has proven there is not infinite energy available to sustain any cycle indefinitely. There is no infinity anywhere in the physical universe. One day it will die. With the utmost of its modern resources and the whole of its authority, science has recreated—creation.

According to mediaevalist E. Curtius, the most quoted phrase in the Bible at the time experimental science was being developed was not from the Gospel but from the Wisdom of Solomon: *Omnia in mensura, numero et pondere disposuisti:* "You have disposed everything in measure, number and weight" (*Book of Wisdom* 11:21). This perception, recorded about a century before Christ, is the cradle of scientific method. This was not, of course, understood as limiting God to any given system of numbers, but rather as making the mysteries of His creation accessible to experiment and reason. Empirical knowledge remains the heart of science, if not the soul. All scientific theories, no matter how intuitively arrived at, must eventually submit to empirical confirmation or be discarded. This however, is no comfort for the pure, Humean empiricist who will admit no datum to science save by the manipulation of quantities. None of the great leaps by science has ever been made by empirical methods alone. The scientist is a thinking creature, not an adding machine. Before there can be a science, there must be a metaphysical conception of reality that validates experimental findings. Science cannot be self-justifying. We cannot believe the truths it reveals unless they fit reality as it is. The whole point of seeking the historical origins of science is to trace the metaphysical view that first made science possible.

We now know that science arose in the historically unique culture of European Christendom. And we know it was at a time when a whole civilization first accepted the scriptural dogma of Creation, a true universe chosen by God and given order as a totality of consistently interacting phenomena. Said Professor Whittaker in a Riddell lecture, "It was never possible to oppose seriously the dogma of the Creation except by maintaining that the world has existed from all eternity in more or less its present state." As the pagan concepts died out, it was at last understood that nature was a created being whose mysteries could be fathomed. Man, cast in the image of a rational God, could by his gift of reason learn the secrets of the world. Under the order of a perfect Lawgiver, the workings of natural law could be sought and trusted.

This view and no other can both sustain Western science and ease fears of a scientific Armageddon. This we must truly understand. A science hacked from its roots will die. A science manipulated by men who deny a moral basis for life could doom us to hell on earth. The only safe passage into a better future is restoring the metaphysical foundations of science.

The Metaphysics of Science

"The modern world began on 29 May 1919 when photographs of a solar eclipse, taken on the island of Principe off West Africa and at Sobral in Brazil, confirmed the truth of a new theory of the universe." With these dramatic words, Paul Johnson began his *Modern Times,* perhaps the most richly factual account of recent history now in print. Johnson continued: "It had been apparent for half a century that the

Newtonian cosmology based upon the straight lines of Euclidean geometry and Galileo's notion of absolute time was in serious need of modification.... In particular, the motions of the planet Mercury deviated by forty-three seconds of arc a century from its predictable behaviour under Newtonian laws of physics. Why?"

That "why?" is the proverbial pregnant question, and we will try to answer it here. My own answer, off the top, is that Newtonian cosmology failed because it reflected a false concept of the universe. The concept that failed was not scientific but metaphysical. Newton, a Christian, and for all his genius, did not suspect the limitations of plane geometry, and defended the infinite universe. Nor could he anticipate the later anti-heroic notion that the infinite universe is "self-explaining." The "infinity catastrophe" had already been formulated in his time: If the universe has an infinite amount of homogenously distributed matter, the gravitational attraction at any point is either zero or infinite—either possibility precludes life as we know it. Newton dismissed this, but we can hardly expect him to have anticipated more than two more centuries of scientific development. Even into our century, Lord Kelvin was defending the idea that space is infinite, and that the amount of matter beyond our Milky Way was inconsequential. In these views, held by great scientists, was recreated the pagan Great Year, of course unwittingly—the self-explaining infinite universe, the creation that needs no Creator. Such ideas are a feast for the anti-heroes who will have no God. It took a stupendous scientific effort to break free and move beyond them. That was what was being tested at Principe and Sobral in 1919. An entire world view was on trial.

Were science nothing more than number crunching, as the empiricist would have it, no such test could arise. Science already had the numbers. It was the scientific metaphysic that was wrong. Unless we have the right metaphysical view of the universe, even our measurements are wrong! So it was that in the fateful experiments, the Newtonian cosmology gave way to Einstein's relativity, or "invariance" principle as he preferred to call it. The new way of looking at the universe, proven by observation, was the old Western way: that vision of creation that had ignited the flame of science.

Cliches notwithstanding, seeing is not believing. We are all familiar with optical illusions, and perhaps other ways our senses can be fooled. A perfectly dry balloon, filled with ice, would feel "wet" to us. Science, in a sense, is the art of cutting through such illusions. It deals wholly with data from our senses, often magnified immensely by instruments like telescopes and electron microscopes. With such tools, we learn that our touch or hearing or sight may not be reliable. Ergo, we need a reliable tool, science, to correct our senses. Thus do we come to trust science to reveal the truth of the material world.

But why are we confident that scientific findings give us an accurate picture of physical reality? Here we come back to metaphysics, and there will be no answer within science itself. This, again, is our pregnant "why." The truth is, believing is seeing—if our metaphysical belief is correct to begin with. We could not identify an apple if we did not first believe in apples. As we have seen, false world views led to stillborn science in all the ancient world, and to measurably false science in the "Enlightened West." In the end, everything depends on what we believe, on our metaphysical view, and only if we are right can we place any trust in science. The great trailblazers of science have all kept in sight a singular conception of the cosmos. As Jaki notes, the plain fact is that "from Oresme through Copernicus, Galileo, Newton, Euler, Faraday and Maxwell, to Planck, Einstein and even beyond, all great creators of science found most useful, nay indispensable, for their scientific creativity, the belief that the universe is fully ordered." "It would have been enough," he adds, "to speak of one belief, the belief in a personal rational Creator. It was this belief, as cultivated especially within a Christian matrix, which supported the view for which the world was an objective and orderly entity investigatable by the mind because the mind too was an orderly and objective product of the same rational, that is, perfectly consistent, Creator."

In his Gifford Lectures in 1927, Sir Arthur Eddington, astronomer and disciple of Einsteinian physics, calmly worked his way through physical or exact science, to reach this question: "Granted that physical science has limited its scope so as to leave a background which we are at liberty, or even invited, to fill with a reality of spiritual import, we have yet to face the most difficult criticism from science. 'Here,' says science, 'I have left a domain in which I shall not interfere. I grant that you have some kind of avenue to it through the self-knowledge of consciousness, so that it is not necessarily a domain of pure gnosticism. But how are you going to deal with this domain? Have you any system of inference from mystic experience comparable to the system by which science develops a knowledge of the outside world? I do not insist on your employing my method, which I acknowledge is inapplicable; but you ought to have some defensible method. The alleged basis of experience may possibly be valid; but have I any reason to regard the religious interpretation currently given to it as anything more than muddle-headed romancing?"

An interesting question, indeed; the more so in that even Eddington mistakes the view of scientism for that of science. There is nothing in science itself that questions the quality of knowledge in other fields. It is, rather, the anti-heroic philosophies that allow no knowledge other than that developed by the scientific method. But science itself was devised from a body of "unscientific" knowledge by theologians. Obviously if the anti-hero is to be consistent, he will have to throw out scientific knowledge as unscientific! But all this begs the previous question: What justifies science? It did not emerge from itself, so if science is held to have value, we must equally assign real value to the other sources of knowledge from which it originated. All the familiar tools of the mind may be cited: reason, careful observation, historical and linguistic analysis, intuition, introspection, empirical investigation, imagination, and plain, scholarly discipline. It may be argued that superior scientific knowledge is validated by method: if the result of a given experiment can be repeated in carefully controlled conditions, it can be taken as true; whereas, say, an historian's thesis is always open to some question. This we may concede, but it takes us no closer to an answer. A replicable result may be a fluke or sheer luck. It cannot be adjudged true without a metaphysical assumption, prior belief, about the nature of reality (and of truth). If we do not live in an ordered universe, the experimental method is itself nothing more than muddle-headed romancing. The scientistic philosophies are engaged in logical theft. They smuggle the whole Christian concept of nature into their claim that science is valid; then they brazenly cite the success of science to disavow all metaphysics!

This flim-flam has grave consequences. Richard Weaver observes,

> Science exists in the form of a set of methods.... What is not so well understood...is the effect of this practical success upon the more general theory of reality and knowledge. Until rather recently it was held that subject matter is prior to method. But in the last few decades, this position has been reversed, and it is now being said, or assumed, that nothing which cannot be found by the scientific method is real, which is, of course, the position of modern positivism.... Here is a complete victory for instrumentalism whereby, in effect, a methodology makes reality as it proceeds with the act of discovery. The effect of this on man's attitude toward the world can be nothing less than revolutionary.... For what it does is rule out the given, the contingent, the inscrutable—in sum, all that is greater than or independent of man. The grounds for that humility which all the great ethical systems have inculcated is thereby withdrawn. Man, with his Method, leaps into the seat of the Creator, which, in the wisdom of poetry and religion, is the ultimate act of pride.

Here, precisely, is the source of anti-heroic infection of our era, and the fever has spread far beyond science. For one instance:

> There, as every observer of the movement knows, subject matter, representing the antecedently real, has been virtually retired in favor of methodology. The teacher is not a man who knows facts and ideas but a man trained in method. It is assumed that there is nothing which the method cannot do. When stubborn facts of the given world—such as inequalities of aptitude or the human tendency toward delinquency—stand in the way of the triumph of the method, they are either ignored or misleadingly reported. For these educational positivists

there is no nature of man, but only some pliable stuff which can be kneaded into any desired shape by the principles of a materialist psychology.

This we have all seen, and it is important for us to grasp how a perversion of scientific philosophy, seemingly so rarefied and distant, comes back to haunt even our neighborhood schools and cheat our children out of their education.

If the logical positivists go to one extreme, Marxists go to the other. The positivist declares that what is not scientific *(Erkenntnis)* is mere subjective experience *(Erlebnis)* which cannot be raised to the level of knowledge—and which, interestingly enough, includes the writings of the positivists. The Marxist, believing that dialectical materialism is the key to science, declares that everything, including mankind, is to be scientific. In reflection of the long-obsolete mechanistic view of science, the Marxist holds to determinism. We are, he maintains, fully shaped by physical forces, history and especially economic factors. This is fatuous—the Marxist is an active participant in "the struggle" by choice—but it is doggedly maintained as official doctrine in the Soviet Union and its satellites. Revealingly, however, Soviet scientists are largely exempt from Marxist dogmas, for the simple reason that science requires freedom of thought. To follow their results and ideas, they have to deny determinist premises. Otherwise they could not do their job, which is largely the vicious business of developing the arms with which the Soviet state terrorizes the world.

It is somewhat ironic that determinism remains the ruling view in this country in all the so-called behavioral sciences. I have argued elsewhere there can be no true science of man because the "subject matter," human beings, have the capacity to change any result by choice. The vaunted scientific method cannot work, and does not. Nevertheless, the pseudo-scientist proceeds on the assumption that men are automata, determined by heredity and environment. The amount of idiocy that flows from this assumption is beyond all measure. Every doctrine that denies personal choice and responsibility, all the fashionable poobah that "society is to blame" or "crime is caused by poverty and bad neighborhoods" and the like, is from this source. It appears we will be a long time getting rid of the blunders of nineteenth-century science.

The matter may be simply put: a false metaphysic produces false science. If science is to have any future, and if its future is to be benign, there is no choice but to preserve and guard its true metaphysical foundations. This is a task, not for scientists themselves, but for philosophers, scholars, and all intelligent laymen who recognize the immense promise science holds for a moral world. Etienne Gilson observes that "the question posed about the possibility of science in general is not susceptible of a scientific answer because this implies the existence of science for its own justification." A defense of science, then, must come from without, and it lies in the Judeo-Christian conception of an orderly ration. Jaki, a doctor of physics and theology, writes, "The answer, which is God, will greatly strengthen the scientist's trust in the existence of an objectively existing, rationally ordered universe which can be investigated by the human mind, a pursuit which is man's exclusive privilege and responsibility. This trust, privilege and responsibility constitute the backbone of the scientific enterprise."

"Discovery," he adds, "is the soul of science. That scientific discoveries are the fruit of the painstaking self-exertion of geniuses is also worth emphasizing in an age in which approval is given to claims that the mind is merely a concept and that philosophy is but talk about talk." The rightful metaphysical basis for science must have room for the mind of man: "Actually, every act of research is a defiance of restraints, and this is what makes men's freedom a nightmare for those who make it a scientific claim that the universe is sheer mechanism, be it physical, biological or psychological. Revealingly enough, during the age of classical physics no physicist of any consequence supported the view that the laws of physics, which were then taken to be strictly deterministic, had discredited the freedom of the will." Said Einstein, "Belief in an external world independent of the perceiving subject is the basis of all natural science." The world is *not* relative to the observer. It is there, given an order by God that is revealed to science as natural law. The independence of the world is assured by the fact that the laws of physics work whether we believe in them or not. The independence of man is assured by the fact that we can, at will, introduce "events" into the workings of nature, and make her do our bidding. All of civilization, from the first stone ax to the Cray computer, is, precisely, unnatural creation by the mind and will of man.

Science emerged from, depends on, and today gives us back the world of Christian conception. The scientist may, at times, become so engrossed by his system that he forgets its limitations and loses sight of cosmology: the nature and innate logic of a cosmos that makes science possible. But, in the end, all science *is* cosmology, and we must come home to it. Scientist or layman, we may all muse with physicist Loren Eiseley: "if 'dead' matter has reared up this curious landscape of fiddling crickets, song sparrows and wondering men, it must be plain even to the most devoted materialist that the matter of which he speaks contains amazing, if not dreadful, powers, and may not impossibly be, as Hardy has suggested, 'but one mask of the many worn by the Great Face behind.' "

Chapter XII
The Rightful Role of Science

The whole movement of scientific philosophy is a crusade.
—Hans Reichenbach

While you and i have lips and voice which
are for kissing and to sing with
who cares if some one eyed son of a bitch
invents an instrument to measure Spring with?
—e e cummings

Many have dreamed of a brave new world built on purely "scientific" principles. At last, they say, men could escape chaos and manage their affairs with rational, objective standards. All conflict and deprivation would disappear. All of us would be made healthy in mind and body, and function as smoothly as so many quartz clocks. All of our needs would be met and our goals fulfilled—nothing easier! "Basically man seeks freedom from hunger and want, adequate warmth and protection, and freedom from disease," surely attainable ends,

317

in the view of Alexander Robertus Todd of Cambridge, a Nobel laureate in chemistry.

One *does* hope we will also get fresh straw in our stalls each day. A genuinely scientific society might be conceived on the principles of animal husbandry; but not one that could be peopled by men. There could be no scientists in it—and no dreamers. It could have no art or music or literature, no honor or courage, no manners, no morality, no faith and no hope. It would be as flat and tasteless as a piece of cardboard. All it could look forward to is inescapable doom. The three laws of thermodynamics, it is said, may be read to mean, first, that we can't win; second, that we can't break even; and third, that we can't get out of the game. It is hard to conjure a more hellish vision. That such thoughts could be entertained at all, much less held up as an ideal, involves not only grave misconceptions about the nature and limits of science but a campaign of philosophical deceit.

In seeking its rightful role, we cannot overemphasize that science is a limited tool, serving limited human purposes. After all, all tools, including science, have specific, circumscribed uses. We would not use a can opener to dig fossils any more than we would use carbon-14 dating to heat soup. It is simple sense that the specialized methods of science, so effective in their intended areas of study, are useless for other, equally important human concerns. We do not weigh a prayer, or measure the warmth of a smile with a thermometer, or consult color charts to declare the dawn rosy-fingered. Our task, then, is to fit the tool, science, to the hand and purpose of its user—man.

There is a rightful and indispensable role for science. If we yield to unwarranted fear; if we do not claim science on its proper basis, we risk losing its immense potentials when we need them the most. Indeed, we risk the very survival of a free, moral order. The civilizing Western vision has spread throughout the world on the strength of our scientific superiority. It has many enemies, whose hordes would pick the bones of the West should their own, war-directed "science" prevail. But while there is peril before us, there is even greater opportunity; to undermine, and finally rid ourselves of, the re-barbarized totalitarianism that plagues our times. The key to this is a free and vigorous science within the larger contexts of a just community and our enduring concern for the moral well-being of all mankind. Science, so understood, can be a force without equal for liberating the oppressed and lifting the downtrodden. Truth can no longer be repelled by guarded borders.

"Science may spark a moral awakening here in this very pragmatic part of the world," Jaki foresees.

> Science may inspire greater rationality in lands where blind will is worshipped. Science may extort more and more freedom from institutionalized oppression. Science may, for the sheer necessity of survival, secure greater respect for thousands of millions of individuals who have been treated in recent decades like so many ants. Science may banish witchcraft from its last strongholds. Science, provided it is not abused, may provide hope for a better future, which will see history coming down not on this side or that side but on all sides—on the side of mankind as a whole.

Mischievous Make-Believe Metaphysics

George Bernard Shaw, sadly surveying the desolation of the Great War, placed the blame for it on the flood tide of anti-heroism. His description is remarkably concise:

> In the middle of the XIX century naturalists and physicists
> assured the world, in the name of Science, that salvation and
> damnation are all nonsense, and that predestination is the
> central truth of religion, inasmuch as human beings are
> produced by their environment, their sins and good deeds being
> only a series of chemical and mechanical reactions over which
> they have no control. Such figments as mind, choice, purpose,
> conscience, will, and so forth, are, they taught, mere illusions,
> produced because they are useful in the continual struggle of the
> human machine to maintain its environment in a favorable
> condition, a process incidentally involving the ruthless destruc-
> tion or subjugation of its competitors for the supply...of
> subsistence available.

Shaw had particular reference to Darwin in terming this an
"English" affliction, but the ideas of mechanistic physics were
equally contributory. Interestingly, those ideas were permanently banished almost at the moment Shaw wrote in 1919,
when Einstein's General Relativity was tested. Yet the
infection spread fueled not by science, in truth, widening
despite science. Its role in the even more "ruthless destruction" of the Second World War was more obvious than in the
First. This, as we have noted, is amply documented, but it
takes no great insight to trace such concepts as *Lebensraum*
(room to live), or the "master race," or the "ruling class" to the
anti-heroic view Shaw related. It is with us still as we near the
end of the century.

There is no doubting the horrors that can be committed
"in the name of Science." Yet there has never been a threat
from science per se. It is but a tool, and we do not seriously
blame the hammer for hitting our thumb. It is, moreover,
amoral by nature (as we shall discuss below), unable to judge
the rightness or wrongness of its own doings. Therefore we
can only adjudge the good or evil of those who use it.

Our problem is false and obsolete philosophies of science. These we have touched on more than once, and need not examine here at any length. The obvious answer, after we see through the fallacies of the old systems, must be to formulate, in outline, a realistic scientific philosophy. It must fully account the limits as well as the potential of science. It must hold true over time: discarding old baggage, seeking the true meaning of current findings, and always allowing for future advances. It must avoid the twin errors of making present knowledge or present method the final word in science—either error holds the truth hostage to future discovery. Only by anchoring the basis of science in a transcendent reality can we reach beyond the narrow materialist schemes of the last century and give science its true bearings in a world of space and time. The rightful basis of science, as we have seen, lies in unrestricted consistency, in a cosmos revealing its design by its regularity and its susceptibility to rational scientific exploration. In the ordered and contingent cosmology of Einstein, man has for the first time transcended the universe by forming a scientifically valid concept of it. Science itself thus, by unimpeachable methods, bears witness to the vision that birthed it, and which animates the West. The "clockwork universe" is gone for good, and with it must go all the disfiguring concepts of men as meaningless apes, or worse, mindless automata, shaped by deterministic forces. Deliciously fitting it is that the mind and will of men, in their finest scientific achievement, threw off their anti-heroic fetters and renewed our birthright of dignity and purpose to human life.

Poor Dr. Einstein. With immense force of mind, he overthrew the old notions of an infinite cosmos derived from plane geometry. Galileo's concept of absolute time had to go. Newton's inverse-square law had to go. Even our conceptions of "matter" had to go. Reality took shape from the position of the viewer. The cosmos is finite, shaped and curved by the gravitational interaction of its substance. For this fantastic feat of intelligence, Einstein's work was greeted with a chorus of chirps from the intellectuals, fairly described by a critic as "a herd of independent minds": "everything is relative." As much as fifteen minutes later, the chirps were saying there are no absolutes and proclaiming the end of those silly superstitions, right and wrong.

The obvious conclusion was that tiresome Christian morality had been vanquished, and that we could make love *or* war as we pleased, without incurring divine wrath. People did a lot of both. But the conclusion had been drawn from cheap philosophy, not from science (which cannot address moral questions). Behaviorism and pragmatism were by then already well advanced, and simply seized on "everything is relative" for propaganda. It was painful to Einstein, who deemed moral relativism a disease and hated having it attributed to his theories. The mistake was unscientific as well. General Relativity was the most absolutist cosmology ever offered in science, and Einstein wanted to call it "Invariance." "It is a common mistake," Eddington remarked at the time, "to suppose that Einstein's theory of relativity asserts that everything is relative. Actually it says, 'There are absolute things in the world, but you must look deeply for them.'" "The only message befitting Einstein...," Jaki adds, "would have been a warning that the absolute is lurking everywhere beneath the relative." The famous formula, $E = mc^2$ is one absolute in the theory (that of energy for mass at rest), and even undergraduate minds have noted that the statement, "everything is relative," is itself an absolute.

Our illusory release from moral law was no blessing. Men allegedly freed from absolute Good and Evil are not made free thereby, but unmade as men. It is no coincidence that literature and art turned black and bitter and jaded in those times, and that Mussolini, Hitler and Stalin rose to power. What is moral relativism but an excuse for evil? Sixty-odd years later, atrocities and terrorism are still so excused.

Einstein was not the only scientific genius victimized by anti-heroic philosophers. About the same time, Planck's quantum theory was likewise claimed for make-believe metaphysics: as a denial of causality. This is akin to declaring that we live in a chaos, not a universe. At rarefied levels, some have indeed questioned whether science any longer need retain the concept of a universe. To those less obsessed, the contradiction should be plain. Without causality, without ordered process in nature, science itself becomes impossible. A "science" that "discovers" its own futility cannot be believed. The creativity of great scientists has always been in proportion to belief in causality and physical law in nature. Planck himself firmly held this view, and shared with Einstein the belief in an ordered external world independent of the observer. Suffice to observe that the one view can only undermine science, while the other has proven its great fruitfulness.

An older and far more troublesome problem was, in effect, introduced by Newton's success. With its mathematical regularity, Newton's universe could be, and soon was, conceived as a machine. This view was so firmly fixed by the early 1800s that developments in exact science were hardly to be considered unless engineers could actually model them in working machinery. (Not until Einstein did we learn that the parts would have to be elastic.) The oneness of the cosmos was established, but at a fearful price. What was its substance, mind or matter? Hegel and the idealists opted for pantheism and in effect pronounced all to be mind. Scientists and philosophers of science almost unanimously chose materialism, saying all was matter, hence subject only to physical interpretation.

A want of rigor is seldom the shortcoming of either scientists or philosophers. The consequences of a materialist cosmos were worked out in full. All natural process was fully determined by physical law. Man, as a product of nature, was equally the result of deterministic forces. " ... mind, choice, purpose conscience, will, and so forth," as Shaw put it, were illusions, "figments." Deterministic philosophies were elaborated by Hegel and Marx, among others, seeing individual men as meaningless and helpless reeds bent by the grandiose forces of history and economics, wherein alone meaning resided. Darwin's theories of evolution seemed to glue it all together: the mechanisms of control and change had been found in nature herself. This was heady stuff, and anti-heroes lapped it up. Man had been freed of moral compunction, and nothing now lay before his march to conquer the stars. All virtue resided in power. The script for the appalling bloodletting in our century was here written.

Determinism, as a working scientific assumption for inorganic process, is one thing. Thinking that determinism disproves thinking is another. The contradiction is so glaring that only a mind obsessed with the "truth" of science can gloss it over. It doesn't help. A mind so enthralled is still thinking.

Science can learn nothing except by processes of mind; facts do not explain themselves. Neither can science reveal any knowledge except to human thought: facts, nature, matter, force, and so on are themselves *ideas.* They exist nowhere except in mind. They cannot be weighed, measured, or discerned by any scientific means. We think, and know we think, by self-knowledge: our only direct access to reality, and one both prior and necessary to the inferential knowledge of external reality developed by science. Mind, in a word, is the ultimate embarrassment to scientific materialism. (If the anti-heroes persist in declaring themselves mindless, we can't complain too much.)

The dilemma is this. Suppose determinism is true. All "events" in nature are determined by previous causes, through "the seamless web of causality," back to the original cause—presumably Big Bang. Evolution implies involution; everything in the present was *involved,* inherent in that primal mass of neutrons (or whatever it was). This, Shaw perceived rightly, is "predestination," and with a vengeance. Having rejected God as First Cause, we must reintroduce all the divine attributes of creativity to primal nature. Our evolutionary rise, our cities, our minds, our un-Darwinian aesthetic and spiritual senses, those "mythopoeic requirements" cited by Wilson, must all have been determined by some original unfathomable dance of the atoms. This was too much for Freud, a resolute atheist, who clung to scientifically discredited Lamarckism (inheritance of acquired features), lest evolution reveal inherent divinity (as du Noüy later insisted it did). If nothing is acquired, everything is involved: including mind.

Suppose further that we apply the methods of exact science to the human brain. We will find the atoms acting in the determined way. We will not find mind. Thought is simply inaccessible to metrics. The dilemma deepens. Either this aggregate of normal atoms is or is not a thinking machine. If it is not, then we have collapsed all science, and can no longer draw on its findings to construct fanciful materialist philosophies. If it is, we have (or had, before Einstein) a tremendous mystery to explain. This collection of atoms is disobeying physical law. It is itself acting as a cause and creating new events in nature—a power we take for granted and use all our lives, but which, to mechanistic science, can only be supernatural. As Eddington put it, "Either the physicist must leave his causal scheme at the mercy of supernatural interference from me, or he must explain away my supernatural qualities." Naturally, the anti-heroic philosophers chose the latter—by dismissing mind, including their own, as a physical "epiphenomenon." This is less a *reductio ad absurdum* than a frantic disavowal of the Christian foundations of the West.

Such was the appeal of this rebellion and the prestige of classical mechanics that seemingly every academic discipline developed a case of physics envy. Studies of man, politics, society, even literature fell over their own feet declaring themselves to be sciences, as exact as physics, with unflinching fidelity to its deterministic assumptions and methods. And here the mischief began in earnest. To treat man as a scientific subject, he must be reduced to measurements, to quantities, with no qualitative aspects whatsoever, including mind. The behavioral "scientist" must form and vigorously defend, against even his own findings, a view of man as a determined lump of matter: the familiar and false view of anti-heroism. This delusion to this day saturates the pseudo-sciences and sets the compass for their efforts. Here is a more recent statement of it, notable for the rigor of its self-abnegation, and the determination of the "social scientist" to march in lockstep with physics over the cliff:

> Determinism is the fundamental tenet of all science. Indeed, it is inconceivable that we could explain or count on anything in—the physical world without relying on the basic assumption that all phenomena are strictly determined....
>
> Dynamic psychology is a science of human thinking and human behavior and as a science [note the planted axiom] must be deterministic. The phenomena of human thought, feeling, and behavior,...must be understandable and explainable in terms of...causal factors.... In such a deterministic science of human behavior there is no place for the fortuitous, or for 'free will' in the sense used in philosophy.... a free will, or a freedom of choice, can be shown [willingly?], on closer inspection and analysis, to be based on unconscious determinism.

And now over the cliff: "Psychotherapy, far from requiring freedom to choose in order to influence patients treated, *itself operates deterministically* to achieve for the patient this *subjective* sense of freedom" (emphasis added) (from "Determinism, 'Freedom,' and Psychotherapy," by Robert P. Knight, *Psychiatry*, August, 1946). This is about as far as you can go with axiomatic determinism. The reader may wish to ponder on his own how Mr. Knight got the subjective sense that he, and not the atoms, had written the article; how a science itself fully determined can have the faintest idea whether it is doing its patients any good (and what is good?); and like questions raised in abundance here. We merely wish to note the stark dogmatism and unscientific posture. What concerns us is the reductionist conception of human life so determinedly decreed. It is surely a wonder that men can see themselves as so many lumps or interchangeable units, in order to call themselves scientists. But it is no surprise such, uh, thinking has escaped the asylum, doing much harm.

Here all the superstitions of anti-heroism foregather, and refuse to be gainsaid by humane letters, history, religious belief, intuition, the words of the wise, introspection, self-knowledge or logical contradiction. All of that is malarkey. All that matters is that "science" has advised us that we are automata, and modern men believe in nothing but science. If there's one little fly in the ointment, it is that "science" has never said anything of the sort. What we have here is a misinformed notion about science, an error compounded when that science became obsolete. That scientific methods are inapplicable to men, and that real science has moved on to non-mechanistic conceptions, is lost on dogged imitators of century-old physics. The behaviorists are well funded, and for decades have churned out truckloads of findings and theories about man which faithfully reflect their deterministic prem-ises. Garbage in, garbage out. Worse, it all comes out in that hideous, bloviated language that bespeaks the incoherence of the underlying thought even as it befouls English. As the flood washes over us, America is turned into a giant experiment for social engineering, on behaviorist principles. Much of the substance of modern liberalism is erected on these very notions of man as the helpless product of genetic, psycho-logical or environmental "forces." Concurrently, the role of responsibility, diligence, character, moral agency, or indeed, any of the qualities of whole and purposeful human life, is denied. "Freedom" is put into quotation marks and written off as a "subjective sense": small wonder liberalism is so blind to totalitarianism and so slow to defend liberty.

This onslaught inverts traditional values and undermines social harmony. Criminals, oddballs, malingerers and
perverts are coddled because they "came from a bad environment." And, of course, the rest of us get taxed to death to pay
for it. The politics is familiar, but what we do not see, and
should, is that the troubles start with misconceptions about
science, and gross misapplication of its methods. A curb to
such abuse must begin with understanding the limits and true
function of science.

A related error bears mention. Seeking order and
arrangement in nature, by hypothesizing such entities as
atoms, is a legitimate and fruitful part of metrical or exact
science. Atoms are good little units, in truth universals, each of
its kind alike and well behaved. Science has to sort and
categorize with such conceptual entities; it cannot deal with
any unique thing or event. The "sciences" of man likewise are
barred from study of the unique. They can only deal with
men—unique individuals all, and that is a scientific certainty—in groups; hence in broad and not-very-useful generalities. The behaviorist is necessarily dealing with conceptual
fictions such as Race, Class and Groups he can devise ("lower-
middle-class white blue-collar urban dropouts"). Such "group-
think" swiftly loses sight of human reality: an error common
to all collectivist schemes. We all recognize one obnoxious
example of it in racism. Too often we bridle at the barbs
without seeing the underlying mistake: that the concept of
"race" is a fiction, or at least so vague as to be almost useless.
The truth is that no two people of any race, class, or other
category are alike. We are not full-time members of categories. We are unique human beings. To no one can we

automatically attribute the imaginary characteristics of equally imaginary aggregates.

Such group-think, the staple fare in all the dubious sciences of man, may well be the leading manufacturer and merchandiser of modern superstition. It dispenses with human beings in favor of purely fictitious interchangeable units, then replaces truth with group statistics (plus or minus *n* percent error). If physics allowed such error we wouldn't have physics, and for that matter if banks did, we wouldn't have banking. "Under the influence of scientific assumptions," says Jung, "not only the psyche but the individual man and, indeed, all individual events whatsoever suffer a leveling down and a process of blurring that distorts the picture of reality into a conceptual average." Therefore, "one of the chief factors responsible for psychological mass-mindedness is scientific rationalism, which robs the individual of his foundations and his dignity." The person is reduced to a "social unit," "a mere abstract number in the bureau of statistics." Rooted here is the modern malaise, the sense of being lost, adrift, purposeless. In this conceptual fog, the value of the individual and of life itself is lost. It is a very short step beyond to the demagogic creation of hated "classes" or "races" and to genocidal slaughter.

Scientific Limitations

A phenomenon termed "humor" is observed among species *homo sapiens*. This phenomenon appears unrelated to mating rituals or survival mechanisms, but clearly is a causative factor to a wide array of unexplained behavioral responses. Specimens aurally or visually affected by "humor" are seen to contort facial muscles or emit an astonishing range of hoots, wheezes, groans, snorts, cackles, grunts, howls or other raucous noises. At times they shake silently, or slap their thighs, or fall down and roll round. Here, obviously is a matter for science to investigate—or is it? Can science take a joke? We shall see.

To appreciate all that science can do, we must understand what it cannot. One thing it cannot do is laugh. But scientists can! The homely world of man has always been wider by far than the broad vistas of science. This sort of thing is lost on those sober-sided *philosophes* and determinists who toil ceaselessly to make the world fit their formulas. George Will reminds us, "The occupational hazard of political movements is terminal earnestness." But we can amuse ourselves with the proposition that science, properly outfitted, can do anything, and will now explore "humor" (and no doubt "explain" it out of existence).

We will need a new science of humor which, at Eddington's suggestion, and with proper classical reference, we may call Geloeology. Of course geloeologists must be found who are themselves devoid of all humor, lest a stray chuckle distort their conclusions. This should not be difficult. One of many candidates who come to mind is the scientist who some while ago "explained" kissing as a craving for salt (perhaps he didn't investigate quite enough at the passion pits). We shall further provide our department of geloeology with a bank of computers and a very large grant.

After years of exhaustive observation and sober, critical analysis, the geloeologists plot and computerize all the characteristics of a "joke" (as unlikely a proposition as any that one could think of, but let it pass). Aiding and correcting this process is the peer review of countless studies and papers published in scholarly quarterlies. At last we come to the test: does the science of geloeology have predictive value? *Is* it a science? An alleged joke is found: Henny Youngman says, "Take my wife—please!" The geloeologists consult their tables and feed the line into the computer. Tapes spin, lights blink, mechanisms hum, and the scientists rush forward to read the computer printout....

...Sorry! I don't know what the computer answered. All I know is that it was wrong. If the printout said, "No, this is not a joke," we'd laugh—at the scientists. If it said, "Yes, this is a joke," nobody would laugh. The time we laugh at a joke is when we first hear it, not later, and especially not when it has to be explained. So whatever the computer spins out is bound to be pretty funny—but not as funny as the whole idea of scientific joke testing. We have an easier test. We laugh when we hear a good one.

There are, I'm sorry to say, weightier matters lurking behind this yarn. The principal test of a scientific finding is that it must be replicable in controlled conditions. This is the "scientific method" itself. Do thus and so, under identical conditions, and you get exactly the same result, any time, anywhere. Exactly to the extent that we believe the universe is ordered, we become confident that this method yields valid knowledge. Western belief gives enormous confidence that this procedure will always work when it is applied to suitable subjects—that is, when it is used by exact sciences to investigate inorganic material or forces. Just as obviously it will not work with all materials or in all situations. It won't work with a joke because humor isn't "replicable": a joke loses its punch on the second and third hearings. Our business then is to draw the line at where the method can and cannot be used. But right away we find a permanent limitation on scientific reach: the whole class of things transient, unique, or otherwise unreplicable in the laboratory is, even in theory, beyond science, or at least beyond the exact methods worthy of the name.

Scientistic philosophy denies that anything is theoretically beyond science; otherwise its pretensions collapse. It does this by simply dismissing as trivial or even unreal that same class of scientifically intractable material—precisely because it *is* beyond scientific methods. For instance, logical positivism, perhaps the most important branch of recent voodoo, scorns as "subjective experience" anything unsuitable for the scientific method. Anyone who has not sold his soul to scientism (and who, as it were, dabbles in the free marketplace of philosophy) might consider this a sadly stunted, self-denying view. Far the wiser perspective is Lewis's, that "the only difference is what many see we call a real thing, but what only one sees we call a dream. But things that many see may have no taste or moment in them at all, and things that are shown to one may be spears and waterspouts from the very depths of truth." Only "things that many see," and not all of them, are treatable by science. "Things that are shown to one" are the clay of literature and art. Can any sane philosophy deny them? Balance is needed. Perhaps it is science, investigating the merely material, that can tell us little or nothing from the "very depths of truth."

Another limitation on "the method" inheres in the consciousness of the subject, and indeed, in that still-mysterious rebellion against mechanism called life. Botany seems safe at first, but we are not *quite* sure that plants do not have some mode of intelligence unknown to us. They do seem to like to be talked to, and to listen to good music (and wilt upon hearing rock, if some experiments are to be believed). Biology gets progressively "iffier" with the increasing intelligence of the animal. Mind is mysterious stuff. In general, the more of it there is inside, the less confident we are (this side of ideological formulas) that we can get at it examining from outside. Misgivings here have a solid scientific basis. Consciousness, or if you prefer, free will, can alter scientific test results, that is, gives less and less evidence of being "determined." The animals observed display personality and individuality, and investigators give them names. Their behavior produces enough surprises to dispel any notion that it is "determined" within scientific exactitude. At the level of human intelligence, for reasons we have touched, empirical science breaks down completely. Humans do not act as if they were determined, and with fewer exceptions than there are professed determinists, do not believe they are either. If sufficiently annoyed at scientific investigators, people can and do say or do outrageous things just to mess up the results. There can be no real science where the "subject" is capable of lying. Scientists, like everyone else, lie now and then, and as it is a special scandal in their own trade, are acutely aware of it.

And here is another wondrous dilemma. We humans all know we can change our minds, falsify, lie, or generally make a total mess of "determined" behavior. Determinists, whether philosophers or scientists dabbling in philosophy, know as well as anybody else that they lied as much as kids as anybody else, and like everybody else know perfectly well when they are telling a whopper. They lie in asserting determinism, by a willful act in defiance of determinism. And they know as they do it that they are lying; almost always consciously, but perhaps for a few, sunk in self-deception, only in their heart. The best minds among them almost always repent and recant—T. H. Huxley, H. G. Wells, George Bernard Shaw, and others. Among the logical positivists, Reichenbach admitted not only to his engagement in a "crusade" ("the whole movement of scientific philosophy is a crusade"), but to being motivated for it by a most unscientific interest in social engineering. Herbert Feigl, noting "Confession, it is said, is good for the soul," made his own: "Undoubtedly we [the logical positivists] *made up* some facts of scientific history to suit our theories" (emphasis added). That is very short of the mark, but it is very human, and enough. (Let those so saintly as to be able to apologize more gracefully, condemn; the rest of us will understand that too.) Even that brilliant logician and anti-heroic, irascible curmudgeon Bertrand Russell was moved at the end of his long life to plead for—are you ready for this?—"Christian love."

One thing I think we might discern from all this is that there is a time in life when the crusading fires have burned low, and when we look at all things with fully human eyes, without a hint of prejudgment. Or maybe it is twice: when we are very young and still filled with that beautifully scientific sense of wonder that leads to discovery, and when we are old, and need no longer harbor illusions. In between, if this be true, we must keep our common humanity uppermost, and love each other, and be eternally watchful not to carry schemes of a scientific heaven on earth too far. No such way to heaven is known or ever will be, and in pursuing any we will find ourselves, like a fish, hooked on the end of a still-human line.

An Elephant Slid Down a Grassy Hillside....

So began another exercise by Eddington, many years ago, into the schemes of exact science. The gentleman had a knack for apt examples, and though science has changed, the nature of the example has not, so we might as well pursue it.

The question posed is how long will it take for the elephant to get to the bottom, and the question in that is, how does metrical science seek the answer? (By "metrical," we mean no more or less than resort to measurement, no matter how magnified measurement may be by scientific instruments.)

We measure the elephant, and find it has a mass of two tons. We measure the hillside, and find it has a gradient of 60 degrees. We must indeed measure every factor that has any bearing on the problem—the shape of the elephant, the density of the air, the coefficient of friction down the hillside, etc. These measurements were and often still are called "pointer readings," meaning that we are not concerned with the elephant's weight, but that the pointer on our scale points to two tons. Exact science deals only in pointer readings, or in collections of pointer readings (tensors). It has no way to deal with the elephant or slope. All factors have to be translated into a usable scientific language, that is, the symbols for the measurements involved, before we can manipulate the quantities and make sense of them. Only with this translation does the problem become science, susceptible of treatment with the hypotheses and formulas that have slowly been accumulated by experiment.

A very curious thing happens in this process. The elephant and the slope disappear. Their reality is lost while scientists wrestle with the pointer readings. They revert to being part of a scientifically unfathomable "other." The elephant is *equal to* the symbols for "mass, two tons," but not *identical* to them. Exact science has no test for "identity." In other words, what Eddington called the "inner, un-get-at-able" nature of the elephant is completely hidden to science. "Whenever we state the properties of a body in terms of physical quantities, we are imparting knowledge as to the response of the various metrical indicators to its presence *and nothing* more." What we learn about is elephant-equivalent sliding through an Einsteinian space–time tube. What escapes us entirely is the intrinsic nature of the elephant.

This is general in metrical science, no matter that the most tractable materials or processes are being investigated. The knowledge derived is innately inferential and subjective. That is, the methodology has access only to the properties and effects of the thing we wish to learn about, while paradoxically foreclosing direct knowledge of the thing itself. We may think of it this way; just as the voice we hear on the phone is not the same as the person on the other end of the line, so too the metrical findings of science are not the same as the subject under study. In the one case the voice must be converted into electrical impulses to be transmitted over the wire; in the other, the "real world" subject's properties must be converted into symbols useful to science. In short, science provides the linkage to, but not direct knowledge of, the natural world. A second layer of subjectivity is innately involved as well in our human senses. Sensory impressions from the outside world are converted into nerve impulses to be carried to the brain before our mind can interpret them; and senses can be fooled. We use scientific instruments to magnify and correct our own senses—but we still have to use our senses to read the instruments. Our scientific conclusions, therefore, are really inferences about inferences, albeit extremely reliable ones. Said Eddington, "...if you still think that this substitution [into scientific symbols] has taken all reality away from the problem, I am not sorry that you should have a foretaste of the difficulty in store for those who hold that exact science is all-sufficient for the description of the universe and that there is nothing in our experience which cannot be brought within its scope."

In physics, successful treatment of the pointer readings is considered to be *complete* knowledge. Scientifically, this poses no problem at all, but philosophically, to say the least, it is less than satisfying and opens old questions. All scientistic philosophy claims exclusive validity for scientific knowledge, and dismisses everything else we may learn by any other means, from literature, for example, as "subjective." Yet in the end we find that exact science, that envy of the behaviorists, can itself produce but inferential and subjective knowledge of the inorganic world. The ultimate "logic" of logical positivism is that there can be no science—and no elephants. Determinists, misappropriating what they suppose is an assumption of physics, conclude erroneously that even the human mind is determined. But in physics, the genuine science, no such claim can be made: there is room aplenty for mind in that impenetrable "other." Thought, indeed, is actually built into the Einsteinian scheme, in the sense that a knowledgeable observer is posited. Thought also vindicated itself magnificently in the creation of relativity and quantum mechanics. It isn't physicists one hears claiming thought is impossible, but sloppy would-be imitators. But to pursue such claims into the arcana of anti-heroic argumentation is sheer bedlam. Suffice to say that contradiction reveals their fallacy. The real mistake was in taking them seriously in the first place. They were, as their proponents have now admitted, deceptions, implements in a war of ideas—a war against the Western order.

Moral Dilemmas of Amoral Science

"He didn't seem like a fanatic Nazi. I think he was a cold scientist." So said Gita Stammler about Dr. Joseph Mengele, whom she had sheltered in Brazil. "He always denied that he had committed any crimes."

A "cold scientist" may believe this, no matter what his acts, and there is no doubting Mengele's scientific credentials. He held doctorates in medicine and anthropology from an educational system far more rigorous than our own. His demeanor was professional, even as he performed "experiments" on children that we find unspeakable. It is conscience, our moral sensibility, that recoils in horror. There are no "crimes" in science.

Science, by definition, is "value-free." This is proper, and indeed necessary, at the operational level. The investigator must be free to pursue the truth independently. No pressures, opinions, value-systems or other extraneous influences may obtrude, lest they promise his work. Science in the service of a political or ideological system is, in effect, abandoning the search for truth in favor predetermined goals and simply ceases to be science. (For example, Stalin decreed a State-serving scientific disgrace, "Lysenkoism," because it was "politically correct.") We automatically suspect findings that

are subservient or self-interested. Only rigorous exclusion of
values protects the integrity of scientific conclusions. In the
end, the only question is, are the findings accurate and
replicable?

Moreover, science itself is permanently disbarred from
addressing any moral question. It has no tools at all to do so. It
cannot weigh good and evil on a scale or search for God with a
telescope; and a good thing it is. We may greatly fear
"scientific" endorsement of "good causes." Demagogues can
paint their most atrocious crimes as "noble"—only "eliminate" the Jews or the bourgeois class, and our future will be
glorious. Given the temper of the times, men could be most
easily lured into such evil by a "scientific" imprimatur—and in
fact in these cases, that is what happened: mass exter-
minations were sanctioned by Darwinism. Mengele believed
this was "science" as firmly as he believed in the law of gravity.
From this view, he was virtually a saint. After all, he was
trying to advance the good of all mankind by experimenting
on a few meaningless specimens—wasn't he? Within science,
there is no moral check on this or on any act, criminal or not,
and no possible capacity to examine moral issues. For this, I
repeat, we must be profoundly grateful, but clearly we have a
dilemma, and a difficult one.

What is the role of amoral (value-free) science in the
larger, moral human community? And how can science be
directed to, or at least held within, morally permissible
enterprise? We cannot really police it from without, any more
than it can generate moral direction from within. Such an
attempt conjures up thoughts of boards of censors, or moral
busybodies, or of a Stalin. And it wouldn't work anyway:
science must be free.

All that is left as a safeguard is the moral convictions of the scientists themselves. For a realist approach, we must clearly take into account the larger human role of the scientist, even as we place science in the larger human enterprise. We need proportion. Anti-heroic notions mislead us by asserting science to be all-important, when it is not. The pursuit of knowledge is not limited to science, and it is not the only good. According to Matthew Arnold, men also have innate devotion to "beauty, moral principles and social harmony." Only by fulfilling all aspects of our nature can we attain a true culture and insure the moral health of the community, including its science.

In other words, the role of science is limited, and must be understood to be, even as its tools are limited. It serves larger human needs, and it does so in response to what itself is a moral value: the pursuit of truth. What it may offer is improving mastery over natural process, and an ever-wider, ever-more universal conception of physical reality. Yet the development of knowledge cannot be isolated from the larger human enterprise or from our other capacities. Scientific knowledge, like any, must be related to the human situation overall. It is a human construct for solely human purpose. As science is woven from human material, a moral element is necessary and inseparable from it.

Conversely, as anti-heroic dogmas attack and weaken moral conviction, they attack and threaten even the existence of science. If it is the duty of the larger community to defend science against this assault, it is likewise the duty of the men and women in science to adjudge such dogmas with moral perception. This, in the end, is our rebuke to a Mengele. None can be made by the anti-hero.

Unscientific Comforts. . . .

I walk to work each day. To me it is a process of the simplest choices, and I get there without incident. In the general view we have discussed, this is a miracle. My behavior has been dictated by the stars. Presumably if one little "quark" misfires in my brain, I would walk to town instead, or stumble over my neighbor's herbacious border. But it never happens. And the pseudo-scientific view that asserts it will, is hardly distinguishable from astrology, and every bit as useful.

Things are not always as they seem. Legitimate science can tell me that my desk is something of an illusion, and that it is almost entirely empty space, pervaded by fields of force. Fortunately, these forces hold my papers up just as well as my comfortable old desk. The world we inhabit is not really an illusion. We just see it from a different perspective than the nuclear physicist, and different vantages are permissible even in science. In the world of human dimension, most of us manage to get along nicely, despite fanciful theories that we cannot.

There will always be such a human world. Science cannot devour it. The most obvious scientific limitation of all, one hardly necessary to discuss, is permanent proof against scientistic follies. This is the realm of the abstract, the immaterial, the spiritual. Science, of course, being limited to metrical investigation of material substance, may never enter. It can treat quantities but not qualities, how but not why, what is but never what ought to be. Beyond that barrier are the things that matter most to us, scientists certainly included. In our private human park are beauty, joy, humor, love; music, literature, art; manners, character, purpose, faith and soul.

One can easily extend the list. This is our world, as much or more than the earth below our feet. This world can be mocked or denied from without, but not invaded. It is ours just for the asking, and always will be.

Epilogue
Reclaiming Our Future

And God saw every thing that he had made, and, behold, it was
very good.

—Genesis 1:31

As personal and private life is lower than participating in the
Body of Christ, so the collective life is lower than the personal
and private life and has no value save in its service. The secular
community, since it exists for our natural good and not for our
supernatural, has no higher end than to facilitate and safeguard
the family, and friendship, and solitude. To be happy at home,
said Johnson, is the end of all human endeavour. As long as we
are thinking only of natural values we must say that the sun
looks down on nothing half so good as a household laughing
together over a meal, or two friends talking over a pint of beer,
or a man alone reading a book that interests him; and that all
economics, politics, laws, armies, and institutions, save in so far
as they prolong and multiply such scenes, are a mere ploughing
the sand and sowing the ocean, a meaningless vanity and
vexation of the spirit. Collective activities are, of course,
necessary; but this is the end to which they are necessary.

—C. S. Lewis

An age may be characterized as much by what it does not do, as by what it does. The great non-event of our times, Solzhenitsyn reminds us, is that men did not abandon religion. Human life—whole and with transcendent purpose—has survived the darkest, most determined assault ever known. Future historians may well mark our time as the dawn of a new heroic age. Some may call it "post-anti-heroic," to mark what we have been though. For it seems certain to me that our posterity will look back upon our era as a nightmare reaching its blackest convulsions in the twentieth century.

The future is taking shape now in our own beliefs and in the courage of our leaders. Ideas and leadership—not natural or social "forces"—are the prime movers in human affairs. We can safely ignore the crystal ball gazers like Hegel, Comte and Marx who professed such divination of human events that the future was transparent to them. According to Marx, socialism would arrive "with the inexorability of a law of nature." These men and their like all batted zero because they left free will and human purpose out of their theories. They tried to turn us into helpless pawns; but we create our own fate. We ourselves do not wish to predict the future but to change it. For this we must understand the present by identifying its dominant ideas and the salesmen and preachers of those ideas. It has been the burden of this work to get outside the anti-heroic premises and habits of thought that have swept over the West, so that we can see them for what they are and learn what has really been happening to us.

We have seen the long-rising tide of anti-heroism, over many centuries, erode and inundate the foundations of Western belief and a civilized order. We have heard the anti-hero claim that his dreary New Order is the promised land,

and brag that our descent into barbarism is "inevitable." And as the flood waters lapped at our last fortresses and cathedrals, it seemed he was correct and that all was lost. For the leaderless multitudes, morale faltered. But always a few men have lit candles in defiance, and through their faith we remember that dawn follows the night.

Our past has not been destroyed. Our faith lives. From our roots and living moral teachings we have a framework of truth and knowledge against which the assertions of anti-heroism can be weighed. Thus we have been able to locate the critical turnings toward an anti-heroic view in centuries past. These departures were not the tug of truth, but errors by philosophers, false assumptions based on faulty or obsolete science, and admitted deceptions by anti-heroes to advance their "cause." We have seen the effects of these errors and lies compound and snowball over the years until they created a complete—and completely false—conception of life and reality. This "new" view, inverting moral law and values, appears in its fullness not a product of thought but of pride and lust or darker urges. It is an evil impulse, destroying knowledge, making the fine arts ugly, turning language into babble, educating our children for the anthill, and unleashing our meanest and most bestial cravings. It wars on the best in us and empties life of transcendent meaning.

I have described anti-heroism as the mirror opposite of the Judeo-Christian teachings and traditions of the West. This is true, especially in practical effect. But in another sense, as darkness is the absence of light, we understand anti-heroism to be a void, the absence of life. Lewis argued that there is no true evil, but only good perverted. An individual may fall into evil by obsession with, and thence misuse of, some virtue or good, for instance, physical love. But anti-heroism, a whole world view, falls into a deeper evil of failing to seek good at all, denying it, mocking it, until life itself drains away into a soulless void.

Anti-heroism, at bedrock, is definable only as a negative. The anti-hero, denied a positive basis for life, takes on many hues, but always at the extreme. The more anti-heroic he is, the more he will gravitate to the opposite sides of life, to the angel or the beast, to the temporal or the eternal, to mind or to body. These opposites seem at war with each other, but in truth both in isolation are anti-heroic, representing pure forms of the two kinds of rebellion against God, fallen angel and fallen man. To Hegel, all was mind; to Hume, nothing was mind; both contribute to the age against life in our time. Beneath it, the two strands are joined in the hand of the prince of the world.

In contrast, the heroic view demands balance between the extremes. The Christian is instructed to keep one foot in the world and one in heaven; to render unto Caesar and to God what is due each; to walk the strait and narrow. All life lies between. Even goodness can be corrupted by obsession. Life should not be some grey, deadly serious thing. Laughter offsets our defeats and joy our suffering, if we know creation is good. The way of life is balance. If few there be that find it, perhaps it is that we take even "religion" too seriously—both in seeking it and hating it.

It is, indeed, another signature of an anti-heroic era that the "search for religion" becomes frantic. The real thing is missing, and we must have something, so come to believe anything, as Chesterton warned. Robert Farrar Capon identifies three such "religions" as predominant in America today:

theme, or narcissistic concern with Self; Gnosticism, the reduction of life to formulas and concepts and slogans; and Angelism, the worship of perfect abstractions, particularly collectives such as Society or Science, each with a capital S. Characteristically, anti-heroism incorporates all three with gusto. But none satisfies a spiritual hunger, and worse, all lose sight of what "religion" means. Says Capon, "...in the profoundest sense—that is, in terms of the Gospel's unique and primary message—Christianity is not a religion at all....its crucial message is the quite irreligious announcement that the religion business is in fact over; that, whatever it was that human beings have been trying to transact by means of it, has finally been transacted once and for all, not by religionists, but by God himself. The claim of the Gospel, in other words, is that it delivers, in full and free of charge, what other religions promise only as a catalogue item available to those who can fill out the order forms correctly. Indeed, it makes the even more bizarre assertion that the delivery in question has actually, if mysteriously, been made—not to this or that coterie of properly-heeled customers, but to the vulgar, catholic, flat-broke bulk of humanity as such...." The modern, he adds observingly, "will buy almost any angelic religion—however moralistic, cramped, sectarian, cruel or bizarre—just to avoid the only thing [he] could be comfortable with: the... promise that, for the taking, every child of Adam has a free bus ticket home."

Those of us who treasure that free ticket home still sing songs to life. But what makes the anti-hero tick? What is his belief, his motive force, at the deepest level? It is unspoken and may or may not be known to him. But something is there; some belief that propels him. I have long pondered this question and find no compelling answer. I keep groping for a positive vision but there is none. It is like contemplating a whole century of Fausts. All I can suggest is possibilities.

An obvious motive, but only on the surface, is revolutionary utopianism. This may be enough to keep anti-heroic foot soldiers in line, but it is completely unsatisfactory beyond that. Utopia-building is a key mark of the twentieth-century landscape, and the one crystalline fact about them is that they all fail. No matter how much force and determination is applied, they always fail. Moscow may seem a sort of paradise to its Party followers (I doubt it), and the system can be claimed to "work" because it is still expanding. But even Kremlin bosses have to buy their luxuries in free countries, and plenty of yuppies are far better off in what is supposed to matter to such minds—material goods. Life is little better than slave labor for the unprivileged 99% in these workers' paradises. Nobody in his right mind can mistake these hellholes for utopia or even potential utopia, or call them good.

A second possibility is Muggeridge's "death wish." This at a glance does not seem like a positive motive, a vision, but in a way it is. The atheist, Lewis reminded us, desperately wants life to end all. The prospect of personal annihilation is far less ominous to him than the burden of moral responsibility in life and—horrors!—throughout eternity. To such, the demands of life as a moral being are too great; existence must have an exit sign so that he can pass untormented into the void. I can easily see this death wish being strong enough to motivate the creation of materialistic sciences and philosophies. With such credentials the anti-hero can support his claim to beasthood where, indeed, death ends all. He can even pretend pity toward us "immature" souls who cannot face death, and say that all of our hopes and values are based on a childish and "unscientific" view of life. But I doubt this pseudo-vision will be any comfort. The anti-hero knows, down inside, he is dissimulating to ease his own guilt, and it turns his personal desperation into callousness and evil. His claims, in the end, are death worship, and materialism, the philosophy of death, is disastrous to healthy human life. It is, in any case, a ghastly and grotesque thing to inflict on others, especially on our children.

A third possibility is outright diabolism—if in fact this can be distinguished from a death wish (I'm not sure it can). Satan worship reemerges in our "enlightened" time, even at the level of popular culture. Bell, as noted earlier, could trace an overt demonaic impulse to the counter-culture of the 1960s and its insistence that nothing be sacred. As symptoms of moral and cultural disease, these manifestations ought to trigger all the alarms. Yet it is the general thrust, if unspoken impulse, of anti-heroism that is truly worrisome. This is where we see the wiles of hell striving against the spirit and pulling us down to the bestial and to the earthbound mire. I can speak with some authority in this. It is impossible to study our descent into anti-heroism, as I have, without developing a swift and sure sense of what diabolism really is.

There is one other possibility to consider, despite my instinct that all anti-heroic heresies involve the acting out of Western myth. If Max Picard is to be believed, the anti-hero may be trying to create a new myth by undoing all the old. Men in all ages, said Picard, are in a "Flight from God." In our times, with the objective world of faith rotting away in the anti-heroic seas, nearly all men become immersed in the

Flight, and even the vision of God dims. The whole force of life seems to become irrelevant, and the many plunge themselves into a hopeless quest for power or trinkets or Self. The Flight becomes strong, a stampede that few can resist. "What the Flight wants," he went on, "is this: to be primal, original, creative, as God is. The category of revolution is used to bring about the original and creative situation [so that things] may be returned once again to the beginning.... The Chthonic, that which springs out of the earth, and, in general, whatever is dark, these are popular. Darkness exists before the light of the created; it is the moment prior to creation. Best of all, one would like to enclose the entire Flight in the darkness existing before creation...."

Here, certainly, is a startlingly apt description of the modern mood. Is this, then, the darkness worshipped in secret by the anti-hero, the limbo before time? Here and only here is a clean nothingness, before life, before the world, beyond death. If man cannot realize his glory, let him at least be given the ultimate annihilation and be unmade. But we are creatures and our story is already long; it cannot be untold. God does not unmake creation, for it is good. A yearning for the void can only be the whisperings of the dark, for the void and the dark are one. They are, alike, the absence of God that is the torment of all human endeavor. For better or worse, we exist in the here and now, and we cannot escape pretending to be anything other than what we are. But this is a blessing, whatever the anti-hero may say about it. One came before us in real time and life to say, "I am the light." These words are our beacon and our hope in the reality we must deal with. Christ alone among men claimed to be present at the creation, and these words were spoken before the making of the world.

No power can unmake them. The power of anti-heroism shrinks to nothing before them. There will be no make-believe escape to the void for the anti-hero, not even if he sells his soul for it. He will learn that the darkness he courts is not pre-Adamite but diabolic.

Look at the "leaders" (anti-heroes never call their Big Brothers dictators) of the proletarian paradises. They are all little Jesuses, pretending to be present at the creation as it were, as Picard suggested. They affect a godlike omniscience to "create" a pseudo-divine order of their own devising. They define morality as obedience to their state and demand to be worshipped. They put posters of themselves on every wall, distribute their thoughts as a new gospel, and build themselves monuments and obelisks. They imprison, torture and kill all who will not believe, in the idiotic hope that crushing dissent will complete their godhood. They seek immortality in carvings in stone. What fools! From the viewpoint of eternity, their empires and stones are dust scattered in an instant by the winds. Even if we have no such vantage, we see only vanity in their works until the appointed end when none is left to see.

In the emptiness of anti-heroism lies its defeat. The anti-hero, proclaiming (falsely) that only experience teaches us, never dreamt the world would learn and recoil from our uniformly appalling experience with his dogmas. Late in this century we are sick to death of anti-heroic pretenses and works. Anti-heroism, denying traditional faith, offers neither a new vision of good to move men nor the courage of leadership. It cannot, in a word, summon the heroic resources that are the true determinants of human affairs. It is dying, as all prideful works must in the end.

Change has long been in the air. The keener-sighted saw or sensed it decades ago and added their strength to it. Recent years have seen an outpouring of scholarship in the heroic mode. The old claims of anti-heroism have been massively refuted in every field, even its strongholds at the fringes of science. In the field of affairs, experience, unfailingly adverse to anti-heroic postures keeps adding up for all to see. The anti-heroes, confronted at last by men both morally and intellectually superior, show signs of disarray, and offer at best confused and cowardly counsel. These changes are beginning to be felt in the political process (always the last to know!). Mind, I put no stock at all in political reforms or the results of an election or two. Nevertheless, we can read in politics a different wind and a new leadership.

As an historian, I am convinced that there are times of historic change or crisis where everything we think or do takes on the utmost importance. These crossroads come but rarely, but there is every reason to believe we are in one now. They grow out of a massive clash of ideas, not some dramatic event on the surface of affairs like an assassination or a plane crash. As such, they are difficult to detect, and we do not always recognize the crisis when it arrives. Yet the moment comes for each of us, and what it involves is a choice between the one set of ideas or the other. That choice is being made by many right now. The old anti-heroic scheme is being abandoned in favor of the renascent heroic vision. I have no crystal ball, but need none to see a more heroic future taking shape. It is merely a matter of reading present ideas. Still, the issue is far from settled, and we have more to do.

Twice before America has been through a sea change of belief. The first was the ferment of ideas that culminated in the American Revolution and free, limited, constitutional self-government. This was a rebellion against excessive governmental authority and an affirmation of the moral worth and self-reliance of the individual person. It extended religious tolerance and liberty beyond the dreams of the Old World. The new government was a piddling affair that minded its own business, kept its books in the black without taxes, avoided foreign entanglements, and issued only gold and silver money. The whole American story was the unleashed energy of free men who crossed and tamed a continent in a century: an explosion of inventiveness, dynamism and construction such as the world had never seen. Freedom worked as no slave system can. Liberty is moral in nature, and the American pioneers and settlers brought their churches to every hamlet and outpost in the land.

Those lessons, so dearly won and so fruitful, began to fade in the late nineteenth century. The shock of the Civil War and various growing pains weakened confidence in the "great experiment." Europe, at the time, was deep into an intellectual ferment almost the opposite of the founding ideas and faith of America. Science and philosophy alike seemed to question the Christian order. The ideas of Marx, Darwin and many others in essence reanimated the old authoritarian European schemes and centralized political power. So it was that a relative handful of professors and intellectuals in America, writing in the last years of the century and the first years of this, imported and drew on European theories in a conscious effort to undo our libertarian heritage and remake America in an Old World mold. This announced the second sea change in our belief.

These thinkers, our first anti-heroes, were dumbfound-
ingly successful. The defense of freedom and moral value had
already weakened, and they had much discontent to play on.
But mostly, their strength was a vision of a new, even
stronger, "scientific" America. Their collectivist ideas spread
from a few seminal advocates—most notably John Dewey,
Charles Beard and Thorstein Veblen—to second- and third-
hand purveyors of ideas in and out of the academy, and finally
reached the teachers and ministers and the working press—
the word wielders. Thence the collectivist mentality spread to
the professions, the business community, the courts, the arts,
the public, and last, of course, to politicians. Other bright
lights in this movement were Frederick Jackson Turner,
Harold Lasswell, Richard Ely, and the sociologist Lester Frank
Ward, who summed up the new doctrines in these words:
"The individual has reigned long enough. The day has come
for society to take its affairs into its own hands and shape its
own destinies." Society of the capital S kind, that is: that
noble-sounding, all-but-meaningless abstraction deified by
the anti-hero then and now.

Of course, there is no "society" being to take things into
its own hands. What this formula works out to is the
imposition of coercive governmental control over the many
by the few elite—"thinkers" either too presumptuous or
stupid to realize it can't be done. But the elitists had their way,
and from that time to this, government has bloated and
American liberty has become an increasingly endangered
species. Follow the dominant intellectual currents from 1900
to 1930 and you will see the dominant political movements
from 1930 to 1980, in living proof of Weaver's famous phrase,
"Ideas have consequences." The consequences in this case

have not been happy. The anti-heroic preachments of a few, long ago, bring us to the anti-heroic confusions and disorders of the present.

The thrust of this second revolution was eloquently summarized by Walter Lippmann in the mid-1930s, long before the results could be felt in every life: "The premises of authoritarian collectivism," he wrote, "have become the working beliefs, the self-evident assumptions, the unquestioned axioms, not only of all revolutionary regimes, but of nearly every effort which lays claim to being enlightened, humane, and progressive.... Throughout the world, in the name of progress, men who call themselves communists, socialists, fascists, nationalists, progressives, and even liberals, are unanimous in holding that government with its instruments of coercion must, by commanding the people how they shall live, direct the course of civilization and fix the shape of things to come."

These axioms, working beliefs and assumptions are anything but self-evident in the light of later experience. On the contrary, opinion swells to a chorus that they are not only mistaken but evil. They are tired ideas, hangovers from excited and rather silly philosophical babbling a century ago. Indeed, the notion that government is some sort of deity able to "command the people how they shall live" is a holdover of barbarism older than history. The theoretical basis for the whole sordid stew has been shredded, especially by the advance of science. And anyone can now see that, in practical effect, the anti-heroic has been dehumanizing and murderous. Even the words and labels have become muddied and useless. I have not spoken of liberal vs. conservative in this book, partly because the words seem to me beyond repair and not long for the world, but more because they are words at the political surface that do not begin to penetrate to the heart of the conflict between heroism and anti-heroism. This is a struggle of mind, imagination and soul, not politics. And it is here the tide has turned against anti-heroism. This marks the third sea change in American belief.

It is, I say again, happening now, and we are all parties to the outcome. If you take the anti-heroic view that there is nothing the individual person can do to control his own destiny, then stand aside. Be the helpless pawn of fate you say you are. But if you long for the sense of life and purpose our era denies; if your mind hungers and your spirit thirsts for something far better than the pursuit of things, or power, or politics, or self, then the time to change is now. Today we are at the threshold of a new understanding that will restore life in the human dimension. Its framework is already in place. It is our business to flesh it out with an affirmation of the heroic, in belief, in thought, in word and in deed.

The right events will not come easily or overnight, but we can all breathe clean air the moment we choose to, by dumping our faith in worldly, political, anti-heroic solutions to worldly, political, anti-heroic problems. The fruits may not be ours to savor, but at least we can restore a decent life for our children and grandchildren. Can any parent do less? Bilbo Baggins, Tolkien's beloved hobbit hero, says at the end, "But I have been too deeply hurt, Sam. I tried to save the Shire, and it has been saved, but not for me. It must often be so, Sam, when things are in danger: someone has to give them up, lose them, so that others may keep them." So, too, we have been deeply hurt by anti-heroism in our time, yet it remains our duty and our joy to pass along the rightness of life to our sons and daughters.

What, in the end, does the heroic teach us? I could fill another book with that! But really, these are matters each of us must learn and grow with, at the old human pace, day by day. The critical choice is to see that it is right, supremely right, and that herein lies the fullness of life we seek. Beyond that one decision, life sweetens in every way. Our vision no longer fixes on fictitious utopias invented by anti-heroes, but upon the timeless truth of man's condition under God. Old words take on new luster: "Where the spirit of the Lord is, there is liberty." We are born free and self-controlling, never meant to be under bureaucratic thumbs in some contrived "command" society. We are free because we are moral and purposeful beings. All community between us is that of voluntary association between free men, and all collectives instituted by force pervert and destroy our friendly and productive personal arrangements. On this fact all anti-heroic schemes founder.

We will come to see, too, that whatever our temporal arrangements, they must be calculated to bring out the very best in us—not, as we have seen in the anti-heroic, to bring out the bestial. There is no new morality. Men cannot invent what is right and wrong; that was given to us, and people of all cultures and faiths have cleaved largely to the same concepts throughout all history. Only with the rise of anti-heroism have men dared declare systematically that wrongs are the new rights, that promiscuity is sexual liberation, that dictators can kill dissenters and women their babies if we use the right words and incantations, and so on. Similarly, infatuated with his deified collective, the anti-hero excuses in the group what is the most hideous crime for an individual. But in his heart, can it be that even the anti-hero knows his wrongs are wrong, and trembles, and seeks the void to expatiate his guilt?

No one need be this way, living in guilt or unhappiness or fear. We are human. We choose our path. We come into this world one by one, each unique, each of us hungry for what is right and good in our own circumstances. The heroic is inborn in us all, for we can see what we should be as well as what we are. What more is asked of us, said the prophet, than to act justly and keep the faith? "Where, then," Muggeridge inquires, "does happiness lie? In forgetfulness, not indulgence, of the self. In escape from sensual appetites, not in their satisfaction.... To life [our glance] upward, becoming aware of the wide, luminous universe outside—this alone is happiness."

"Living thus in the twilight of a spent civilization," Muggeridge said elsewhere, "amidst its ludicrous and frightening shadows, what is there to believe? Curiously enough these twilight circumstances provide a setting in which, as it seems to me, the purpose which lies behind them stands out with particular clarity. As human love only shines in all its splendour when the last tiny glimmer of desire has been extinguished, so we have to make the world a wilderness to find God. The meaning of the universe lies beyond history as love lies beyond desire...." *Pace,* my friend, but the world is not quite wilderness yet, nor civilization spent. And to seek God, as Pascal said, as you have reminded us, is to find Him. That choice remains to us. It is the choice that has come alive again today.

Ponder one last time the import of anti-heroism's dark and ferocious drag down to the earth—and Chesterton's exuberant reply: "The Christian optimism is based on the fact that we do *not* fit in to the world. I had tried to be happy by telling myself that man is an animal, like any other that sought its meat from God. But now I was really happy, for I had learnt that man is a monstrosity. I had been right in feeling all things odd, for I myself was at once worse and better than all things. The [anti-hero's] pleasure was prosaic, for it dwelt on the naturalness of everything; the Christian pleasure was poetic, for it dwelt on the unnaturalness of everything in the light of the supernatural. The modern philosopher had told me again and again that I was in the right place, and I had still felt depressed even in acquiescence. But I had heard that I was in the *wrong* place, and my soul sang for joy, like a bird in spring."

Is this not every man's tale in this time of woe? Yet, courage: for by the power of choice given us, we can put the nightmare behind us. Let those who will claim their status as beasts of the field and things of the earth: that is the modern nightmare. The rest of us with a taste for life will find it in our monstrosity, strangers to this world, creatures with a ticket to the eternal free for the asking. In the words, "Thy will be done," is our life and our joy and our heroic vision. We have only to accept them to find the serenity we thought lost in a World Without Heroes.

Index

George Roche, a nationally known author and lecturer featured in *Readers' Digest, Time, Newsweek,* the *Wall Street Journal,* and on *Firing Line,* the *McNeil-Lehrer News Hour,* and the *Today Show,* is president of Hillsdale College in southern Michigan.

Formerly the presidentially appointed chairman of the National Council on Educational Research, Dr. Roche is the author of eight books on education, history, philosophy, and government, including *America by the Throat: The Stranglehold of Federal Bureaucracy* (1985), and his first novel, *Going Home* (1986).

George Roche and his wife, June, live in Hillsdale, Michigan. They have four children: George IV, Muriel, Maggie, and Jacob; and a grandson, George V.